Electric Words

ACL-MIT Press Series in Natural Language Processing
Aravind K. Joshi, Karen Sparck Jones, and Mark Y. Liberman, editors

Electric Words
Dictionaries, Computers,
and Meanings

Yorick A. Wilks,
Brian M. Slator, and
Louise M. Guthrie

A Bradford Book
The MIT Press
Cambridge, Massachusetts
London, England

This book was set in Times Roman by Asco Trade Typesetting Ltd., Hong Kong and was printed and bound in the United States of America.

First printing.

Library of Congress Cataloging-in-Publication Data

Wilks, Yorick, 1939–
  Electric words: dictionaries, computers, and meanings / Yorick A.
Wilks, Brian M. Slator, Louise M. Guthrie.
     p.   cm.—(ACL-MIT Press series in natural-language processing)
"A Bradford book."
Includes bibliographical references and index.
ISBN 0-262-23182-4 (hc)
  1. Natural language processing (Computer science)
2. Computational linguistics. I. Slator, Brian M. II. Guthrie,
Louise M. III. Title. IV. Series.
QA76.9.N38W55   1995
413'.0285'5—dc20   94-49362
                                                       CIP

Contents

Preface

It was only 20 years ago, a long time in this field but short for most things, that "computing and the lexicon" was a topic that raised only yawns from much of the computational linguistics community. Dictionaries themselves were the books you would find only on the desk of those who couldn't spell. They were known to be prone to error, like all human endeavors, and a reasonable attitude to them might have been that of Johnson to his own great dictionary, as he put it, "insensitive to praise or blame." Such books just were what they were, and that did not, for most of those in computational linguistics, include being an object for research or computation.

How it has all changed, as government agencies and large corporations compete to get their hands on large lexicons to speed the growth of their natural language processing (NLP) systems; national needs are appealed to, lexical knowledge bases have something of the cachet that recently attached to real-world knowledge bases. Of more interest, perhaps, the continuity of dictionaries and lexicons with the exploration of fundamental issues to do with the expression and representation of meaning has again been recognized.

How has all this come about? First, it has been through dissatisfaction with the trivial size of most NLP systems and a realization that this could not continue if there were ever to be serious NLP applications. Then there was growing respect for the content and consistency of real dictionaries; not that they were perfect but because, unlike much academic linguistics and philosophy, their authors had taken real concrete decisions about meaning every day, just as judges take practical moral decisions every day, while ethical philosophers continue to debate and discuss.

None of that proves that the meaning representations in dictionaries, even if they can be extracted, are the ones that humans use or that NLP systems need. But suddenly it all seemed worth a try, and the large and colorful subject matter of this book came into being. Looking back, many researchers were slow to recognize the pioneering efforts of those who first investigated dictionaries computationally on primitive machines: Olney, Amsler, and Walker. To Don Walker, in particular, we dedicate this book.

Acknowledgments

We thank all those who offered helpful comments on earlier drafts and provided helpful material, especially Becky Bruce, Nicoletta Calzolari, Jim Cowie, Thierry Fontenelle, Richard Fowler, Patrick Hanks, and Paul Procter. Many thanks for our discussions over the years are owed to the Natural Language Research Group at the Computing Research Laboratory, New Mexico State University. Tremendous help with the final production of the book was given by Bea Guzman and Venus Rauls. One of the authors thanks the Master and Fellows of Trinity Hall, Cambridge University, whose fellowship allowed him to write his part of the book.

Electric Words

Chapter 1

Introduction

Dictionaries and computation are two subjects not often brought together in the same book, or even in the same proposition until recently. The aim of this book is to explore the growing relations between them and, in particular, to investigate whether what is found in traditional dictionaries can be of service to those concerned with getting computers to process and, some would say, understand natural languages like English, Japanese, Spanish, and so on.

Artificial intelligence (AI) will be a subject never far from the concerns of this book. Most of its adherents have claimed that coded knowledge of the real world was required if machines were to understand language in any serious sense. The problem was always how to get it: there were no suitable sources and no time to handcraft it in. A recent advertisement for an Oxford dictionary reads: "So if your dictionary doesn't know who John Major is, isn't it time you swapped it for one that does?" That shows that the distinction between dictionaries and encyclopedias may be harder to draw today than when Todd could write in the preface to his revision of Johnson's great dictionary ([1755]/1827) that "he who makes [dictionaries] must often write of what he does not understand." Dictionaries, like encyclopedias, are now of some immediate interest to anyone who shares the knowledge-directed goals of AI.

Patrick Suppes used to say, 25 years ago, that he would only be interested in machine translation (MT) when programs could process a whole book. In fact, they already could and did when he said that, but his remark was in the right spirit. Although MT, by methods now considered superficial by most who work in AI, processed large volumes of text by the mid-1960s, those AI researchers who aimed for something deeper, for a modeling of what most people would call "understanding" a text, wrote programs that processed only a few sentences, a fact often disguised in their theses, papers, and books. Reputations have been made from the processing of little more than a single sentence. In a moment of great honesty 5 years ago, a group of AI researchers on natural language processing (NLP) admitted in public (in answer to Bran Boguraev's question) how many words there really were in the vocabularies of their systems. The average of the answers was 36, a figure often taken to be a misprint when it appears, though it was all too true. Remedies for this situation, which, whatever it was, had little to do with science or engineering as normally understood, have been to move to a larger scale and more empirical methods; they have ranged from the use of neural or connectionist networks in language understanding to a return to statistical methods for the analysis of texts, as well as attempts to increase the size of lexicons for computational systems by attempting to extract meaning (together with syntactic and other kinds of grammatical information) from existing dictionaries available in machine-readable form. This form is usually the computer tape from which the dictionary itself was printed, although, as we shall see, the very earliest efforts in this tradition (in the mid-1960's) required a special keypunching of whole printed dictionaries from the text.

Those earliest efforts involved little more than word frequency counting, but they were very important. They were not, as they were often treated, the most boring and unintellectual parts of computational linguistics. Matters have now gone far beyond mere counting, and have begun to intrude into the difficult province of meaning itself, and the question of how it can be formally expressed. This is perhaps the most interesting area for the authors of this book and we shall give it full coverage for, if anything useful comes from it, there will be consequences far beyond merely increasing the size of language-processing systems by automatic methods.

The issue here can be understood by analogy with the studies by philosophers like Wisdom (1961) and Hart (1961) of legal decisions taken in the courts. Their activity was not thought quite right by many philosophers of ethics, for whom their subject was a wholly a priori one, having nothing to gain from *empirical* evidence. Wisdom argued that, whereas ethical philosophers argue endlessly in the abstract about moral matters, courts, especially appellate courts, where written justifications of metaphysical and ethical issues are regularly given, actually take concrete decisions with far-reaching effect. Philosophers argue about the principles of causation, for example, but judges take reasoned decisions about what caused what in particular cases.

One can argue that lexicographers, too, take concrete decisions about meaning and its expression (indeed, thousands and thousands of them, under commercial time constraints!) while philosophers and formal semanticists argue about principles with little concrete effect. Note that, in neither of these areas, are we suggesting any sort of Wittgensteinian, or directly democratic, approach to either meaning or law such as going out and asking people what they think words mean. Psychologists know that you do not successfully elicit people's tacit knowledge of meaning, or anything else, by just asking them directly in a survey. Judges, rightly or wrongly, believe they are eliciting and expressing the common meaning of concepts and so do lexicographers. If that is so, then in the case of lexicography it may be a serious contribution to a theory of meaning to attempt to formalize and refine what the lexicographer's craft actually contains, quite independent of any practical computational or technological benefit.

Johnson defined lexicographers in his own dictionary as "harmless drudges" and, until recently, computational lexicographers were thought of rather similarly by their colleagues in AI and the more fashionable parts of computational linguistics: syntax, semantics, pragmatics, and so on. That perception has changed in recent years, partly because of the renewed emphasis on scale in computational linguistics itself, and partly because of a return to empiricism in the field and the realization that, even though dictionaries are only fallible human products, they may be the place to look for large-scale facts about meaning.

From the beginning of computational linguistics there was a desire, both practical and intellectual, to subject computational systems to empirical tests, ones where standard statistical methods might be be brought to bear, and where it could be seen whether the hypotheses of researchers worked outside very small handcrafted domains. If we exempt, for the moment, early MT work with its large handmade lexicons, then to do that almost certainly required that linguistic information be made available on a large scale by the use of automatic methods, and an obvious first place to look was existing dictionaries. Did they have content that could be made available in some automatic manner to computational linguistic programs operating on texts? One could put that question as, "Can existing dictionaries yield up information that helps understand texts with computers?," where "yield up" is taken to mean subjecting the dictionary to the same kind of analysis (or parsing) techniques applied to ordinary texts so as to get information from them. We look at a range of such techniques in the body of this book.

A range of other interesting questions and assumptions then arose: even if the content of standard dictionaries could be extracted in some way, was the information, which presumably helped human language users when consulting a dictionary, the same as or close to that needed by a language-understanding computer program that did not use language in the same way as people? All kinds of vaguely Wittgensteinian worries and quibbles collect about this point, especially the feeling that knowledge may be inherently related to the task for which it was collected and may not be transferable to the solution of another, quite different, task.

Almost everyone concedes both that dictionaries contain a great number of items of knowledge about the world, such as that oats is a cereal fed to cattle, and that the distinction between knowledge of language and knowledge of the world is shaky at best. But the basic question remains as to whether information that can be extracted from dictionaries, automatically or by humans, is also the kind that meets the AI demand for computer-usable, or *tractable*, world knowledge. "Tractable" in this sense is a word that is important for us in this book.

As interest in computational lexicography revived in the later 1980s, some researchers (usually coming from AI or lexical semantics) found more intellectual questions could be investigated by its methods than had been suspected: questions about the empirical basis of semantic relations and whether the structures implicit in dictionaries, odd though they were (at least in the sense of not being simple hierarchical trees) had any formal properties at all, such as significant graph-theoretic properties. We devote considerable space later to discussions of the range of possible structures lurking unseen within dictionaries.

There was also plenty of drudgery, as Johnson himself had promised; the new computational lexicography required the conversion of dictionaries on magnetic tape, as supplied by publishers, into forms such that computer-usable information could be extracted from them. Boguraev (and see Amsler 1982) emphasized just how much detailed and painstaking work is needed to strip away all the typesetting dross on a tape for computational purposes, so as to get at basic information that can then be processed into some form of standard database, and he became something of a folk hero in the trade for these efforts.

These tapes turned out to contain all the craftwork of traditional lexicography in electronic form, all its panoply of type sizes, italics, meaningful colons, and sense subdivision conventions. Yet again, and by a curious historical serendipity, computational interest in dictionaries revived at just the moment when some publishers, particularly in Britain, were making dictionary formats—the formats for their readers that is, not just the format on computer tapes—more purely formalized, as regards both syntax and the defining vocabulary used to define word senses. It is a curious historical coincidence that dictionaries like the *Longman Dictionary of Contemporary English* (LDOCE) (Procter 1978), and later the *Oxford Advanced Learners Dictionary* (OALD) (Hornby 1963), and the Collins (COBUILD) seem almost to have been designed for computational linguistic investigation even though, in fact, their radically new formats were designed for learners of English with only limited facility in the language.

This book aims to cover all these issues at appropriate levels, not only the drudgery but also the highest-level theoretical claims about semantics and dictionaries, the products provided by the publishers, as well as the politics of funding agencies and companies that are now making support of these lexical investigations a higher priority than ever before. A major theme in what follows is the reinvestigation of early computational work on dictionaries and thesauri in the 1960s, dismissed by many at the time as pedestrian but now seen to be highly original and interesting, and which did not come to fruition largely because of the puny level of computing power then available.

Another core section of the latter part of the book is a comparative survey of the work now going on in many centers across the world on the central task, as we see it, of extracting usable structures from dictionaries for computational linguistic purposes, and the way those structures differ from, or interact with, structures derived from standard texts (or corpora, as they are called in opposition to dictionary texts). And this leads naturally to a further question: how far future dictionaries can be constructed by means of corpus analysis, which is to say by defining, or refining, word senses against their actual occurrence in very large volumes of natural text, as surveyed by computer.

Machine-Readable Texts and Dictionaries

Dictionaries are special texts whose subject matter is a language, or a pair of languages in the case of a bilingual dictionary. The purpose of dictionaries is to provide a wide range of information about words: etymology, pronunciation, stress, morphology, syntax, register, and, of course, to give definitions of senses of words and, in so doing, supply knowledge about not just language but about the world itself.

Researchers in computational linguistics (CL) and AI have viewed dictionaries in two quite different ways:

1. With theoretical interest, as a tool or database for investigating the semantic structure of natural language

2. With the practical interest we noted, as a resource for overcoming the "knowledge-acquisition bottleneck," in Byrd's phrase: how to acquire formal meaning and knowledge representations automatically in large numbers for further CL work

It is important to note that the two aims are quite independent; one could have either without the other. We, as authors, happen to have both interests and, indeed, substantial prejudices about how both should be done. In this book we continue with the now conventional usage of "lexicon" to mean a set of formalized entries, to be used in conjunction with a set of computer programs, and keep "dictionary" to mean a physical printed text giving lexical information, including meaning descriptions.

There must be no doubt about the commitment to sheer size, to quantity (and quality) of data, if these enterprises are to be other than intellectually trivial. Suppes's remark noted earlier about MT and the whole book has now become a methodological distinction (usually attributed to Miller 1985, but also to be found in Amsler 1982), namely, the contrast of the *demo* and *book* approaches to CL lexicons, where the former implies handcrafting on a small scale and the latter supports quantity, no matter how achieved.

The standard objection to the demo approach, apart from the fact it produces only small numbers of vocabulary codings, is that the entries are made, consciously or unconsciously, with a particular application in mind and so are, in some sense, experimentally circular when an analysis algorithm is applied to them; they necessarily contain what is required to show the desired behavior. The problem with this criticism, if true, is that it applies equally well to handcrafted versions of the book approach. Miller's own WordNet system (1985) is the largest formal lexical structure so far built explicitly for computational and psychological use. It was intended to show the virtues of the book approach. But if the act of entry handcrafting is *itself* part of the problem, then size will not cure it. The same could (and certainly has been) said of the Cyc project at Microelectronic Computer Technology Corporation (MCC) (Lenat, Prakash, and Shepherd 1986; Lenat and Feigenbaum 1987), which aims to hand-code 1 million entries from an encyclopedia into a logical formalism, an enterprise which will take an estimated 2 person-centuries of work. We believe this is a mistaken approach because it wastes precious human resources and makes dubious theoretical assumptions, despite Lenat's claim that their work is theory-free. Cyc has certainly been presented by Lenat as a resource for NLP as well as more straightforward knowledge-based reasoning tasks, and hence falls under the same category as WordNet, that is, a very large version of a handcrafted book approach (both Cyc and WordNet are discussed further in chapter 8).

The difficulty here is not simply solved, because dictionaries are themselves paradigms of large-scale handcrafted books of vocabulary entries, and are well known to be fallible. Hence it is not obvious that any automatic procedure, applied to a dictionary, will produce data any more reliable than that base. Again, automaticity does not confer reliability, any more than "book" scale does. It is here that we reveal a prejudice (and it may be no more) in favor of automaticity in lexicon building: the hope that large lexicons can be extracted automatically from machine-readable dictionaries, (MRDs), and that the very process of extraction (and the opportunity that provides for imposing uniformity and consistency) will provide better, more defensible, entries, ones which may be able to avoid the biases associated with handcrafting on whatever scale. Our prejudices are now out in the open and the problem will be to justify them in the course of this book.

Standard dictionary and encyclopedia entries, even though constructed in a principled manner over many years by professional lexicographers and encyclopedists, are designed for human, not computer, use. By preferring to use them, as a basis for NLP rather than specialized lexicons like WordNet, we are effectively introducing an explicit "serendipity" assumption: that a particular type of structure will suit our purposes better, even though it was constructed for a different purpose than the one we have in mind. This is a very strong assumption, probably inconsistent with the commonsense one that knowledge is normally collected and arranged for particular purposes, and is inextricably connected with those purposes. This is a view normally thought of as "instrumentalist" if not merely commonsense. But we shall indeed question it in this book.

One aspect of our defense will be that dictionaries contain much more information than they appear to. In that way they are quite unlike the explicitly formal lexicons such as WordNet or Cyc, which contain exactly what they appear to and (hopefully) what their makers intended them to. We shall demonstrate that statistical techniques are able to extract from existing dictionaries quite different (though not inconsistent) structures from those the original lexicographers intended to express. We shall contrast what one might call the lexicographers' conscious (such as the explicit definitions) from their collective unconscious (other associative information that our techniques reveal and that we shall describe in due course). These associative techniques (see chapter 7) are closely related to statistical techniques that could be applied to any text corpus to elicit associations of word use, clusterings of senses, and so forth, that the individual authors had no means of knowing they were employing.

The area we are now entering is the new and interesting one of the intimate relationship between computation over dictionaries and over text corpora. New dictionaries are now being explicitly constructed by reference to computation over corpora (Sinclair 1987b). We also discuss the degree to which word sense distinctions can be made by statistical methods alone, applied to corpora, as well as "hybrid" methods such as the extraction of core meanings automatically from existing dictionaries, as we noted, and then tuned, or refined, against texts to give the particular qualities, features, or what you will, of special text types.

This notion of tuning, which we discuss in detail below, is one way of escape from another well-known trap in this area, that of how to choose a text corpus to represent a whole language. At the moment the air is full of discussion of the building of national text corpora in various languages all over the world, all chosen on impeccable grounds, but which are, in the end, academic and political choices as to what texts are most acceptable as representing a particular language. No one seriously suggests collecting a corpus on purely quantitative grounds to represent the state of a language in the demotic terms of the quantity and type of the actual words produced by writing or speaking, and as read by whole populations.

On such a criterion, the *New York Post* would have to be represented by a far larger part of a corpus of modern American English than *The New York Times*, as would *19* or *Honey* as opposed to *Mind*, in Britain. But if a "properly balanced" corpus is in fact a chimera and there are only corpora for particular purposes and particular topics, then the notion we mentioned, of word senses as extracted from dictionaries for their "cores" (a notion we make precise later) and then "tuned" against a particular corpus for whatever task or subject area we have in mind, may produce a viable and defensible notion of word sense. One would hope to have, by such a method, a notion that what one might call a sense definition is not merely static, which is what one might call any sense definition tied only to a dictionary of past stable usage.

So confused has this struggle over corpus choice become that an observer can see within it the return of Chomskyan arguments long thought banished from an empirical and nonintuitive linguistics. It will be remembered that part of Chomsky's criticism of empirically gathered linguistic data was that the data had, in the end, to be subject to the test of linguistic intuition (1986). The corpus movement (including the grammar projects of Quirk, Greenbaum, and others, and the lexical computation movement itself) was designed to take us away from all that wrangling over intuition and the starring of made-up sentences (Quirk et al. 1985).

But it has not quite worked out as expected, for even the data collectors are now sometimes prepared to say in public that if the corpus they have collected does not happen to contain the sense of the word they want, and one that their intuition tells them should be there, then they will massage the corpus boundaries until it does contain it. One should not laugh at this; intuition will not just go away in the face of data, and we are rediscovering, in empirical linguistics, no more than the great Kantian truisms that intuition without data is blind, and data without intuition are meaningless.

The methodologies that we advocate, and seek in the work of colleagues, in this book are what is becoming known as hybrid: an inspiration that is not Kantian at all, but in tune with the more general move in AI toward a compromise between quantitative and symbolic methods. We see this combination as the best approach to what is, in effect, the Holy Grail of this book: a *neutral, machine-tractable, dictionary (MTD)*.

Machine tractability is a basic notion that we want to contrast with machine-readable, a goal easily achieved with a tape reader. Machine tractability means much more: first, it means all the cleaning-up operations on tapes that Boguraev describes, but it means, in addition, the conversion of an existing dictionary to a form that is appropriate for further CL tasks (Boguraev, 1989). Such a dictionary normally contains a full range of types of linguistic information, but, as we noted, we choose to concentrate on the semantic and pragmatic, while mentioning the others. We restrict our goal, for the reasons we gave, to MTDs that are automatically extracted, and not explicitly constructed by hand. The notion of an MTD arose within the context of our work at New Mexico State

University (NMSU), described below, and we want to reemphasize the notion above, since the term has been used by some (e.g., Nomura 1993) to mean *any NLP lexicon whatever*, which loses some of the force of "tractable."

The term "neutral" begs another set of large questions. We rejected earlier the idea of neutral, "purpose-free," corpora and handcrafted lexicons (like Cyc and WordNet) but now bring the term back for an extracted MTD. The reason is this: it is a commonsense observation (which does not prove it true, of course, and it has been strongly questioned by Atkins and Levin 1990) that all dictionaries contain much the same information about the meaning of a given sense of a word. If that is true (and we discuss it in detail later), then one might go on to assume that that common information could be put into a neutral form so that it could be transformed subsequently into any linguistic format to suit the needs of a particular program.

If there is any element of neutral content in computational lexical semantics (as opposed to the multiplicity of formats and notations dependent on particular linguistic theories), then we hope to locate it in terms of our own work and that of others described in this book. It is a worthy goal, whether or not it can be reached.

Chapter 2

A Short History of Meaning

Meaning is a large and traditionally difficult topic, but since dictionaries claim to capture the meanings of words, we cannot ignore it. Moreover, much computational linguistics, and especially within the AI tradition, has claimed to be computing meanings in one way or another.

One might say that lexicography is a "craft theory of meaning." Todd noted in the nineteenth century that a lexicographer must write of what he does not understand, but lexicographers cannot in *general* be writing down the meanings of words they do not understand (Johnson [1755] 1827). The interesting question is how and why did the notion arise that one could write down not only word lists of parts and wholes but then move on to explaining or describing the meanings of words? This is an extraordinary shift, from the earliest thesauri, or word treasuries, that listed such items as the detailed parts of a bishop's armor, or the estates of a lord, to word lists that were explanatory synonyms. Here is one of those historical-cultural shifts, full of philosophical signifiance in the European tradition of thought, where words come explicitly to refer to one another in an organized manner.

One may then ask a second question. In Hanks's (1991) terms, "How is a lexicographer to know what any word means?" And, one might add, how does he express it when he does? That is the very heart of the craft and we must not expect a detailed description of what is a pure skill, to be learned, not discussed. Hanks's answer is that the lexicographer has three sources of "craft knowledge":

a. A corpus of texts, well chosen of course, a tradition that begins with Johnson's six Scottish amanuenses copying the works of the best contemporary authors

b. His knowledge and intuition as a native speaker, the only source for most recent linguists but here just one among several

c. The tradition of consulting previous dictionaries and grammars

It is (c) that ensures, at worst, plagiarism, but, at best, the continuity and consistency one expects in a legal system of precedent. In this book we shall be concerned with all three and what can be done to systematize and automate their interaction. Hanks and his colleagues have done much to show that systematic computer access to large corpora (under [a] above) undermines entrenched evidence of types (b) and (c): for example, that "take" in English rarely occurs as a verb with any of the contentful senses found under its definitions, but almost always as the vacuous auxiliary in a phrasal verb, as in "take part," "take a break," etc.

As we shall see later in this book, the craft of dictionary description is not a fixed thing but has itself been subject to influences from the "theory of meaning." Hanks (1987), for example, has argued forcefully that in the eighteenth and nineteenth centuries lexicographers came under the influence of logical doctrines of composition, substitutability, and the role of definition, and it is from these that he, along with Sinclair, sought to rescue the discursive pre-Johnsonian tradition of definition in COBUILD by means of a style in which meaning definitions are associated explicitly with particular selectional preferences of the word being explained. But all that is for later, for now we must turn to those theories of meaning themselves.

The function of this chapter is to look quickly at the systematic study of meaning, so as to see which parts have been taken up in craft and computational lexicography, and which parts rejected. We shall be as brief as possible, and will, at every stage, try to keep in mind that we are discussing meaning only in the context of symbolic expressions and manipulations that a lexicographer or computer might carry out.

Meaning as Nonsymbolic

A. The protoreferential theory of meaning, that meanings are the actual objects out there in the world that words refer to, sometimes thought of (e.g., by Wittgenstein) as being the oldest one in the book, that of the God of Genesis. It is almost impossible to hold that the meaning of words really are physical objects, for fear of coming under Swift's stricture in the *Voyage to Laputa*:

many of the most Learned and Wise adhere to the new Scheme of expressing themselves by Things; which hath only this Inconvenience attending it; that if a Man's Business be very great ... he must be obliged in proportion to carry a greater Bundle of Things upon his Back, unless he can afford one or two strong Servants to attend him. (Swift, 1726/1983, p. 235)

The view is often adapted in more modern semantic theories to claim "abstract objects" as the meanings of words, which in turn become algebraic constants in a calculus, with the effect that this view becomes indistinguishable, when put into operation, from a "meaning as symbols" theory (i.e., [K] below).

B. The manipulative or action theory of meaning, whose best exemplar is something like the fact that the meaning of "tying your shoelaces" can be nothing other than the action of tying shoelaces itself, that is, something you do not explain (with words) but *show*. More complex versions distinguish between who it is whose action or behavior constitutes meaning, namely, that of the hearer or the speaker. The "speech act" tradition in philosophy and linguistics belongs here too, whether its proponents would like it to or not, insofar as it has nonsymbolic content.

C. The verification view, that meaning is processes of verification, is a theory that is now a little out of fashion, but contains an important strain of empiricism. In this view the meaning of a sentence (and it is a view of *sentence* meaning) is simply the procedures that could be carried out to see if it were true, with the implication that, if there are no such procedures, it has no meaning. A version of this, within physical science, was called operationalism (Bridgman 1936).

Intermediate Cases

These are all, to some degree, abstract procedures that play the role of meanings, and the intermediacy comes from the problem of deciding whether the explanation of meaning lies in the procedures themselves or in their symbolic representations.

D. The procedural view of meaning (Woods 1978), a view normally stated only in AI, but with strong references back to operationalist and verificationist procedures in science. Computation is the only area in which any reasonable form of distinction can be made between procedures executed or carried out and their formal description. This notion, of "execution," is crucial in computation, and is why one may look to the subject for insight into the role of procedures in explaining meaning.

E. The functional view, often ascribed to Frege. It is the claim that meaning is a functional mapping between intensional logical descriptions (usually expressed as truth conditions) and worlds of which they may or may not be true. It is thus a mapping of truth conditions to worlds and can be thought of as a procedural version of (I) below. The functions are purely abstract procedures and, unlike computational functions, are never actually "executed."

F. The connectionist or subsymbolic view of meaning (see extended discussion in Partridge and Wilks 1990). This view of the meaning of word symbols is that they are "grounded" in subsymbolic activity in brains or artificial networks. Just how this transition to the symbolic from something nonsymbolic takes place has not yet been made clear, at least not in terms of symbols.

G. The information theoretic view of meaning. This is an old theory but has returned recently in connection with statistical applications to texts and dictionaries. It is essentially a "code" view of meaning where having meaning consists in an agent making choices (of symbols) among the available candidates: for example, the letter *a* has meaning in English just insofar as it has been chosen from among 26 candidates, and hence its "meaning" is different in Italian where only 20 choices are available.

H. The meaning-as-stereotypes view: the notion that the meanings of terms are not captured by necessary and sufficient conditions, as is implied by some of the other views, especially the truth condition view ([I] below), but are rather expressed as a stereotypical individual, who may not meet any set of necessary and sufficient conditions at all. This can seem a form of referential view (to a stereotypical individual) but is normally interpreted in terms of descriptions. Putnam (1977) has given a defense of such a position and it is the view of meaning with the strongest psychological tradition of support (Rosch 1976).

Meaning as Symbolic

I. The truth-conditional theory of meaning, often associated with Davidson (1970), claims that the meaning of a sentence (and it is again a theory of sentence meaning) is the conditions under which it would be true. These are normally taken (if this position is to be distinct from [C] above) as formal conditions, not procedures to test the conditions against the actual world.

J. The meaning-as-deductive-relations theory. In its crudest form this takes the view that the meaning of a sentence is what it implies or what is deducible from it. A recent, odder, version has surfaced in AI (Hobbs 1987) where meaning is what implies the sentence in question, that is, what it follows from. The best-known version is Quine's (1960) "meaning holism" where the meaning of a sentence is a function of the whole set of relations it enters into with all other sentences of its type (e.g., as embedded within a scientific theory).

K. This can be crudely put as "meaning is other words or symbols." It is the one closest to craft theories of dictionary meaning, and lurks beneath many other theories of meaning, and is found explicitly in Wilks (1975a–c). It is certainly present in Wittgenstein's (1953) "Words have the meanings we give them and we give them meanings by explanations." At other times he expressed a version quite close to Quine's (see [J] above), that sentences are given meaning by their place and function in arguments and justifications; the best-known simplification of that was "meaning as use."

One could also put here "lexical-field" structuralist views of word meaning that claim that words take their meanings from their relations in a field of related words (e.g., "brown" has meaning in English by relationship to other named colors—a matter that varies from language to language and not with respect to the external world). This is a view quite different from other words or symbols functioning as explanation.

It will already be clear that there is no right taxonomy of meaning, and the 11 types distinguished above are also interrelated and could, with time and care, be reduced to a smaller number. Conversely, subtypes have been packed together above and the number could have been considerably larger. The theories could have been separated by word vs. sentence-based theories of meaning, but, as will become clear, that distinction is not as firm as one would hope, if only because sentence forms can be set up precisely to express the meaning of a single word, as in "Chrysanthemum means a flower originating in Japan," etc.

We discuss in some detail below those theories from the list above that have most relevance to a dictionary and text theory of word meaning. We shall not attempt to adjudicate between them here, since each rests on some firm intuition that confirms its value and permanence, but our prejudice will be clear: that any computational-based theory of lexis has to come down in practice (and had better therefore in theory as well) to some form of (K) above, that meaning is other symbols, and those always turn out to be words.

A. Meaning as Reference

One mentions this theory normally only to dismiss it: the view that the meanings or reference of words are things. We all have this deep feeling that sometimes we can and do successfully point to things and refer to them, but those experiences seem the exception rather than the norm after we are 2 years old, and are therefore too thin to be a ground of all meaning. One sends the theory off with some quote from Wittgenstein (1953) such as:

"That philosophical concept of meaning (i.e. as referring or pointing) has its place in a primitive idea of the way language functions" (§2).
   "So one might say the ostensive (i.e. pointing to) definition explains the use— the meaning—of a word when the overall role of the word in language is clear" (§30).

The sentiment in the last quotation was the one picked up and developed by Quine in his *Word and Object*, where he argued, in the situation of an anthropologist confronting an unknown tribal language, that the people observed as always saying "Gavagai" in the presence of a rabbit (even if they pointed as they said it) could not be said determinately to mean or refer to a rabbit as they did so: we might not know enough about what part of the rabbit they referred to, or that it was, in their coherent but quite different belief system, the spirit of their grandmothers to which they intended to point. Quine's point was our lack of access to the role of the word in their whole language, and the imagined situation of the anthropologist, or linguist, wholly outside the language and culture served to reinforce that point. Quine extended this to a wider indeterminacy, of meaning, and so of translation. One could not know either, in any manner that Quine would consider determinate, that a word uttered in such a context was not a name at all but some form of far more complex action, as in Austin's (1962): " 'Bull' or 'Thunder' [which] ... could be a warning, information, a prediction ..."

   There were simpler, less global, but more traditional objections: the objects we see and refer to in the here and now are only a small fraction of the entities, dead, imagined, abstract, fantasied, or conjured up only by the vague mention that we introduce into almost every sentence. It is inconceivable, the counterargument goes, that an account that is based on real tangible objects should also happen to serve as the ground of meaning for the majority of sentences when those are unavailable for one reason or another. The basis of meaning, it concludes, cannot rest on the minority of cases of physical presence.

   This old struggle, now seldom seen in action, may seem far from the concerns of lexicography and dictionary meaning, since objects are never introduced into dictionaries. Yet, pictures of them increasingly are. What was once an idiosyncrasy of German and French dictionaries is now standard for explaining in a diagram, quicker than a description can, where the parts of a car fit.

There is an eccentric variant of (A), sometimes held by those in areas related to our concerns, namely, that terms refer not to the external objects they name but to associated brain areas, for example, "the ANIMATE area of the brain." A theory of this general sort has been detected by some critics in Fodor (1975). Schank (1975) at times seems to have espoused a grounding of his primitive actions (see [K] below) in terms of brain hardware. The theory is, in a sense, irrefutable, but also quite vacuous since nothing whatever turns on there actually being such brain parts. They have the same status as the abstract referents that ground formal semantics, as noted above, though appearing more scientific. Yet the claim has no actual connection to neurophysiology at all.

B. Meaning as Physical Manipulation, Action, or Behavior

The stage may be set by an initial quotation from Longuet-Higgins (1972, p. 1173): "Not only should we think of the production and comprehension of natural utterances as processes describable in algorithmic terms; but that our utterances themselves should be thought of as pieces of program whose effect is to modify one another's behavioral predispositions." The meaning of an English sentence, in this view, is a program or procedure that runs in a hearer. The essence of the Davies and Isard (1972) view is a development of this: that the meaning of what I say is all that happens to you, or what you do, on hearing it.

This position has a great deal in common with a version of speech act theory (Austin 1962, Searle 1969), which was an outgrowth of another view of Wittgenstein's, namely, that language behavior and physical behavior in general were not wholly distinct. Wittgenstein is said to have been converted from his earlier view that language displayed an underlying logical form during a train trip with the economist Sraffa, who flicked his fingers from under his chin in the Italian way and asked Wittgenstein, "And what pray, is the logical form of that?"

Austin did much to develop this continuity of saying and acting by considering the performances available to users of a wide range of English verbs, much wider than many would have expected. A key notion for Austin was convention (developed further by Lewis among many others) in saying as in acting: "Conventional procedures having a certain conventional effect." It is clear here that we are dealing with acts, actions of speaking and not procedures in the sense of section D below). Austin contrasted his view with that of (essentially symbolic) truth conditions as bearers of meaning (cf. chapter 3, section I). "I am running" is true in just those circumstances where I am actually running but, says Austin, "I apologize" is not like that, and is more like running itself, a real action. We cannot ask whether "I apologize" is true or false; it is something we do. We can ask that of "I am apologizing" but that happens not to be a way of apologizing.

Grice (1957) pursued a related line by distinguishing a "natural" use of "mean" which he contrasted with a non-natural use, one where humans convey or give meaning by actions: "Spots mean measles" is the former because nature does not mean anything at all. But "The white smoke means a Pope has been chosen" refers to an action that has or gives meaning.

Davies and Isard's view is simpler for discussion than speech act theory proper because it transfers the whole analysis to the hearer/receiver: what is meant is what goes on (a) internally (in the brain/mind/machine) and (b) externally (behavior). Thus it is not at all a simple behavioral theory of meaning (as would be "the meaning of my command is your response"). Its attraction is to ask us to consider saying "wash the dishes" to a person and to a robot dishwasher. In the latter case we might agree that the English sentence was no more than a command in a very high-level programming language. Why then, Davies and Isard might ask, treat its meaning and function differently in the other situation?

This a/b distinction can also be seen in the work of Winograd (1972) where an English sentence is translated into a piece of MICRO PLANNER formalism (say "here are 10 blocks on the table") and this code is in some sense (a), the internal intensional, or unrun procedural, meaning of the sentence, and when that piece of program is run, it produces the names of the 10 blocks and thus the external behavior (b) is just the declaration of the result.

Once a program is compiled, the question arises as to whether the listener should run it. Should he pass the salt? Should he tell the speaker when he last saw his father? (Johnson-Laird 1978).

Johnson-Laird does not actually say that questions have no meaning if we cannot form up programs for answering them definitively. He admits that some questions may not translate to executable programs and, indeed, so many examples come to mind, from "Is Fermat's last theorem true?" downward.

If I say to you, "Pass the salt," and you do, is it plausible to say you are running my program? Moreover, the procedure you form up, if you do, may be very odd in many ways; it may cause you to knock over the pepper while reaching for the salt, or cause you not to move a muscle but merely to glower. Worse still, you might not understand English and be thinking, "Is this broken French?" Are all these possible meanings of "Please pass the salt" in English? Again, surely not. The fundamental problem here concerns the inner reference of a procedure: the abstract referents reached when the program is run in a mind or brain (such as Winograd's block names B1, B2, etc.) and the outer reference of procedures (the real physical objects reached, such as the chair I sit on) when we identify things in the world. The logical words "denotation," "reference," "extension" are all contaminated with both sorts of entity. Davies and Isard conflate the location of both sorts of referent into meaning, as well as the procedures themselves; the inner abstract referents are found in (a), and the real-world referents (of doctrine A above) in (b).

A possibility we shall need to consider in the next chapters is that it may be possible to conflate two views of meaning here by allowing that meanings can be expressed in other symbols, whether logical items in formal structures or just words, but that the meanings of the basic definitional predicates, or PRIMITIVES, must themselves be expressed through experience, such as physical manipulations of the world, as doctrine B requires. An example would be the explanation found in telephone booths in various European countries as to how to use the phone. The purpose of the explanatory text is not really to explain how to use a phone to someone who has never seen or used one before. It is to show the differences of use in the country you happen to be in. The text assumes you already understand all the "manipulative primitives" such as HOLD-RECEIVER-TO-EAR or INSERT-COIN. These themselves are not explained but assumed as known from real experience. It could be argued that dictionary explanations may be in the same position. For example, "having," and "taking" are not really explained in dictionaries, even though their headwords appear there, for they are given only vacuous definitions and are assumed understood from the experience of everyday life.

C. Verificationism

This is a philosophical doctrine of sentence meaning, widely considered refuted, but which never quite goes away for good. In its (Ayer 1946) older forms it was stated as, "The meaning of a sentence is the method of its verification," and it was intended to meet the philosophical needs of empirical science. The knockdown argument against it, known to every generation of philosophy student, was that the principle could not give meaning to itself, for it was unverifiable, and therefore represented more of a methodological choice than a proposition with meaning defensible in its own terms.

A version of Winograd's program as a manipulative theory, presented at the end of section B above, is also very much in the spirit of verificationism, or those versions of intuitionism in mathematics that claim that we cannot know the meaning of a statement unless we know its proof. Fodor argued against Johnson-Laird's procedural theories (see [D] below) as no more than old-fashioned verificationism: that the meaning of a sentence is the set of procedures for its verification or falsification. But Johnson-Laird's case is not quite that, as we shall see in a moment, for verificationism equated meaning to real world procedures, squinting down microscopes and so on, while Johnson-Laird's procedures are both those and others in the head or computer, which is what makes them even odder than classic real-world procedures as explications of meaning.

D. Procedural Semantics

This is an essentially AI theory and has argued, in various ways, that the meanings of symbols, chiefly in computations that express intelligent functions, are themselves procedures, rather than any kind of entity. Versions of such a theory have been put forward by Winograd (1972), Woods (1978), Johnson-Laird (1978), and Wilks (1981), and the notion has been attacked by Fodor on the grounds that all such theories are in fact grounded in the bottom-level machine code of actual computing engines, which really provide the referential entities in question. This was strongly denied by some of the theory's proponents listed above, by making use of the principle that the semantics of different "program levels" are independent, and so the semantics of one cannot be a semantics for another.

The roots of such a procedural theory of meaning in AI are many, and everyone will prefer his or her own; one appropriate source would certainly be Wittgenstein's notion of application as essential to the meaning and function of structures: "We cannot compare a picture with reality if we cannot lay it against reality as a measuring rod" (Wittgenstein 1953, §43).

The importations of Wittgenstein into this discussion are not random or unmotivated; his original anticipation of speech act theory (1953), unlike that of Grice and Searle, had no formal semantics hidden at its core. However, procedural semantics (PS) as a home-grown AI approach to meaning is not just a revamping of the meaning-as-use (see [K] above) theories of the followers of Wittgenstein that were once opposed to the theories of contemporary formalists, and for two reasons:

1. Meaning-as-use was essentially a behaviorist theory where mind was concerned (Ryle 1949) and had no interest at all in whatever mechanisms underlie behavior or performance, whereas PS is also a possible account of such underlying mechanisms.
2. PS, like truth-conditional semantics, is essentially formalist.

One could say that the genesis of PS is an attempt to answer Lewis's (1972) criticism that the use of items like CAUSE, ANIMATE, GOAL, etc. in a language of representation is mere "markerese": the translation of one vague language, like English, into another vague language. He claims to offer a translation into something quite different: of English, say, into truth conditions (view I below) which can be evaluated in terms of the entities denoted, including truth values (truth and falsehood), and so provide the link between the representational system and the real world. This and only this, Lewis would say, deserves the name semantics.

One version of PS would be Johnson-Laird's discussion of the "procedural meaning" of terms like chair: "Consider how we might represent the meaning of a word like chair. The intension of the word chair must include a statement of function. The function, we are told, is to be unpacked in terms of possibility: an object serves the function of a chair because among other things, it is possible to sit on it and rest against its back." (Johnson-Laird 1978, p. 372).

Let us leave possibility on one side for a moment. The question that the passage will have raised in many readers' minds will be whether the writer has implied that the procedural meaning of "chair" is a procedure that recognizes chairs by taking into account their possible functioning, as well as their procedural properties. In short, is the meaning of a word such as "table" more than a set of procedures for determining its extension? Johnson-Laird explicitly asserts that it is: "It is necessary to distinguish between the concept of a table and the perceptual routine for identifying a table." (p. 381).

An issue worth passing mention at this point is the degree to which Johnson-Laird's claims for PS are purely formal, in the sense of not having material consequences in terms of real procedures (whether external or internal to the organism or automaton) but are merely predilections for a particular way of *describing* what one does. In this sense of "formal," Winograd showed that a classic form of the procedural-declarative controversy was purely formal in that, at bottom, it came down to a choice of ways of describing the same real procedures (Winograd 1973). Johnson-Laird (1978) refers to that dispute and claims to be taking up an intermediary position, but the upshot of that dispute is that to call what one uses procedures as opposed to declarations is a purely formal matter. So if this doctrine is to have concrete content, then either we must be equating meanings with concrete *executed* procedures in some device and not merely with formal *descriptions* of procedures, or we are equating meaning with procedures no matter what their explicit form of description, but with the provision that they could be carried out. In practice this would be ensured by their being expressed in a standard form of programming language or pseudocode.

E. Fregean Functionalism

Behind most recent intensional logics for natural language such as Montague's (1974) is the Fregean view of meaning as a special kind of function: one that maps, in the classic manner, from intensional symbolic descriptions to states of affairs in possible worlds. This last notion is one Montague has used but is not essential to the basic functional notion; for earlier philosophers, it would have been a mapping to the real world. There are more and less procedural versions of such logics, Hintikka's (1973) being much more so. Nonetheless, all such routes to a theory of meaning, serviceable or not, seem to go via some form of formal semantics in the Frege-Tarski tradition. In Montague's intensional logic, the mapping procedure to the possible worlds is a set of abstract procedures and certainly not concrete computational procedures in the sense of (D) above. The purpose of identifying the meaning with the function itself is to avoid the difficulties we have seen in identifying it with either (or both) of the referents (view A) or the form of the truth conditions (view I below).

F. Connectionism

Connectionism is the cluster of AI theories which assume very simple computing units, connected in very large numbers, and "learning from experience" by means of shifting aggregated weights in a network. This development may offer a way forward in many areas of AI, including the computational semantics of natural language. Connectionism subscribes to many of the standard antilogicist arguments by arguing for (1) the integration of semantics and syntax (not a parallelism of syntax and semantics as in Montague grammar, but of their inseparability); (2) a continuity between linguistic and other forms of world knowledge (and again, not in the sense of simply assimilating the former to the latter as some logicist and "expert-system" approaches do); and (3) and a type of inference that is not reconcilable with the kind offered by logic-based approaches.

Moreover, connectionism has stressed such notions as "competition" between representational structures where the stronger, more connected, one wins, a notion to be found explicitly in computational semantics systems such as preference semantics (Wilks 1975b, c, 1977). An important difference, as regards lexical ambiguity resolution in particular, arises between so-called subsymbolic or distributed approaches within connectionism (Smolensky 1987) and those usually called localist (Cottrell 1985, Waltz and Pollack 1985; see also discussion in Partridge and Wilks 1990).

This difference bears very much on the issue of representation. In a subsymbolic approach to computational semantics one would not necessarily expect to distinguish *representations* for particular word senses; they would be simply different patterns of activation over a set of units representing subsymbolic features, where similar senses would lead to similar patterns. On the other hand, localist approaches to computational semantics have assumed distinguished word senses in their symbolic representations at the outset and have then given weighting criteria for selecting between them. This difference is crucial in disputes about whether there are or are not mental representations of word senses, and whether, if there are, one might expect to construct machine models of them. Mainstream AI remains, at the time of writing, still firmly committed to the notions of symbol manipulation and explicit representations.

G. Meaning and Information Theory

The information-theoretic approach to language structure goes back to early results on the degree to which natural languages are redundant methods of conveying information. At every level of language structure we could make do with fewer symbols than we in fact use; commercial speedwriting and advertising systems make do with shortened words. Everyone who has written a telegram or wire, where words are charged individually, knows how many can be taken out so as to leave the message intact. Information theory is the formalization of such notions of the dispensability of symbols because some of them are predictable from others. Its main field of application has been the transmission of phone messages where every bit costs money.

The classic application in NLP was Markov chain redundancies (Mandelbrot 1961) applied to word sequences in English. If we think of a sentence as words emitted from a device in linear order, where the probability of each word emerging is a fairly simple function of the words that have already emerged, then one can imagine driving the generating device with probabilities gained from very long and laborious computations of actual sequencing in large corpora. The key to the matter is the length of the chain. So if the chain is very short, so that each word produced is driven by a table of sequences of two words and their pairwise likelihoods in English, then after "the," say, almost any English noun would be equally probable and sound equally natural.

One could continue this process, pair by pair, but we know that the result would soon sound odd because the later members of the chain would have no natural tie to preceding elements more than one item back. It all sounds like a party game, and it was against this view of language, among others, that Chomsky's (1981) initial campaigns for a formal theory of language were directed. However, there was always the suspicion that if only the probabilities were from long enough chains, sequence redundancy would be sufficient, so that, in a parody of this view, a novel might be no more than a Markov chain 75,000 items long! In fact the joke shows the problem clearly because, as far as word items are concerned (as opposed to counting typical sequences of larger structures, such as noun phrases, by type), it is hard to compute useful Markov chains of more than a few items: the computation effort is simply too great and the number of exact recurrences in a corpus is too small.

This methodology was extended conceptually to deal with questions of meaning by Carnap and Bar-Hillel (1952) though without any practical consequences. However, a striking practical demonstration has recently been given at IBM, where Brown and colleagues (1991) have produced a system to translate between English and French based entirely on statistical associations obtained within and between long stretches of parallel English and French text from the Hansard report of the proceedings of the Canadian Parliament. They have obtained results of about 45% of new sentences translated correctly, a figure far higher than many would have expected, and they may go much further.

All this forces one to think again about the relation between statistical information theory and language processing for tasks that seem to require the processing of meaning, such as translation. In one sense there is nothing at all about meaning in this approach; questions of meaning are essentially replaced by questions about quantitative symbol choice. Meaning is a matter of choices and the likelihood of any given choice as opposed to the others available at the same point. Information theory has analogues to certain symbolic views to be discussed under section K below. Lexical field theory assigns no meaning to words as such, for they have meaning by qualitative contrast to others in the same field or sets for example, north is what is not south, east, or west. In preference semantics (Wilks 1975a), having meaning is to have *a* meaning as opposed to others, and the appropriate meaning is that which sums up the likeliest set of choices.

Church and Hanks (1990) have, in recent years revived, a statistical measure called mutual information in connection with lexicography: it is the quantitative association between word pairs as a measure of similarity of meaning, together with a related measure of meaning contrast. So, for example, they took a standard statistic of mutual information to show, with respect to a large corpus, that "strong" and "powerful" tend to co-occur with different sets of successor words. Halliday (1980) had pointed out long before that although the words appear intuitively close in meaning, we only say "strong tea or coffee," never "powerful tea or coffee," and used this fact to argue the role of collocation in meaning analysis. The idea goes back to the much-quoted Firth (1957) maxim: "You shall know a word by the company it keeps."

Mutual information statistics show, but do not say, that "strong" and "northerly" have strong overlap of information in a "wind" context; together, the two words say less than either says alone, because the second is highly predictable from the first on a large number of occasions. Having made the choice of "strong," then, the choice of "northerly" is the most probable and hence carries the least information. This is, of course, a sense of "information" not easily combined with commonsense notions if, for example, the words closely associated with either "strong" or "powerful" as immediate successors do not overlap very much (though some counterexamples, depending on the corpus, might be "resistance," "inclination," "hatred," or "desire"). If such overlap were to be a criterion of similarity of meaning, then "strong" and "powerful" would seem to have little to do with each other, although we intuitively feel them to be closely related in meaning. In later chapters we explore the relations between these empirical notions of "mutual information" and notions of meaning that we can understand. The test, as always, will be whether crucial empirical results follow that assist with any of the practical language-processing tasks that we have defined. In the end, as Hanks puts it (1991, p. 37): "Explanations come out of the head, not out of the text" (see chapter 6).

H. Meanings as Stereotypes

It has been observed by many writers that the definition of classes, and hence of the meanings of their names, by necessary and sufficient conditions for membership is inadequate over wide ranges of phenomena, and showing this was a main feature of Wittgenstein's philosophical program:

One might say that the concept of game is a concept with blurred edges ... But is a blurred concept a concept at all? ... Is an indistinct photograph a picture of a person at all? Is it even always an advantage to replace an indistinct picture by a sharp one? Isn't the indistinct one often exactly what we need? (Wittgenstein 1953, §71).

All this is now believed by some to have been put into operational terms by theories like "fuzzy logic." Putnam's approach was different: it accepted Wittgenstein's point about the inadequacy of definition (as yielding meaning) and, like him, sought to identify meaning with stereotypical examples of concepts. Thus, for Putnam a typical lemon would be yellow, ovate, wrinkled, and so forth, even if many of those in the store were actually green. Putnam argued that the price to be paid for this use of commonsense stereotypes as bearers of meaning was that the stereotype no longer served to pick out a class in the world as a classic Fregean intension was supposed to (see section E above). A great deal of empirical psychological research has been done (Rosch 1976) to determine how far humans identify word meanings with stereotypical exemplars.

Mellor (1977) has argued that Putnam is fundamentally mistaken in that the Fregean association between intensional description and a class of entities in the world is not so easily broken; "water," Mellor argued, picks out (as a stereotypical transparent wet, drinkable, stuff) both water and heavy water. This shows that they are a natural kind, whatever scientists, who know the correct formula for heavy water, may have to say to the contrary. Nonetheless, there clearly is a role for the stereotypical, the conventional, the default, or the preferred in the establishment of a meaning. Hanks (1978) and many others have argued that dictionary description is in fact always about the typical, rather than an attempt to give necessary and sufficient conditions for being a thing of a certain type.

There is, however, another strand in Putnam's arguments on these issues, one that does much to weaken the power of his arguments about commonsense stereotypical meaning, but one that has other interesting connections to dictionary expressions of meaning. For reasons we cannot go into here, Putnam holds that scientists have in their possession real necessary and sufficient conditions, ones that do in fact serve in the proper Fregean manner to pick out extensions in the world. The average person has access only to the normal stereotype that does not, as we saw with water, pick out a natural kind class reliably. Putnam calls his placing of scientists in this elite position concerning meaning (and not only science) a "division of linguistic labor." Mellor has argued that all this is quite misguided and that scientists simply have a different stereotype, in addition to the commonsense one.

The relevance of this here is that there is, as has been often noted (Hanks 1978), a style of dictionary entry which is, in effect, Putnamian in that it defines a common concept in a scientific, rather than a commonsense, manner, and thus allows the scientific stereotype to leak into common use, in just the way that Putnam did not want for fear of bad philosophical consequences from the breakdown of the division of linguistic labor. So we have, for example, in the *Collins Dictionary*, "the duration of 9,192,631,770 periods of radiation corresponding to the transition between two hyperfine levels of the ground state of cesium-133," which turns out to be the definition of a second. Hanks complains that it defines but does not explain, which is not quite right; it explains perfectly the technical grounding or definition of seconds, *PROVIDED YOU ALREADY KNOW WHAT IT IS THAT IS BEING DEFINED*. But that, of course, is what many seek in a dictionary and they would not be satisfied by the definition above.

Grace Murray Hopper, toward the end of her life, was fond of appearing on the lecture and talk show circuit with her own explanation of time. In her case, time was equated with the speed of electricity, and she would hold up nine inches of copper wire to explain the word nanosecond. In terms of this discussion, hers was no more effective a method than the cesium 133 explanation. But hers was visual and more memorable.

Chapter 3

Symbolic Accounts of Definitional Meaning

I. Truth Conditions as a Theory of Meaning

In chapter 2 we referred to Winograd's well-known "blocks world" (1972) or SHRDLU program," which can be used to illustrate a practical AI version of a truth-conditional theory of meaning. Running a SHRDLU program can locate *referents* that are real external things (had the program had a real, external, arm, let us say) as well as abstract entities, ones supposedly corresponding to the real ones. In Winograd's SHRDLU (1972), running the formal structure constructed as the meaning representation of, say, "a big red block" locates (or fails to locate) a referent "i" (an entity within the system itself), but never the referent "e," which is to say a block, hard and shiny, out there in the real world, because the program in fact had no such arm.

But the formal meaning structures in themselves correspond exactly to what are usually called truth conditions: statements of the necessary and sufficient conditions under which a sentence is true. A component condition in SHRDLU would be (EQUDIM X), which is true if and only if some entity filling the X variable is equidimensional, such as a cube.

The truth-conditional theory of meaning is often associated with a full representational logic, in the tradition from Leibniz to Frege, including notions of compositionality and substitutability of formal items. But truth conditions considered purely as a theory of meaning can be abstracted away from any logic or representational theory, as we find in the work of Davidson. It is also, of course, a symbolic theory, whatever additional views Davidson may have on reference, because truth conditions cannot be conceived of apart from symbolic expression.

Davidson's thesis (1970) is as follows:

I suggest that a theory of truth for a language [gives] the meanings of all independently meaningful expressions on the basis of an analysis of their structure ... a semantic theory of a natural language cannot be considered adequate unless it provides an account of the concept of truth along the lines proposed by Tarski for formalized languages ... by a theory of truth I mean a set of axioms that entail, for every sentence of the language, a statement of the conditions under which it is true. (p. 177)

The requirements for a (Davidsonian) theory of truth for a language L are as follows:

1. For every sentence S of L there is a T sentence.

(T) S of L is true if and only if p.

2. The T sentences are all TRUE.
3. The T sentences are all PROVABLE.
4. From a finite number of axioms (recursivity condition).
5. The metalanguage should contain the object language.

The set of T sentences for the language as a whole (i.e., for all S) fix the meaning of the "true" for L. p is a logical description (or logical form) of S. Note the equation of logical form and truth conditions, but the claim itself can be understood and assessed without any actual logical forms being displayed. p must be componential: its structure must be such that the whole is composed of the truth conditions of its parts.

Here is the key move: Davidson believes T (a "truth" sentence) to be equivalent to M (a "meaning" sentence) as follows:

(M) S of L means p.

Which is to say, the truth conditions p are the meaning of the sentences of language L, and this for Davidson is how we understand the sentences of our own language. There are classic objections to this move, of which the best known is that necessarily true sentences can be added arbitrarily to the right-hand side, for example:

"Snow is white" is true if and only if snow is white and hats are hats.

This is reasonable as a truth condition because "hats are hats" is always true and the biconditional therefore holds. Hence it is a plausible T sentence even though a very implausible M one, that is, as a statement about the meaning of "Snow is white," which has nothing at all to do with hats. But there are much more fundamental objections. Consider some examples of Searle's (1969):

1. (1)   Bill opened the door.

2. (1)   Sally opened her eyes.

3. (4)   The carpenter opened the wall.

4. (3)   Sam opened his book to page 37.

5. (4)   The surgeon opened the wound.

6. (13) The chairman opened the meeting.

7. (13) The general opened fire.

8. (12) Billy opened a restaurant.

Searle's case is that "open" has the same "literal meaning" in 1–5, but in 6–8, "it is at least arguable that the word has a different sense or meaning." The penalty for denying the sameness of meaning for 1–5 is "being forced to hold the view that the word 'open' is definitely or perhaps infinitely ambiguous" (Searle 1969). He goes on:

> In each case the truth conditions marked by the word "open" are different, even though the meaning is the same. What constitutes opening a wound is quite different from what constitutes opening a book, and *UNDERSTANDING* these sentences requires *UNDERSTANDING* each differently. (Searle 1969, p. 23, emphasis added)

But if that is true, then the semantic content is not sufficient for understanding, because it is not sufficient to determine the truth conditions by itself. Here Searle is clearly using "semantic content" to mean roughly what one would get from a dictionary definition of the sense that 1–5 share (if they indeed do). He reinforces his position with examples like "Bill opened the mountain" where, he says, we grasp the meaning of the words involved, but have no idea what the sentence means (where "mean" now is more like his earlier use of "understanding"). "If somebody orders me to open the mountain, I haven't the faintest idea what I am supposed to do" (Searle 1969).

His conclusion, drawn from both types of example, is that understanding is achieved against a background of "human social practices" (Searle 1969). "We know how to open doors, books ... and the differences in that background of practices produce different understanding of the same verb." For mountains we have no such practices, though "it would be easy to invent a background that would give a clear sense to the idea of opening mountains ... but we have no such backgrounds at present." So easy is it, in fact, that all readers of Ali Baba and the Pied Piper of Hamelin have had this background for some centuries. Searle's case is that this background is not, and cannot be made, part of semantic content, and that it is not representational in nature. His reason for this is in terms of an infinite regress of the items in the representation (Searle 1969).

It may seem churlish to criticize Searle, since he is so plainly right about the inadequacy of truth conditions as providing a basis for a theory of meaning. But the consequences of what he says are very important for our overall goal of understanding lexical sense meaning, so let us pursue the case a little, remembering that Searle's views on this issue have been influential (and are closely related to Lewis's [1972] notion of convention in meaning specification) on contemporary lexicographers.

We have added parentheses to the right of each sentence number containing its sense number in the *Shorter Oxford English Dictionary*. This method (which does not depend strongly on the dictionary chosen) does not produce results that agree with Searle, that 1–5 bear the same literal meaning or that 6–8 all bear different ones. If it is objected that this is mere dictionary positivism, not to say authoritarianism, we should add that we went to the dictionary armed with strong intuitions, as strong as Searle's no doubt, that "open" in sentences 1–5 bears at least two distinct senses: the difference is that between (a) moving something in a conventional manner to allow passage (doors, eyelids) and (b) breaking into some space by making an opening (walls, wounds).

The *Oxford English Dictionary* (OED) makes this distinction more elegantly, and adds a third for books. Moreover, saying this need not bring down on one's head Searle's penalty of the "infinite number of meanings," for the OED provides a·sorting frame of some 15 (transitive) senses of "open" into which one could probably, with a little protean cut and thrust, squeeze all such examples. Whatever Searle meant by sense or literal meaning, he did not mean truth conditions, for these were equated by him with a fuller understanding than mere meaning could give. One is therefore entitled to ask what he did mean by "literal meanings," and to show that whatever it was, it is not to be found in dictionaries, a natural habitat for such entities.

Things are actually worse than this for, so slippery are meanings and truth conditions, that one who held Searle's intuitions about the relationships and divisions within the examples 1–8 could argue that "open" in 1–5 had the same meaning in the sense of the same truth conditions.

Truth conditions can be stated at many levels of generality and it is only a matter of ingenuity to state one general enough to cover 1–5 but not 6–8. In the case of our (and the OED's) intuitions as to the division of the examples (one on which 1 and 2 form a sense class) we could write the skeletal truth condition down. The fact that opening doors is different from opening eyes no more shows that the activities correspond to different truth conditions than does the undoubted difference between opening your eyes and opening anyone else's eyes. In saying this we do not for one moment wish to defend any identification of meaning and truth conditions, but only to point out that neither his, nor our, nor the OED's intuitions on the classification of examples 1–8 bear strongly on that issue.

Let us return to Searle's opposition of "background as social practice" to "background as representations." Although he is opposing sense meaning favorably to truth conditions (a view we share) Searle seems prepared nonetheless to identify truth conditions with these fuller "backgrounds." In a throwaway line Searle identifies Schank with the latter (representational) view, though many of Schank's co-workers in AI have presented strong versions of the former (practice or performance) version. Searle's sketched case against the representation version is implausible. The "infinite regress of terms" argument has a certain period charm, the problem being that it should also apply to representational languages like English in which Searle chooses to write; dictionaries give representations for words, but those words require representations, etc., so as Searle puts it, "we would never know where to stop." But, of course, we do; we stop where we do and when we like. Why should formal representations not do so too? Searle does not take the primacy of practice as seriously as he sometimes claims. At one point, quoted earlier, he argues that faced with an instruction to "open the mountain" he would not know what to do. But why should he, to achieve adequate everyday understanding? Faced with "The engineer adjusted the flow and damp rate of the nuclear generator," we may feel rather the same, but understand the sentence as well as the journalist who wrote it. Practical engineering competence cannot be a requirement for understanding in these matters. Moreover, when Searle writes of opening the mountain that a background could easily be provided, yielding understanding, he must mean a representational one (of the sort the two well-known fables give). If in fact he meant a rock mining and tunneling course, he would emerge from that still no wiser about what to expect after reading the command "Open Sesame!" in the old fable.

J. Meaning as Deductive or Inferential Relations

This view of sentence meaning is often opposed to truth-conditional meaning using a term such as "meaning holism," which is in turn identified with the doctrines of Quine, although it can be found rather earlier in Wittgenstein's form of holism embodied in such remarks as "To understand a sentence means to understand a language" (Wittgenstein 1953 §199).

The basic insight is that the truth of sentences is established not in isolation but as part of a complex system of inference. "Rats carry plague," "God is good," "This particle has spin 1/2," are all sentences whose meaning cannot be assessed apart from the world of knowledge and inference in which they are embedded.

Davidson (1959) denies this criticism, and argues that truth conditions also require logical relations between sentences. But for him this could only be deduction, which is not adequate since scientific theories (giving meaning to their component sentences) have rarely been fully deductive. In any case this denial is incompatible with his "direct recognition" view of truth conditions and their adequacy. Quine also believes that meaning is a notion derivative from truth but, unlike Davidson, he has no hope of a theory of truth for natural languages.

K. Meaning as Equivalent to Symbolic Structures

This is the core doctrine for us since it is the one closest to lexicographic assumptions and practice. The disadvantage is its breadth, since it includes within it, in some form, virtually all the doctrines of meaning within AI and linguistics.

Within AI a basic topic has always been that of general considerations, drawn from particular calculi, as to the form that machine representations of language and knowledge should take. In that enterprise no firm distinction has been drawn between the formal representation of a language, such as English, and the formal representation of knowledge of the world, independently of the language in which it is presented to a machine. The early history of AI is grounded in theorem proving by machine, and in particular Robinson's (1965) resolution method for a mechanical logic. The first substantial claims concerning the use of first order logic as a general representational language for human knowledge are in McCarthy and Hayes (1969).

That work established a school in AI for which first order predicate calculus was the natural representational device for language and knowledge, and it functioned as a representational language, largely divorced from the claims noted above about the formal semantics of that representational language. A later representational development in AI was the advocacy of a more sophisticated representational system from a logical point of view, not just first order calculus but the associated Tarskian model theory as well. This was forcefully argued by McDermott for some time (1976) though he later recanted (1987).

That approach foresaw no particular problems about natural language as such. One could describe it, perhaps a little unfairly, as viewing natural language as a side effect within the general scheme of purposive behavior by intelligent agents; language had no particular interest of its own. That view survives now in the age of expert systems or, more generally, "knowledge-based systems," where the view is often put, that if only a program had a full knowledge representation in the particular area of expertise under examination, then no problems of language understanding could arise, because to have the appropriate knowledge, appropriately coded, is also to understand whatever natural language describes the situations in question (Shagiro and Neal 1982).

Some influence was also felt in AI from the specific proposals of Montague's (1974) model-theoretic semantics for English, and that influence is seen in Hobbs and Rosenschein (1977) and Hirst (1987), though it can be doubted whether their computational and procedural work was actually dependent on the model-theoretic description they used. A persistent problem in AI is the difficulty of knowing whether, or the extent to which, a program actually functions in terms of the representation and notation used by the author to describe it. Or whether, on the other hand, the real functioning notation at the program level is largely independent of the published "theoretical" descriptions.

This problem cannot arise within logic itself; it is the existence of independent levels of formal translation into programming languages, sometimes several of them in a real implementation, that makes this gap possible. In some senses this "semantic gap" is necessary and inevitable, and Scott and Strachey (1971) showed that the semantics at different levels of expression of the "same program" were independent and indeed incommensurable. But more serious, and contingent, surprises are found in cases like Riesbeck's program (Schank 1975) to implement Schank's conceptual dependency notation, where the notation used in the program is independent of, and maybe even inconsistent with, the Schank notation it was said to implement. It is facts like these that make it hard to be clear what theory or notation a given program is "really using," and hence in what representations the meaning is considered to lie.

It is important to stress that most work in AI on the representation of natural language over the last 20 years has also been an implicit critique of the logic-based approach in that it has deliberately avoided such formalisms in favor of local ones such as conceptual dependency (Schank 1975) and preference semantics (Wilks 1975a), as well as many other variants on Fillmore's (1968) case grammar representation (see survey in Lehmann 1992) These formalisms were often considered ad hoc by the logically oriented or, as in McCarthy's view, were considered as no more than a transitional formalism between a natural language and a proper logic representation.

The question may then be asked: If AI theories of natural language do, by and large, reject logical formalisms, then what theory of meaning can they have or express by means of "local formalisms?" Insofar as there can be said to be a distinctively AI theory of meaning, it would probably be one of (A) the claim that there can be no serious theory of meaning at all independent of a (computational and symbolic) theory of beliefs, goals and plans, or (B) a contextualist theory of meaning, that symbols used in language or computation are given significance by their symbolic environments and by the processes that manipulate them, and those processes are, in their turn, also part of the symbolic environment.

View (A) would certainly (with the "computational" proviso removed for the last two authors) not be far from the views of certain contemporary philosophers critical of an independent theory of meaning: Fodor, Quine, and possibly Stich (1983).

View (B) is rarely expressed in any explicit way, but simply assumed; it certainly underlies almost all work in computational semantics that has not made some explicit appeal to a model-theoretic semantics. Schank's (1975) conceptual dependency school has made such an assumption for 20 years, even though, as we noted earlier, Schank himself (1975) occasionally argued that the symbols expressing his "primitive actions" such as TRANS, PROPEL, etc. were additionally grounded in, or referred to, particular brain items or areas.

Much the same contextualist-proceduralist assumptions were present in Wilks's (1977) work on preference semantics, which was another "coherence" view of meaning in terms of neighboring symbols and the strength of network relationships among them. This version was in fact expressed in explicit and philosophical terms (Wilks 1971) as the claim that "meaning was other words," a notion in direct descent from Saussure, where words themselves could always be unpacked endlessly by further explanations and quasi-definitions. In that view, to have meaning, for a sentence in context, was to admit of resolution to one and only one interpretation, itself symbolic. This claim had the consequence that radically ambiguous sentences, bearing many unresolvable interpretations (e.g., Chomsky's "Colorless green ideas sleep furiously"), were indeed meaningless, though not for the reason Chomsky suggested.

In spite of these apparent differences, the proponents of doctrines of meaning within AI and linguistics are not really disputing about the central issue of meaning and symbolic meaning; it is the latter, embodied in representations, that constitutes meaning, even if promissory notes are issued on formal semantics by some and on procedures by others.

The most radical critic of this whole view has undoubtedly been Quine who attacked the whole notion of there being any firm grounding for the mutual equivalence of strings of words in terms of any property we could call meaning. This was an original form of skepticism in the tradition of Hume. Quine did not argue that we never do translation adequately from a string in one language to a second string in another, only that there can be no independent, noncircular, rational ground for believing that yields an equivalence of meaning.

So he argued, all attempts to prove synonymy of word meaning, so as to build up sentence meaning, will always turn out to rest on substitution of different substrings in a single context without change of meaning, and that in turn will, sooner or later, require the identification of a special class of sentences that are said to be true by meaning alone and can be seen to be so without any knowledge of the world, such as "all red hats are hats" or "all bachelors are male." Quine argued strongly that there can be no defensible criteria that separate such sentences as true in virtue of meaning (or analytic) from those that are true because of how the world happens to be (or synthetic sentences). We shall see later that firm criteria of substitutability based on statistical analysis of texts can be produced and in such a way as to question Quine's claim, a fact first pointed out in this connection by Sparck Jones (1986).

Quine investigated the possibility of an approach to identity of meaning, or sentence synonymy, via behavioral criteria like those in the scenarios of primitive anthropological linguistics of the American structuralist type. That methodology actually proceeded by a method of word substitution to build up alternative utterances, but Quine had declared that taboo, so he pursued the possibility of a purely behavioral definition of the similarity of sentences. It will surprise no one to know that he found that inadequate: the thesis of the "indeterminacy of translation" holds that for any apparently synonymous utterances there will always be a potential infinity of other assumptions (which can be equated with the possible beliefs of the utterer one is seeking to understand with the "translation") which will fit the evidence. Hence there can be no determinate translation.

All this is true but quite vacuous; it interferes with the reality of translation, human or mechanical, no more than Hume's radical skepticism about causation interfered with physics. Davidson (1970) has attempted to mollify it with his principle of "charity" by which we understand well enough to survive in the world by assuming, charitably, that our interlocutors have much the same beliefs and goals as we do. And of course that is the basis of much computational pragmatics in AI and elsewhere (e.g., Ballim and Wilks 1991).

On the other hand, Chomsky has always been an unrepentant "representationalist" about language, believing that there is a separable area of study concerned with the formal representation of natural languages. That view aligns him with the majority of AI researchers in the area, and against connectionists, as well as those described above as having a wholly "knowledge-based" or "expert system" view of language representation. However, Chomsky never allowed his views to have any direct consequences for either natural language computation or for the psychology of language, except that he has also held (1981) that some form of "universal grammar" (not to be confused with the grammar of any particular language; it is the general form of all possible language grammars) is coded in the human brain at birth. The key matter at issue between Chomsky and much of AI research, as it is between certain groups of AI workers, is the modularity of knowledge and, in particular, whether there is a specific form of knowledge of language.

There is sometimes a confusion of terms here, in that Chomsky (along with Fodor and others) uses "module" to distinguish gross faculties, whereas in AI the term has a more empirically founded usage to denote any self-contained body of code that can be evaluated without reference to other such modules. The principal question, about the modularity of language as opposed to world knowledge, is not easy to answer, but can be thrown into sharper relief by recalling the extreme position mentioned above, that of believing that "language is a side effect." That is to say, that language is merely one among many alternative ways of achieving human ends, and often no more than a side effect of other processes, as when we shout "ouch" on being hurt. This view is perhaps the strongest of those that fall under the term "functional" view of language, adopted both by philosophers (e.g., Searle 1969) and by Schank (1975), among others in AI, with his emphasis on the roles of expectation, goals, and plans in understanding language.

In replying to Schank, Chomsky rejected all functional views of language and insisted on a language function, organ, or, in Fodor's (1983) term, a module, and found it necessary to write explicitly that "language is not a task-oriented device" (Fodor 1980). This is an extraordinary remark, devoid of any general support in that paper or elsewhere in Chomsky's work, and all the more strange coming from one who has recently adopted the manner of speaking of the "language organ" and its similarity to other organs of the human body. For to speak of organs and their development, let alone of genetic endowment, as Chomsky also does, is to speak of their function.

However much it may be the case that many humans talk for fun and without purpose, what person who accepts that language has evolved can doubt that language is in its origin and essence task-oriented? Chomsky is thus an extreme example of "meaning as symbols or representations," separating himself even from those aspects of theory (B) above in which actions, goals, intentions, and so on are themselves symbolically represented. But that language is "functional" does not exclude the possibility of a specific language module either.

The history of lexical meaning representations in linguistics proper, through Katz and Fodor (1963) to Weinreich (1966), Gruber (1965), Givon (1967), and Jackendoff (1990) appears very different from that in representational AI (e.g., Simmons 1973, Wilks 1975a–c, Schank 1975, Pustejovsky 1991, Hirst 1987, etc.), but that difference is misleading.

The content of such representations, and the primitive atoms in which they are expressed, are always strikingly similar. Consider the following sample structures (figures 3.1 and 3.2):

The differences here are far less striking than the similarities; attempts to express in coded formulas an analytic explanation of word meaning, whose primitives need not detain us here, and whose debt to case grammar is obvious in all cases. The differences, apart from mere arbitrary

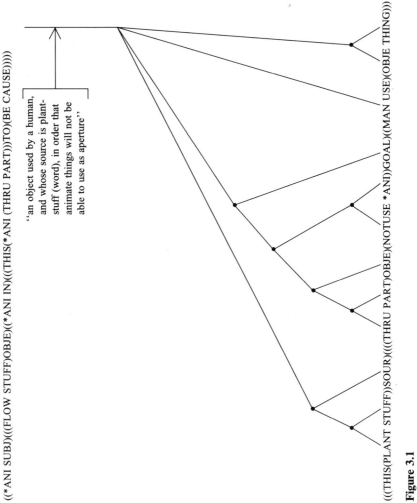

Figure 3.1
Wilks's formulas for "drink" and "door."

Jackendoff:

drink

V

---------<NPj>

[event CAUSE ([Thing]i' [event GO ([Thing LIQUID]j'

   [path TO ([Place IN ([Thing MOUTH OF ([Thing]i)])])])])}

Pustejovsky:

door (*x*, *y*)

Const: aperture (*y*)

Form: phys-obj (*x*)

Telic: pass-through (T,z,*y*)

Agentive: artifact (*x*)

Figure 3.2
Jackendoff and Pustejovsky semantic structures.

notational variation, which accounts for most of the superficial difference, are chiefly imposed by the overall theories within which these structures are intended to function. So, the Katz-Fodor structures were intended to function within the implicit procedures of a mature transformational grammar (Chomsky 1965), while the Jackendoff structures are intended to function with some later version of Chomskyan syntactic theory (Chomsky 1965).

The three more computational structures are intended to play roles within parsers of certain types: Wilks is probably the one most dependent on a certain procedural element, then called preference semantics, in that the structure above for "drink" is intended to capture the stereotypical aspect of what it coded. So in this case "drink" (as an action, not an object) was said to *prefer* an animate entity as its agent, although in the

parsing process other nontypical agents could be accepted as less preferred within an overall "most-coherent" structure. This was a deliberate
attempt to escape from the "necessary and sufficient" conditions or definitional approach embodied in other systems, such as that of Katz and
Fodor.

There is a sad historical footnote worth adding here: AI and linguistics
approaches are often now presented as joint approaches within some
overall Cognitive Science. The above structures show both how true that
is, in terms of overall similarity of appearance, but also how false. Jackendoff (1990), for example, despite the close similarity of his structures
(let alone his "preference rules") never acknowledges his debt to Schank,
who was investigating closely related structures within a different theoretical paradigm long before. Cognitive Science has, in a sense, encour-
aged the mutual reading of literatures but with some unspoken license to
pillage rather than join and attribute, as is normal in scientific progress
(Wilks 1992)

These traditions of analytic explanation are thus close to at least part of
the dictionary definition tradition, which has appeared more and less
conventional, analytic, and formal, at different times. Hanks (1978) has
pilloried the analytic tradition in lexicography by quoting definitions like
the following from *Webster's Third New International Dictionary*:

door: ... a movable piece of firm material or a structure supported usu. along one
side and swinging on pivots or hinges, sliding along a groove, rolling up and
down, revolving as one of four leaves, or folding like an accordion by means
of which an opening may be closed or kept open for passage into or out of a
building, room or other covered enclosure or a car, airplane, elevator or other
vehicle ...

One could compare and contrast this with a computational linguistics definition of door in the formulas above, where the Wilks formula is glossed
as "an object used by a human, and whose source is plant-stuff (i.e.,
wood) in order that animate things will not be able to use the aperture."

The moral here is that once you get into defining things, in whatever
formalism or language, you probably come out with something similar,
however far apart the apparent purposes and paradigms. The odd feature
of the *Webster's* definition that Hanks draws attention to is not so much
the analytic tone but the attempt to cover all the real-world disjunctive
activities in which doors function (e.g., cars, elevators, etc.) and this is
almost certainly a mistake because of their open-endedness.

In all these cases, there is a representational aspect, in which the meaning is implicitly or explicitly claimed to reside in the equation to other symbol strings, whether those are plainly words (as in dictionary definitions) or other symbols that look like words but are assigned some special "primitive-like" status, a topic we cover in depth in chapter 4. The underlying claim here is summed up in the classic Wittgenstein assertion that we give words meaning by explanations and that is precisely the lexicographic tradition as well. Murray (1884) refers to giving "explanations of meanings" as the role of the lexicographer. In Wittgenstein, however, there is another aspect, namely, that explanations also involve a non-symbolic, procedural component showing how things are, how they function. Many lexicographers would reply at this point that that is precisely what they have tried to embody in the wide range of explanatory methods tried out in recent years: pictures, typical examples, explicit usage advice, etc.

The symbolic meaning view remains unsatisfactory, at least in the English-speaking philosophical tradition, because almost no one is prepared to adhere to or even state whole-heartedly doctrines that appear in Europe as idealized text-based theories (under names like "structuralism") of meaning that one could sum up as "there are only words, words lead you to words, and you never get out." This can seem too extreme, even if one suspects it is true for large areas of intellectual life. It is certainly true of dictionaries themselves, for they are necessarily circular. Sparck Jones (1986) investigated (see chapter 6) just what the sizes of "dictionary circles" were that brought you back to your starting point by following defining words back through their definitions, and so on. The minimal dictionary circle of two members (of which the reported case was "gorse" and "furze," which simply define each other in some dictionaries) is un-illuminating, but larger ones cannot all share that property else dictionaries would be of no use.

What is inherently suspicious about all forms of the theory under discussion is:

a. It is left to some other quite different theory to show what and where are the "pegs" by which the great web of language hangs onto the world, as it surely must, somehow, somewhere.

b. The equation of meaning to symbolic entities, of whatever sort, in logic, language, etc., fails to show how the language we use connects to subsymbolic, quantitative, biological processes in the organic entities which we in fact are, and which provide the substrate for all our overtly symbolic activities, whether speaking, writing, reading dictionaries, or whatever.

The problem (a) is the one much emphasized by formal logicians who consider they understand the connection of symbols to the world, although, as we saw, they never offer anything beyond more symbols, nor can they. The way out of this dilemma probably lies in the proper engineering of manipulative prostheses that give direct access to bits of the world corresponding to at least some symbols (in the manner of theories B and D in chapter 2). And this is a scientific and engineering issue, in the way that (a) is a metaphysical one, so we may be guardedly optimistic about an outcome at some stage.

Chapter 4

Primitives in Meaning Definition

Linguistic primitives are atoms, usually corresponding in appearance and spelling to words in a natural language, such as English, and said to name basic concepts underlying human thought. They are made use of in knowledge representation programs and, more relevant for our purposes, in programs for representing and analyzing the meaning of natural language expressions. The notion of primitive is historically close to that of atom; both are entities of which other, more complex, entities are formed (in this case, definitions or symbolic knowledge representations) and which cannot themselves be broken down or defined.

Some notion of primitive is essential to any notion of formal or computational meaning description; even the restricted vocabulary of 2000 defining items in the *Longman Dictionary of Contemporary English* (LDOCE) is certainly a primitive set in our sense, and every dictionary has an (implicit) defining vocabulary smaller than its total set of defined words, so the possibility of a functioning dictionary requires some notion of primitive (Procter 1978). If it is then objected that that covers any defining vocabulary whatever, we agree, but this argument is essential because, as we shall see below, many of the opponents of primitives are opposed to any form of meaning definition or explanation, a position that undermines not only dictionaries but our whole enterprise in this book. Our position on primitives is that words and primitives are not distinct, but primitives are a purpose-defined specialized subvocabulary.

The issue is also one of great antiquity and can be traced back to the "categories of being" of Aristotle, and more obviously to the universal characteristic: the language of universal atoms of meaning with which seventeenth century philosophers believed that problems of reasoning could be definitively settled. The same issue underlay the various thesaurus projects—culminating in Roget's *Thesaurus*—to classify the universe (as synonym lists) in terms of a number of hierarchically organized categories. Again, we would maintain, the same general motivation led Ogden (1942) to draw up a limited vocabulary, called "Basic English," within which, they believed, the whole of literature could be more economically expressed.

In AI, primitive-based systems made their first appearance in the 1960s with the system of Wilks (1968), and later, Schank's system for verb decomposition (1973) and the systems of Norman (1975) and Joshi (1974), but the advocacy of such entities as essential to a computational analysis of natural language structure can be traced back at least to Masterman (1957).

A simple example of a primitive would be Schank's TRANS (later subdivided into MTRANS, PTRANS, ATRANS, and now, ATRANS1 and ATRANS2), which he considered to be a name for the single concept underlying all such acts as buying and selling, on the ground that they involved the physical TRANSfer of some entity in space, later modified to a more abstract notion of legal transfer, ATRANS. The justification for seeking such a commonality between apparently different actions or entities was the same reason that had been given in linguistics: that such a generalization would aid perspicuity in processes and substitute a single rule (using the primitive) for many, based on the corresponding surface words that TRANS was to represent. When discussing primitives it is important to bear in mind that those who advocated their use were not, in general, discussing the efficacy of particular atoms in the vocabulary of a language of representation, but of the complex formal structures of which the primitives were part, for example, conceptualizations and scripts in Schank's work, and formulas, templates, and pseudo-texts in Wilks.

TRANS is untypical of primitives in that it does not look immediately like an English word (though in fact it is short for TRANSfer). It has been argued that since primitives appear to be English words (usually written in uppercase), then that is what they are. Zwicky (1973) has argued that there are no primitives that do not have obvious "translations" into, or correspondences with, English or another language and, in that sense, there cannot be "secret, or incomprehensible, primes."

However, that was strongly denied by Katz (1966), Postal (1970, p. 113) and Schank (1975). As Katz puts it, "although the semantic markers are given in the orthography of a natural language, they cannot be identified with the words or expressions of the language used to provide them with suggestive labels" (p. 156). In other words, Katz considers that primes really exist, quite independently of the words used to describe, locate, or interpret them.

The issues in linguistics arose from the introduction of a semantic component into a Chomskyan generative grammar by Katz and Fodor (1963). This required what they called "semantic markers"; entities like HUMAN would be attached in a lexicon to the sense of "bachelor," meaning an unmarried man, but not to the sense meaning a young seal at a certain phase of its development (but to be attached to the third, meaning the holder of a first degree from a university). Later, within a group known as "generative semanticists," entities called "underlying verbs" were postulated as part of the meaning of words; thus STRIKE would be part of the underlying structure for "remind" as it appears in "Max reminds me of Pete" (Postal 1970). Thirdly, and simultaneously with the last tendency, Fillmore (1968) suggested that verbs should be derived from structures that incorporated cases, like AGENT, whose names were then used very much like those of other primitives.

If we ask what can be in a linguistic primitive set, then certain very general restrictions suggest themselves on the membership of a natural set of primitives (or markers):

a. Finitude: a primitive set should not, for example, contain the names of the natural numbers. More seriously, the set should be considerably smaller than the set of word meanings it is to encode.

b. Comprehensiveness: the set should be adequate to express and distinguish the senses of the word meanings it is to encode.

c. Independence: there should not be markers, X, Y, Z, in the set such that there is some function F such that

$$X = F(Y, Z)$$

This will not be easy to achieve if the primitives are hierarchically organized. If, for example, the set contains ANIMATE and HUMAN, it would then be nonindependent if there were any marker like RATIONAL in it, of which one might hold that HUMAN = ANIMATE + RATIONAL

d. Noncircularity: there should not be nonindependencies such that two markers or primitives can be mutually defined, as in

$$X = F(Z, Y) \quad \text{and} \quad Z = F(X, A)$$

e. Primitiveness: no marker subset should be such that it could plausibly be replaced by a smaller defining set, as in

$A = F1(P, Q), B = F2(P, Q), C = F3(P, Q)$

But these desiderata for a set of primitives bring us no closer to a satisfactory definition of what a primitive is.

Here is a provisional definition:

A *primitive* (or rather a set of primitives plus a syntax, etc.) is a reduction device which yields a semantic representation for a natural language via a translation algorithm and which is not plausibly explicated in terms of, or reducible to, other entities of the same type (e.g., structures of symbolic atoms).

This definition leaves open, as it is intended to, the serious question of whether or not primitives are explicable in terms of, or reducible to, entities of some quite other type. This is a serious question because most attacks on the use of primitives (Charniak 1975, Bobrow and Winograd 1977, Hayes 1974, Lewis 1972) take the form of demands that they be explicated in terms of some other type of entity altogether, just as most bad defenses of primitives take the form of offering some very weak equivalence between primitives and other types of entity (e.g., referential objects, brain parts, abstract denotations, etc.).

Sampson (1975) likened the role of primitives to that of English pound notes with their inscription "we promise to pay the bearer on demand the sum of one pound [i.e., in gold]". The currency promises gold, but in fact one gets only more currency for it at a bank, never gold. In the same way primitives may seem to promise access to something else, but all one ever gets by way of explanation of their meaning is more primitives, provided that their set is at least somewhat nonindependent, so that such an explication of one primitive by others can be given. There is no more trouble about that situation than there is in the present financial situation where we happily accept currency for currency at the bank, and just as in dictionaries we accept definitions of words by more words and never hope for more.

It is worth noting the ubiquity of primitives in closely related areas: the propositional calculus has connectives AND, OR, IMPLIES, and NOT, which constitute a primitive set on the above definition or, more correctly, any two of them constitute a primitive set that can define the other two. Although they are reducible to the single connective "/", the Sheffer stroke, that requires considerable effort and inconvenience. It was only later, when the truth tables were derived by Wittgenstein and Pierce, that the possibility of independent explication of the primitives arose. Only then could one give some answer to "What does AND in the propositional calculus actually mean?" Thus, if one accepts the truth tables as "giving the meaning" of the connectives, then they are no longer primitives in the sense of the above definition. Within AI, the variable SHOPPER in Charniak's supermarket frames and the basic unit PERSON in Bobrow and Winograd's KRL-O language are both primitives. They can be bound to particular shoppers or persons, but nowhere in those systems is one told what a shopper or a person is. Nonetheless, those authors would strongly deny that there are primitives in their systems, which again shows the difficulty of agreeing on what constitutes the use of a primitive.

Hayes (1974) produced a number of arguments against primitives, such as his demand to know what STUFF actually meant (where STUFF is the name for substance in Wilks's system). This is, in effect, the demand for reduction to another type of entity, in this case a model theoretic semantics (MTS) of a primitive system. Hayes's demand is that of the most famous attack on primitives: Lewis's accusation that Katz and Fodor's system was mere "translation" without any semantic underpinning:

Semantic markers are symbols; items in the vocabulary of an artificial language we may call Semantic Markerese. Semantic interpretation by means of them amounts merely to a translation algorithm ... to the auxiliary language Markerese. But we can know the Markerese translation of an English sentence without knowing the first thing about the meaning of the English sentence, ... The Markerese method is attractive in part just because it deals with nothing but symbols. (Lewis 1972, pp. 181–202)

Part of the shamelessness of the accusation, of course, is the suggestion that MTS provides something other than symbols at the end of the road! Hayes's position is closely connected to the demand for MTS of programming languages, but an important difference between the two areas (programming languages and the real world) is that there is no reason to suppose that the sets and objects yielded by the semantics of a program will be the same as the sets and objects in the real world that would be the direct denotations of primitives, such as would be determined by an MTS for the area of knowledge in question, for example, people or aircraft. Hayes seems to assume that the two formalizations (of a program that modeled some aspect of the real world and on MTS of the corresponding representation) would yield the same result, but they need not since the requirements for being an adequate set of objects for a program semantics are only that they support a formal input-output equivalence for the program, and many sets might do that. But, if the two sets of denotations are not the same, there will be problems for anyone who, like Hayes, believes that such denotations are the "real meanings" of the primitives, for which set would then be the real meanings?

The demand for an MTS of a primitive system can be put in one of three analogical ways: (1) as being like an MTS for a logic, (2) for a programming language, or (3) like the axiomatization of a scientific theory. In all three cases there is clear historical evidence that the basic systems were pragmatically useful before there were axiomatizations of them. So a demand that some MTS of primitives be given *before* such devices have any useful role in AI programs is inappropriate: the usefulness of logic over more than two millennia could not in any way have depended on there being, or not being, a formal semantics for it.

What would it be like to satisfy the demand for a MTS for semantic primitives? Heidrich (1973) has attempted to provide one for a fragment of generative semantics analysis, and in particular of the analysis of "seek" as TRY-to-FIND, where the two uppercase "underlying verbs" may be considered as primitives for the argument of this chapter. Heidrich gives, as the denotational meaning of "seek," sets of pairs of seekers and sought things. One of these sets will be that of pairs of humans and the zoological objects they are in fact seeking, a set of which can be written

((Human) (Zoological Object))

If John is in fact seeking a unicorn then the pair

(John, Unicorn)

will be in that set of pairs. Similarly "find" can also be expressed as a set of pairs of finders and found, of which a subset will be that of the human finders and the zoological objects found, and which can also be written as above, although it will not be the same set of pairs because not all things that can be sought can be found, unicorns being the logicians' preferred example.

Lastly, "try" is defined as a mapping from actors (the triers) to actions (the action tried). Thus, TRY-to-FIND will be written

((Human) ((Human) (Zoological Objects)))

where the object on the right of this pair is

((Human) (Zoological Object))

that is, the pairs which are the denotation of find. The point of the whole system is to give a guarantee that "seek" = TRY-to-FIND by defining an operator O such that:

O((Human) (Zoological Object)) = ((Human) ((Human) (Zoological Object)))

which is to say that every seeking of a zoological object by a person is a pair that is also in the pairs that are the meaning of TRY-to-FIND.

The heart of Heidrich's system is the guarantee that can be put as the claim that, for any sentence like "John seeks a unicorn," the corresponding sentence "John tries to find a unicorn" will be synonymous with it. That is to say, a guarantee that is not given by any inference rule:

(X) (Y) (X seek Y implies X try to find Y)

The thesis of this chapter—and we shall come to an exposition of it in the final section—is that any such guarantees must be misguided, for they are wholly inappropriate to the subject matter, natural language. On the contrary, "seek" and "try to find" are more or less equivalent forms of words, so much so that we might indeed use those on the right as part of a reduction language in the manner of generative semantics primitives. But there is no guaranteed equivalence and usage does not assume there is, hence no operator like O can guarantee anything, because there is nothing to guarantee. It is not merely that we can and do use "seek" so that it is not equivalent to "try to find," as in "we seek your leader" (which is more like "we want to find"), for the point would hold even if we could—quite contingently, and without guarantees—always use "try to find" where we use "seek." The serious point is that the value of such a discovery of equivalence would not be enhanced at all by the postulation of an O operator or by the notion that the synonymity rests upon or requires any selection of individuals in another calculus of markers as the "proof" above implies.

Escape Arguments

By "escape arguments" we mean attempts, by both advocates and enemies of primitives, to explicate them in terms of some other kind of entity. In that sense, the claim that semantic primitives were really the words they appear to be and no more would not be an escape argument. Nor would claims (a) that primitives are justified by the overall performance of the linguistic or AI system in which they function, nor that (b) primitives mean exactly what the rules of the primitive language allow them to mean, and no more or less. Both of these are claims to which we shall return, but for now we shall stay with "escape arguments." Katz has given a number of arguments concerning semantic primitives of this general type. In *The Philosophy of Language* he argued that primitives were psychologically real and the content of ideas (Katz 1966, p. 177).

Later, Katz withdrew the claim about psychological reality, and argued instead that primitives referred to abstract concepts (Katz 1972, p. 88). The latter is, if anything, a weaker claim because it offers less for possible refutation. The former can at least be discussed in terms of what people think their general ideas are, but the latter cannot. There has been some ingenious work within psychology proper on the status of semantic primitives, mostly in their support, and this too may reasonably be considered under the general heading of "escape arguments" (Johnson-Laird 1974, Miller and Johnson-Laird 1976, Johnson-Laird and Quinn 1976).

However, the psychological approach suffers from certain handicaps in that, given its assumptions, it is very difficult for it to eliminate alternative yet plausible hypotheses. So, for example, Johnson-Laird (1974) contains an examination of recall experiments in which subjects correctly recalled the substance, though not the surface form, of sentences. Now this is indeed general supporting evidence for a theory of semantic primitives, but it cannot confirm it over and above, say, a hypothesis that meaning is stored in terms of a theory whose primes are, let us say, binary numbers, or some other arbitrary, uninterpretable, secret primes.

There are strong considerations suggesting that there cannot be secret primes. The most ingenious of these is Zwicky's "substance theory" (1973) that depends on an analogy with notions from chemistry, and in particular the correct view of early chemists that the primes of chemistry were themselves substances in the world (like carbon) and not secret attributes that did not manifest themselves. This might seem a strong and plausible methodological assumption. There are also general philosophical considerations to the effect that there is no reason to believe that primitives and words are distinct, and that we cannot really conceive of a secret reduction language for our natural languages. However, and this is the present point, these considerations are not psychological ones, and we do not see how experimental psychology is to rule out the secret primes hypothesis.

To return to Katz for a moment: he also produces two other, quite different sorts, of argument. One is that primitives function within a linguistic theory as scientific entities, like "force" or "neutrino" functions in physics (1966) or as "number" in mathematics (1972) or, in another variation due to Chomsky, that they are items in a scientific descriptive metatheory: "The very notion 'lexical entry' presupposes some sort of fixed, universal, vocabulary in terms of which these objects are characterized, just as the notion 'phonetic representation' presupposes some sort of universal phonetic theory" (Chomsky 1965, p. 17).

These arguments are quite wrong, and not defenses of primitives we would wish to endorse for a moment; the analogy with scientific entities and metatheory breaks down as soon as it is pressed but, whatever they are, they are not escape arguments in our sense. They are, in fact, quite the opposite, since they are denials of the possibility of independent explication of primitives. The point of notions like "neutrino" is that they cannot be explicated independently of the theories in which they function. The weakness of this argument, of course, is that the *experiments* of science that indirectly explicate concepts like neutrino are not available to linguistics in any straightforward sense. However, some general functional explanation of primitives of this sort—though of an engineering rather than a strictly scientific sort—may well be a reasonable one.

Another persistent strain of argument in Katz is that markers refer not to merely psychological entities but to innate ones in some stronger sense. As Bierwisch (1970) puts it, " ... all semantic structures might finally be reduced to components representing the basic dispositions of the cognitive and perceptual structure of the human organism." Schank, too, has taken a position along these lines, and incorporates explicit symbols, such as long-term memory, into his conceptual diagrams as names of psychophysical entities. In this view there is some stronger commitment to the universality of primitives than in the merely psychological view. Moreover, this commitment should be an additional constraint on what can count as a primitive since, if primitives really refer to entities that are innate or even hardwired into human brains, then such empirical notions as the atomic weights of elements would not seem plausible candidates as semantic primitives describing the elements! The general weakness of this "escape view" is that it claims that there is some correct set of primitives open to discovery. Even if that were true, there is no conceivable way, here and now, of setting up any correlation between that right set and the primitives in actual use in linguistic systems.

And supposing the "right set" were one day discovered, how would we reconcile that with the fact that, as Goodman (1951) puts it, "the terms adopted as primitives of a given system are readily definable in some other system. There is no absolute primitive, and no one correct selection of primitives." If, say, Schank's primitive actions were located in the brain's hardware, would that necessarily constitute an "escape justification" of them superior to that of the alternative primitives in terms of which they can easily be expressed? The Schankian PROPEL, for example, seems to be paraphrasable as Y CAUSE X TO MOVE, and INGEST as Y CAUSE X TO MOVE INTO Y. But we need not pursue this choice between possible escape arguments, since the route via cognitive hardware is no more concrete or real than that via psychological-cum-mental introspection, or even abstract concepts.

Putnam's Argument

It may be of interest to note a version of the primitives-vs.-facts dispute within philosophy, or rather as a philosophical attack on the marker system of Katz, one we touched on earlier (chapter 2) in our discussions of stereotypical meaning. Putnam (1970) argued that Katz's definition of a word sense as a conjunction of markers is wrong on several grounds. First, because it is simply unrealistic when we look at the ways meanings are actually defined in dictionaries: not only by markers, but by synonyms, facts, and even illustrative quotations, etc., a point also made by Bolinger in 1965. Many of Katz's primitives or markers are of the type Putnam criticizes, as when (unmarried) appears in the lexical entry for "bachelor," but many are not, at least in the more developed forms of his work. In the entry for "chair" are forms like (something-with-legs) and (something-with-a-back) and these have the same content as complex descriptions in ordinary dictionaries. One quite legitimate criticism of Katz is that he never gives either a characterization that determines what would and what would not count as a marker, and that he never gives any syntax, as Bierwisch (1970) does, that would allow one to characterize such complex markers in terms of an inventory of simple ones. Nonetheless, he certainly does have markers with complex content.

Moreover, it is not the case, as Putnam alleges (Bierwisch 1970), that for Katz the predication of a marker to a word sense is always analytic. Much of Katz's motivation in all this work is the provision of an algorithmic explication of the notoriously obscure philosophical notion of analyticity, which is to say "how can language forms be true purely by form?" as "a red hat is red" is usually held to be. But Katz never claims that "A chair has legs" is analytic, in any sense, in virtue of the presence of (has-four-legs) in the lexical entry for "chair." The notion of analyticity has to come into this discussion, because it is an important tool—though in quite different ways—for both authors under discussion. This becomes clear when we see that Putnam's alternative proposals are to postulate a stereotypical individual and that meaning "definitions" should take the form of the statement of core facts about the stereotype, as in "A tiger has a striped skin."

Yet the opposition to all forms of analyticity is implicit in the use of "fact." The opposition is in fact false because, as we saw, Katz's notion of marker is so broad that the predication of (something-with-legs) of "chair" is just a notational variant of a Putnam core fact "A chair has legs" about a stereotype chair. That is to say, not all Katz markers are equivalent to analytic predications, and many of them are equivalent to the assertion of facts. Hence the opposition Putnam saw between his proposals and Katz's was based on the particular examples from Katz he discussed.

Moreover, the notion of stereotype may well have drawbacks that Katz's views do not. A stereotype man surely has two legs, and therefore "A man has two legs" should be a Putnamian core fact, one that may not always be true, but a reasonable guide to experience. It will have just the same status as "A man is an animal." It is, of course, just the distinction between these two facts that Katz wishes to keep central—and which Putnam cannot—namely, that the first "fact" may let us down from time to time, but the latter almost certainly will not. It was just this distinction—one which may well have its role somewhere in lexical systems that Katz, like all believers in the analytic-synthetic distinction, wished to maintain. One should also note the relevance of this dispute to the issue of a reduced language of semantic description. There is a clear suggestion that Katz's marker language is not coextensive with ordinary English (i.e. it does not simply contain the whole vocabulary of English) but that the language of core facts might well be.

Charniak's Argument

Charniak's "case" (1975) discusses the concept of case in AI systems of representation, but it also presents at least one very general argument against the use of primitives, even though its particular target is case primitives. Charniak is among those who demand some explication of primitives in terms of something else, but he is prepared to consider explicanda for primitives much more congenial to AI than those proposed by logicians. What he proposes are, in effect, procedures to be associated with a particular primitive "meaning (CASE) = The set of inferences one can make about X, knowing only that X is in case CASE," where CASE is some primitive such as TO, FROM, INST (instrument), etc. He argues that no existing primitive-based systems have such inference rules, but that they might well be useful.

He proposes one, using the direction primitive TO: "TO (LOC, EVENT) IMPLIES that X (where OBJECT $(X,$ EVENT)) is located at LOC." However, he proposes four conditions that such a rule must satisfy to be useful:

1. The rule must be independent of the nature of EVENT.

2. TO must be a possible case for more than one primitive action, for, if it were only to appear with, say, action MOVE, then it would be no more than the name of some argument of MOVE, since MOVE could be written MOVE (X, Y, Z) where, say, Y might be always the "direction toward" argument.

3. A case primitive in the rule quoted above must not be ridiculously specific, as would be a direction primitive UP-TO-THIRD-FLOOR.

4. There should not be a better way of doing things that would invalidate any of the above three conditions.

Charniak then suggests two such better ways:

4a. Having only a single movement primitive in a system whose aspects would be distinguished by cases (in that circumstance the primitive FLOW, e.g., would be replaced by a new more general MOVE, but the movee would always be (FLOW STUFF), a liquid). Charniak argues that doing this would invalidate condition 2 and so (case) primitives would no longer confer "benefits" on the system.

4b. Charniak argues that the result of the proposed TO-inference-rule for "move" could place an additional subformula indicating that the mover ends up at a new location.

Doing this, says Charniak, would violate condition 3 against very specific cases.

But it should be noted that if case primitives can be reduced to "argument n of action primitive P" descriptions, then it is quite irrelevant whether or not condition 2 holds. Case primitive TO is no less reduced if it is "argument place $n1$ of $P1$ and argument place $n2$ of $P2$" than if it is only the first clause! Reducibility—if it is a vice, and we believe it not to be in this form—is no worse if TO functions only with a single action primitive. Thus, condition 2 is idle in conjunction with Charniak's much more general argument. Condition 3 has the right flavor, but no clear force. We are given no idea of how specific a case primitive may be before it becomes ridiculous. Condition 4 is where Charniak believes the heart of his argument to be, and where he makes use of conditions 2 and 3, but it too seems to lack all force.

Charniak's Condition 4 has value only if suggestions 4a and 4b are in fact better ways of organizing a primitive-using system, but he gives no strong reasons for believing that they are. In suggestion 4a, with a single movement primitive, we would have a very restricted system, just as a language with only one movement verb would be (think of baby talk using only "go"). Suggestion 4b might violate condition 2 but that is idle anyway, as we saw. Charniak's arguments are not against primitives as such but only for a tradeoff between primitives of different types, so that, in his view, an effective use of case primitives might lead to a single verb primitive. What his suggestions show is nothing radical but only that more bizarrely constructed primitive languages would be clumsier to use for meaning description.

Toward a Clearer View of Semantic Primitives

What follows is not intended to be systematic, but only a sketch for a position justifying the use of semantic primitives in a system for describing meaning content. The first basic claim here is that semantic primitives are a useful organizing hypothesis, in Zwicky's (1973) sense. They enable useful generalizations to be made. Charniak's TO-rule serves as an example, but all primitive-using systems contain many more complex ones—but this does not require that they lead to *universal* generalizations across language boundaries, or even that more than one language be translatable into a given primitive system.

We need not expect that such generalizations lead to conventional linguistic observations at all, only that they yield a more perspicuous language for meaning description. The linguistic debate over whether or not "kill" can be represented in a system of primitives as CAUSE-to-DIE or CAUSE-to-BECOME-NOT-ALIVE (Morgan 1969, Chomsky 1970) has shown that there is no agreement over whether or how such proposals can lead to any conceivable observations of real sentences that will settle the matter.

The continuing appeal to the above pairs not being fully equivalent (Pulman 1983a) in the sense of biconditional entailments (true in all conceivable circumstances) has led to endless silliness, from Sampson's (1975) claim that words are "indivisible," so that no explanations of meaning can be given, let alone analytic definitions, and even to Fodor's (1975) use of nonequivalence to found a theory of mental language rich with innate but indefinable concepts like "telephone"!

The second basic claim of this chapter is that a primitive-using representation language can be essentially a natural language. This in no way implies that it is not a suitable language for formal lexical systems, but only that users of primitives should cease to claim (as Katz and Schank, e.g., do) that the similarity between primitives like CAUSE and English words like "cause" is mere chance, and of no theoretical significance. On the contrary, it is the heart of the matter, because the alternative view, what Lyons (1968) has called the "conceptual substance" view, that there is a real conceptual substance independent of language into which precise and clear conceptual translation can be made, is contrary to common sense and the whole weight of Anglo-Saxon philosophical and linguistic tradition.

The counterclaim made in this chapter is consistent with what Zwicky (1973) has called the substance theory of primes—that every semantic primitive can appear as a surface word in a natural language. This does not require that the same "word" as it appears in the primitive and surface form must, in any definable sense, "have the same meaning." It is simply a claim that the link between the two cannot be broken, even though it is often essential that the two usages do differ, as in the linguistic equation of "kill" with CAUSE-to-BECOME-NOT-ALIVE. The latter can only be a representation of "kill" if CAUSE is taken to mean "reasonably immediate cause." For, if it can cover causation at any distance in time, then the nonequivalence of the two forms is obvious, and your birth could certainly be said to kill you.

It must be conceded that a defensible sense of equivalence of two such forms does not, and cannot, give an identical quantity of information, whatever that may be taken to mean. Different languages are simply more or less specific on certain points, a fact that any practical sense of meaning equivalence must learn to tolerate. In Kiswahili *mguu* happens to mean both "leg" and "foot," for its speakers do not draw a conventional boundary where we happen to. Any English-to-Kiswahili translation from a sentence using "leg" or "foot" may be considered (by the English speaker, but NOT the Kiswahili speaker) to lose information.

There is simply not a correct level of "granularity" in the world that language captures. This point is constantly missed by critics of primitives who believe that there is a right encoding level if we could only find it. Thus, Pulman (1983a) attacks a formula of Wilks (1975b) containing the item "(MAN PART)" on the grounds that, in context, it is a vague translation of "brain" and might as well be "foot." Well, the Kiswahili argument should be conclusive here: if it is specific enough for its purposes, then that is sufficient, because there is no right level of specification. In fact, in the system he criticizes, any level of specification can be given, but the point here is more general, for encodings do not depend on a right level for their utility any more than other languages do, vis-à-vis English.

The view being defended is not that the semantic representations, as illustrated in chapter 3, are really English. It is rather that the facts we accept about natural languages are also facts about any primitive language, namely, that it has no unique and correct vocabulary, no more than English has, that there may be many adequate alternative vocabularies for it, just as there may be many vocabularies for English.

Ritchie (personal communication 1985) has raised the question. If the primitive language is also a natural language, then what set is formed by the union of it and English? If the primitive language has English word names, then the answer is English, with some words having primitive senses in addition to those they have in standard English.

If the word names are in another language, then Ritchie's question has no more sensible an answer than "what is the union of the vocabularies of English and French?" A more satisfactory analogy than set theory is provided by the elusive Wittgensteinian notion of the game. A form like CAUSE plays different roles in English and the primitive language, just as one rugby player may play both Rugby Union and Rugby League at different times—there is no problem, and he is not required to be a schizophrenic. The clearest consequence of the thesis that the primitive language is also a natural language is that there can be no direct justifications of individual primitives (what we called "escape moves" earlier) any more than there can be *direct* justifications, or meanings, given for the words of English. There just is no nonlinguistic realm into which we can escape from language, and from the normal explanations of English words. That is simply fact.

This does not exclude the association of inferential procedures with particular primitives as partial explanations of them, just as we may explain "cause" in English to someone by producing examples of causal inference or, as the Wittgensteinian would say, samples of the proper use of "cause." The third, and final, claim of this chapter is that we should pay more attention to the structure of real dictionaries when thinking about primitive languages. This point has been raised many times, in reply, for example, to Katz's very rigid views of the semantic dictionary entry, as compared to the function of actual dictionaries.

One final point should be made here about a possible justification (noted above) of primitives on the grounds that actual statistical analysis of large dictionaries reveals that their definitions are, in fact, in terms of a restricted subvocabulary to a large extent, and that this is close to a natural set of primitives: cause, human, object, move, substance, and so on. It might be argued that this fact, far from supporting the claims about primitives made in this chapter, has the opposite effect, for this "defining subvocabulary" for *Webster's Third*, say, has all its members actually in the dictionary as well, whereas the primitives of AI description languages, for example, are not, in general, defined in terms of the other primitives. Hence, we have a clear difference between the primitive language and English as defined by *Webster's Third*.

But this difference is more apparent than real, because it is a fact of observation that the dictionary definitions, in *Webster's* say, of members of this "defining subvocabulary" are curiously unsatisfactory. Looking up "substance" or "object" in a dictionary (provided you know the language, and are not a foreigner looking up an unknown lexeme) is unrevealing, precisely because hundreds of entries in the dictionary assume you already know the meaning of the word. In that sense, such words function in very much the way the vocabulary of an explicitly primitive language does.

Although they appear in the dictionary, they are, in a sense, without definition; their organizing role in the whole language is what matters. Wierzbicka (1989) has argued explicitly that no attempt should be made to define such words. Sparck-Jones (1986) has recently published (though the work was actually written much earlier) claims that go further and present computational classification procedures that range over a large dictionary and produce a candidate set of primitives, not by simply taking the most frequent words in definitions but by considering abstractly what features in the dictionary would enable word senses to be clustered into synonymous groups. Again, the standard primitives emerge as the most promising candidates for such features. We discuss this approach in relation to more recent computational systems in chapter 6.

In sum, then, the claim of this chapter is that primitives are to be found in all natural language–understanding systems—even those that like Bobrow and Winograd argue vigorously against them. Explicit use of primitives is preferable, and effort should be concentrated on making the systems that use them work, and not on justifying the primitives directly and independently, for that may not be possible, even in principle. However, such systems should be as formal and perspicuous as possible, although it may be necessary at certain stages to take an inductive, or descriptive, approach to the primitive language—to discover its generalizations, just as one might with a natural language—rather than attempting to fix all its possible well-formed strings and interpretations in advance. Finally, it is most important not to imagine that a useful representational system can only be achieved if certain vexatious philosophical problems—concepts, reference, correctness of the primitive set, and so forth—are cleared up first. If the analogy with the normal functioning of a natural language has any force, then that cannot be necessary.

Chapter 5
Wordbooks as Human Artifacts: Dictionaries and Thesauri

Wordbooks are fallible human products, whether written basically by one man, like Johnson's dictionary, or, as is now standard, by a large and fully computerized team, relying on a corpus of many million words of prose as a source for word contexts. Johnson famously answered the woman who asked why he had misdefined *pastern* with "Ignorance, madam, sheer ignorance," and his preface shows he was well aware of the possibility that he had made many mistakes in the whole work. Later, Horne Tooke made lists of "non-words" in Johnson's dictionary—many hundreds for the letter *a* alone—and Todd, in his revised edition, corrected large numbers of the definitions and textual citations (Johnson [1755] 1827). The only issue for the work described in this book is whether there is sufficient consistency in dictionaries to make them a useful source for natural language processing (NLP). If there is, then Johnson was, in a sense he never imagined when he wrote the words, a "slave of science."

Dictionaries have odd sources, historically, and it is not clear if they can be separated from thesauri with the neat definition we now use of thesauri as "inverted dictionaries," which is to say, words organized so as to be found via their meanings, rather than, as in a standard dictionary, a list of meanings indexed by a word name. The earliest word lists were neither of these, but were essentially inventories such as dialect word forms in Hellenistic times or, in the Middle Ages, lists of castle furniture, armor, and so on, and it is quite unclear whether one would want to call those lists protodictionaries or protothesauri.

Today, we can usefully distinguish at least five species of the genus dictionary: (1) the standard dictionary, (2) the classic thesaurus, (3) bilingual dictionaries, (4) style dictionaries, and (5) concordances. We shall be much concerned in this book with the differences between them.

The Standard Dictionary

This is garden variety, where the word senses of a single language are explained by some method or other: sometimes by definitions or just synonyms, sometimes by illustrative quotations from literature (as in Johnson's dictionary, or by means of the earliest literary source—usually called a dictionary on historical principles—as with the OED) or by made-up example sentences (as in LDOCE, sometimes) or by real sentences from a corpus of contemporary texts (as with COBUILD).

We shall explain later in some detail the structure of these modern dictionaries named by acronyms. Sometimes, as in French dictionaries traditionally, though the practice has now spread to dictionaries of English, the sense is illustrated by drawings or diagrams. In addition, there may be a mass of material having to do with pronunciation, etymology, hyphenation, social register of usage, and associated grammatical and spelling information. Note that dictionaries of English have always assumed some notion of sense division—that a word can be used with quite distinguishable meanings or senses. We return to that issue below to ask how firm that assumption is.

Within this major group it is now standard to separate modern descriptive dictionaries for native speakers (such as the *Concise Oxford Dictionary*, the *Random House Dictionary*, or the *Collins English Dictionary*) from dictionaries for foreign learners (such as LDOCE, COBUILD, or the *Oxford Advanced Learners Dictionary*). As this book bears witness, the latter group have been of the most interest to those involved in the construction of computational resources precisely because they give a great deal of syntactic, semantic, and pragmatic information that is not thought necessary for a native speaker. Another way of putting this is that dictionaries of the first type are usually seen as "decoding" tools for unknown words, whereas the latter are designed (explicitly in the case of COBUILD) as "encoding tools" to assist in generating English.

In concentrating, as we shall in this book, on work done using widely available commercial dictionaries, often designed for learners, we are of course ignoring one substantial tradition of monolingual dictionaries, one that is very important culturally outside the English-speaking world. Those are the national dictionaries, representing a cultural repository, created by scholars attached to a national academy. These are important projects but not ones that have figured in the work described in this book, largely because so much of the recent work has been on dictionaries for

English, the only major language that lacks an academy of any kind to keep it in shape.

The Classic Thesaurus

These are dictionaries in reverse, descending in English from the great nineteeth century thesaurus of Roget. A thesaurus, or word treasury, is essentially an organization of lists of partially synonymous words, and is most often used by crossword puzzle solvers or students seeking variation in usage. Modern college thesauri are organized alphabetically and are distinguishable from dictionaries only by the fact that they do not claim to explain or define the sense of a word but only to provide synonyms. In some cases that is all that can be done to explain a word, even in a dictionary, but the purpose of the thesaurus is not primarily to explain meaning. In some languages, such as German, there is a tradition of providing verb books that distinguish superficially similar verbs (in terms of prefixes, etc.) from one another and give their valency or case patterns. It is not clear whether such a book would be a thesaurus or dictionary on the description given so far.

However, the alphabetized thesaurus is not at all the original article. What Roget did was to design a tree of types of entity in the world based on a classic Aristotelian notion of genera and species, dealing not with natural objects only but also with oppositional concepts like MOTION and STASIS. The lists of words were organized under such headings and subheadings, and it is that device which gave sense to the notion of accessing words via their meanings, since tracing down the tree was intended to locate meanings independent of the ultimate word lists themselves. As we saw in chapter 4, it is far from clear that such meaning primitives as MOTION can be distinguished from the words of the dictionary or thesaurus themselves, nor is there any real need to do so. As we shall see later below, thesauri have played a special role as a tool for the computational analysis of language.

Bilingual Dictionaries

These are correspondence lists that seek to relate two languages to each other at the level of equivalence of individual word senses. However, and this is a matter for discussion later, they are not simply a subspecies of monolingual dictionaries but rather a different kind of object. Their role is not to explain meanings, since the final target string they yield for a source/known language word may be incomprehensible to a user, even though useful. Moreover the user already knows, in that case, what the source language word means.

This is not generally the situation when the bilingual dictionary is used the other way round, starting from a word in the target/unknown language. In that case its meaning is provided, although what is given is not an explanation in the sense discussed earlier, but an equivalent. This difference is not mere hairsplitting; a bilingual dictionary will not normally give an explanation of meaning because what it gives is intended to serve as an equivalent for a translation process, and explanations are normally given only in those cases where a language lacks a more compact form. So, one might find "pleasure at another's pain" in a German-English bilingual dictionary for *Schadenfreude* simply because there is no English equivalent.

But that is the exceptional case. Normally, one would look up *cabillaud* in a French-English dictionary and find "cod" for insertion in a text. One would certainly not want or expect an explanation such as "large edible North Atlantic fish." Bilingual dictionaries are thus asymmetric; there is no reason at all why the two directions of a single dictionary should contain either the same words or the same division of word senses. Either or both directions might explain differences in a referent, for example, when giving the German equivalent of "satchel" in English (the bag that British schoolchildren carry) it might or might not be appropriate to add that, although the objects have an identical function, they are quite differently designed.

Style Dictionaries

An extension to what used to be called grammar books, these, such as Fowler's *Modern English Usage* (Fowler 1926) or Horwill's *Modern American Usage* (Horwill 1935), have a special role, most particularly because they both give opinions on usage as well as rules, and also because they provide large numbers of negative examples as well as positive ones. At the same time they do not always claim that the negative examples are ungrammatical in any strong sense, only that they should be avoided on aesthetic grounds or on those of communicative ease. A popular paperback version is the long-lasting standard, Strunk and White (1979).

Concordances

These are literary artifacts that do not give explanations of meaning but index words against their occurrence in a corpus usually drawn from one work or one author. In that sense they are special scholarly tools and are, in effect, a subspecies of the standard dictionary, leaving out all information except the text citations.

There are also specialized forms of several of the main divisions above, particularly technical versions of mono- and bilingual dictionaries for subject areas such as aeronautics or nuclear technology. When these are reduced to simple technical equivalents, with none of the (unnecessary) sense divisions of usage guides, and when extended from two to many languages, they are normally called terminology banks.

One might argue here that, although not normally considered part of the lexicographic tradition, one cannot separate that tradition from the tradition of creating miniature artificial languages of definition. These were discussed in abstract form in chapter 5, but they have their own lively history, through the symbolisms of Dalgarno, Wilkins, and Leibniz, up to Ogden and Richards' Basic English (an admirable survey and discussion appears in Sparck Jones 1986). Some of these were designed, explicitly or implicitly, as we saw in the last chapter, as languages of primitives for giving definitions of more complex concepts. A dictionary (at least of the standard type) is a compendium of exactly such definitions where the "primitive set" is whatever the union of all the words used in all its definitions happens to be. If this is a set approaching the size of the language itself, the term "primitive" loses all meaning, but in fact it never does (see below, on *Webster's Third*, Revard 1968), and in carefully controlled dictionaries like LDOCE (see below) the defining set is deliberately restricted, in that case to about 2000 terms, so that the term "primitive" begins to seem plausible. Our case will be that this "artificial primitive language" tradition cannot be separated from the mainstream of lexicography itself.

Are There Psychological Constraints on Dictionaries?

The question may seem absurd, but before tackling two substantial forms such constraints might take—the "reality" of word senses and the relationship of dictionaries to a possible "mental lexicon"—let us clear away some preliminary considerations. In chapter 3 we touched on Fodor's so-called language of thought (LOT), one of whose supporting arguments was the purported impossibility of definition (e.g., that "kill" cannot be defined in a necessary and sufficient manner by "cause to die"). One can accept that argument while denying that any important consequences follow since virtually no useful definitions, outside mathematics, are in terms of a necessary and sufficient set of conditions. On that one observation however, Fodor supports the great edifice of the LOT, which is said to be such that its concepts exist psychologically but not in any definitionally reduced form, so that the whole vocabulary of LOT is a primitive set in the sense of chapter 4 because it cannot be reduced by definition.

Of course, if Fodor is right and there is a LOT in his sense, that fact might be expected to have some effect on what definitional activity humans could in fact perform, as when writing and using dictionaries, since, for him, explanatory definitions of sense are not possible, in either LOT or natural languages. Since Fodor offers us no details of the hidden LOT, other than that it is essentially like a natural language in Chomsky's universal terms (see chapter 2), these questions may not need answers. As we saw, the whole LOT trick rests on the absolute denial of definitions, whereas, as we have argued, as explanations they serve us perfectly well in real dictionaries and real life.

Are Word Senses Real?

Is it permissible to assume a notion of "word sense," unexamined and direct from traditional lexicography? What evidence have we that such a notion has any empirical foundation or can be the basis of a serious computational semantics? What all existing dictionaries do is to set out for each word of English, such as "play," a claim that it has, say, eight senses that are then described and distinguished and, most likely, are grouped into sets of senses, some of which are distinct enough to be called "homographs," although that word is never given any precise definition.

What is the status of such a claim? Is it more than the arbitrary segmentation of the word's occurrences of use by a lexicographer? The point can be put most clearly by asking whether there ever was any lexical ambiguity until dictionaries were written in roughly the form we now have them, and, if not, perhaps lexical ambiguity is no more or less than a product of scholarship: a social product, in other words. Translation between languages, as well as more mundane understanding tasks, had, however, been a practice for millennia before such scholarly products and therefore cannot require them. If any reader finds this position bizarre, even as a discussion point, let the reader ask what empirical evidence he or she has that there were word senses before the publication of dictionaries. Perhaps the conscious puns of classical literature are the only positive evidence to hand.

A certain kind of cognitive psychologist may find this position tempting, and Antal (1963) argued that, whatever the range of *reference* of a word, nothing could require us to say that it had more than one sense. Such a view would also be very much to the taste of most formal semanticists who have never found the idea of lexical ambiguity interesting or important. For them, it is a peripheral phenomenon, one that can be dealt with by subscripting symbols as play1, play2, etc. (as Wittgenstein first did in his *Tractatus*) and claiming that there is, in any case, no real ambiguity in the world itself. Symbols can indicate disjoint classes of things and that fact can best be captured by disjoint (subscripted) symbols.

The answer to this position is that, however well people translated "ambiguous words" before the advent of dictionaries, the processes they went through cannot be modeled by a computer without some explicit representation of lexical ambiguity. All practical experience for 25 years has confirmed that, and it is at precisely this point that the psychological research on the reality of word sense ambiguity is so important (Van Petten and Kutas 1989; Gigley 1989; Burgess and Simpson 1989; Simpson and Burgess 1989; Prather and Swinney 1989; Tanenhaus, Burgess, and Seidenburg 1989), although, in a later chapter (chapter 11) we shall discuss a statistically based theory of translation that does deny precisely this.

The psychological and computational evidence, even if true, concerns the need of sense distinction representations and computational processing; it does not establish the need for sense distinctions as found in conventional dictionaries. Doubts about them are increased by what one could call the arbitrariness factor: different dictionaries may give 1, 2, 7, 34, or 87 senses for a single word and they cannot all be right. Worse yet, those different segmentations of usage into discrete senses may not even be inclusive. Sometimes different dictionaries will segment usage into senses for a given word in incommensurate ways; perhaps "play3" (the third of three) in dictionary A cannot be associated with any one of the eight senses of "play" in dictionary B.

The best answer to this last objection is extensibility; a dictionary is plausible only if the methodology that set it up can be extended to capture new senses not already in the dictionary, on the basis of, say, textual material. In that way different dictionaries could, in principle (though it might serve no practical purpose), be tuned to "sense compatibility" by the use of text corpora, just as people can come to agree on their sense intuitions if shown the same texts, even when their initial intuitions about the senses of a word differ.

Such a position is not far from the one Dreyfus (1979) has defended: that modeling intelligence, in any of its manifestations, must inevitably be by means of extensible, or learning, systems. In the case of natural language understanding, that task is often subcontracted out to "metaphor understanding." We discuss that phenomenon further below in connection with dictionaries, but the notion we have introduced here is the fundamental one that dictionaries cannot, if they are to have any serious status, be fixed and frozen with respect to word sense distinctions, any more than they can with regard to the inventory of word names itself, which we all know to be in constant flux, with words dying and being born every day. We return to this in connection with metaphor and "novel usage" below, and in chapter 6 consider experimental results that could be said to confirm the empirical basis of word sense distinction.

A traditional question arises at this point, but not one to which we need give an immediate answer, namely, is the sense extension of words merely an empirical phenomenon, one that may or may not take place in particular languages, or is it, on the contrary, inevitable and a necessary part of the use of a symbolic system to cover a changing and unpredictable world? One can divert the question from the global to the individual at this point: whatever is the case with a language as a whole, the language of an individual must, as an evolving process, learn how to interpret new or metaphorical uses, and it is that inevitable process, at the very least, that work on metaphorical use seeks to model. As to the broader question of a whole language, even if one's intuitive answer is with the latter alternative, that is to say, the inevitability of coping with change, that cannot now be demonstrated and, for the moment, we rest with Wittgenstein's (1953 §133) "it is not our aim to refine the system of rules for the use of our words in unheard-of ways."

Kay's Mental Lexicon vs. Concrete Dictionaries

We now turn to a different kind of problem that some have detected in dictionaries, one that bears some relationship to Fodor's LOT. Kay

(1989) has objected that computational research on dictionaries (of the kind that is the core of this book) may well be fundamentally misguided because those dictionaries are social products, a point we fully concede, and can have no ascertainable relationship to the true "mental lexicon" which one can, without too much distortion, think of as the core of the LOT. Kay's claim is that dictionaries are *psychologically* inadequate.

More particularly, Kay is asking whether the goal of an "abstract" dictionary—one that is "neutral" between particular linguistic theories and which could be a resource independent of its notation—can usefully be pursued independently of the task of making the true mental lexicon concrete, which would mean something like a program or database that was able to express whatever the true mental lexicon (in heads) of a particular language actually is.

He points out that the actual structures of the brain/mind may well not separate out a word sense lexicon from the mass of real-world knowledge it stores as well. He is surely right about that, for there is no reason at all to believe the mind is conveniently organized in modules like a linguistic, or any other, theory. Moreover, Kay argues, the information to be found in conventional dictionaries can at best augment particular deficiencies in our mental lexicon but cannot possibly supplant it, nor can it be a source from which a serious lexical knowledge base could be built, precisely because it lacks that mass of real-world knowledge that the mental lexicon presumably has: "Many researchers, especially members of the artificial intelligentsia, will claim that the sheer [*sic*] amount of information in a typical dictionary entry is simply too little to support the kinds of inference people base on them" (Kay 1989), p. 38).

It will be obvious that Kay's critique strikes at the overall aim of the research that forms the body of this book. We are assuming, as does much of the research described in this book, a principle of sufficiency that states that, whatever the truth of the claim, it is at least an experimental question worth examination—whether the knowledge extractable from an existing dictionary, or set of them, is sufficient to allow NLP to some required level. After all, whatever the mental lexicon may turn out to be, we have no evidence yet, apart from hunches, that a computational entity isomorphic with it is required for NLP. It might be, for example, that the mental lexicon contains far too much (e.g., perhaps a memory of every single use we have ever made of a particular word) and therefore demonstration of its differences from dictionaries may be irrelevant.

Kay's demonstration continues by considering the entry for the main sense of "give" in Hornby (1963):

"allow (sb.) to have; allow or cause (sb. or sth.) to pass into the care or keeping of" [where sb.=somebody and sth.=something].

This is a classic "vacuous" entry for a core, or primitive, term of a language: exactly the type of word for which we showed (in chapter 4) that its meaning could not be given by the same method as the words it is used to define. Kay comments on the fact that it is hard to make the definition fit actual examples of the use of "give," and that that fact has led to precisely the sort of AI-style semantic entries which we exemplified in chapter 3, ones in which variables are named, and where some of the possible inferences are explicitly drawn as to the purposes and results of actions. Kay then has no difficulty in showing that such more explicit entries, which specify the agents of actions as Hornby's entry does not, will be overspecific because if one specifies the agent of giving as a person, then such an AI-style definition will not cover "The machine gave him back his dime."

Kay's targets have multiplied and become muddled in this argument. While showing that Hornby's entry is too vague, in that it has no explicit participants for the action specified, Kay also wants to show that more specific AI-style entries (where those *are* specified) are not good candidates for a mental lexicon either, because they are too specific and rule out forms like the machine-giver.

His central discussion is contradictory because, a little like Wittgenstein at his worst, Kay wants to attack all proffered formalisms whatever, while at the same time arguing that real dictionaries cannot offer much for the construction of any concrete (i.e., computable) form of the mental lexicon for practical purposes because they are vague. Nothing in his conclusion actually follows because he leaves out the distinction we have stressed, here and in previous chapters, between existing usage data, however expressed, and the inevitable novelty of new but comprehensible usage. In previous chapters we talked of notions like "preference" (chapter 3) that specify preferred usages but permit and attempt to interpret others that do not conform to constraints. Earlier in this chapter, we claimed that extensibility and the ability of a lexicological methodology to deal with novelty computationally was a way out of this conundrum. It must be remembered, in all this, that Kay's argument is based on a joke because he has no idea whatever what the actual nature of the mental lexicon is. His guess is simply no better or worse than anyone else's.

When contrasting dictionaries and lexicons, Kay writes: "the lexicon will have to be a much larger compendium of information than the dictionary" (Kay 1989, p. 39). That may well be true, but not for the reasons he gives. One is as likely to find boundary-breaking cases ("The machine gave me change") in dictionaries as in lexicons if they become established. Lexicon users (people with brains) clearly have access to some preferential metarule for accepting the extension of sense, but that fact does not make any dictionary-lexicon contrast that assists Kay's distinction, since people are not dictionary users in the same way as they are lexicon users. Dictionaries do not come with such metarules for very good reason; they merely record and are not directly connected to any processing mechanism. In our view, then, the dictionary-lexicon distinction is not just one of size or quality of data, as Kay seems to think, but it is rather that the human lexicon must be essentially connected to, or contain, a process for dealing with new senses, ones that break previous constraints; it cannot be merely a record of that language user's past.

Kay allows or sees none of this; for him the ideal lexicon and dictionary must both cover all possible usage in advance, and their inadequacies can be shown by failure to do so:

"Much of what needs to be done in order to construct the concrete lexicon is essentially anthropological in nature because it consists in mapping the ontology of the culture and articulating the relationships between that map and the vocabulary of the language. The notion of giving is not given by the physical world; it is enshrined in our culture and, presumably, many others. (Kay 1989, p. 40)

The spirit here is precisely that of Wittgenstein with his emphasis on the role of culture and very general facts of nature in the structure of language. It is an attitude that can very easily be merely negative and opposed to any actual experiment or activity, since the task is hopeless. Wittgenstein, however, unlike Kay, appreciated fully that knowledge of language cannot, in principle, capture all the possible ways in which a word can be used: "It is only in the normal cases that the use of a word is clearly prescribed" (Wittgenstein 1953, §142).

Not even Kay's main case follows on the evidence he gives. Elegant though it is, his argument does not show that structures proposed by researchers (whether they are called dictionaries or models of the mental lexicon is ultimately unimportant since we have no independent access to the mental lexicon, but only the models and structures we write down) cannot be associated with procedures to cope with unforeseen usages, nor does he show that dictionaries cannot have arbitrary amounts of cultural and real-world information attached. His illustrative use of Hornby's dictionary was a deliberately anachronistic choice in that regard:

"I have several reasons for supposing that the concrete lexicon will not be a dictionary in the usual sense and will not serve the makers of dictionaries very much except as an abstraction. One is that it will be impossible to achieve the level of specificity that it will require without large amounts of technical terminology and specialized notational devices. It is therefore likely to be accessible only to people with specialized knowledge and training. The second reason is similar ... it is that the concrete lexicon will in some ways be deceptively—often quite misleadingly— simple. The sense (give1) (sense 1 of "give") is defined to be (cause1 to have1) where (cause1) is sense 1 of "cause." ... Ignoring the subscripts, the idea that comes across is disarmingly simple, but the subscripts are crucial to the intention. (Kay 1989, p. 41)

Kay goes on to argue, correctly, that *dictionary* entries (the above quote being about the mental *lexicon*, of course) for such primitive words are agonized over by lexicographers but not read by users because that is precisely where they need no assistance. He concludes that a start should be made on the construction of the concrete lexicon but. "I do not believe that dictionaries will contribute much to the enterprise or that it can be accomplished in any important measure by processing dictionaries automatically. ... In the lexicon, giving is simple once you know about having" (Kay 1989, p. 41).

Again, his feeling here is far stronger than his argument. The subscripted objects above are (unfortunately for Kay) no more than modified forms of the AI-style lexical entry of chapter 3, yet Kay seems to be arguing both that a concrete lexicon should be *simple* (i.e., it should not have subscripts) and that it must have them because the definitional items are themselves ambiguous (hence "the subscripts are crucial to the intention"). Kay is onto a very important phenomenon here, but totally fails to bring it out clearly, and we believe that when it is brought out fully, his pessimistic conclusions are not demonstrated at all.

What he has shown is that the primitives or definitional items IN ANY SYSTEM are always themselves ambiguous words, hence the subscripts that attempt to mollify or eliminate this. But Kay has a feeling that a real mental lexicon cannot consist of ambiguous items ("... in the lexicon, giving is simple ...") and indeed this fact is one of the deep mysteries surrounding any LOT: how can it contain *un*ambiguous items if, as Fodor always insists, it is also to be language-like, and under the same universal, formal, constraints as a natural language when all natural languages (necessarily, one might suggest) contain ambiguous words? Saying that is no more than to observe there are more things and actions in the world than there are words to name them.

The concrete lexicon, on being written down, must therefore have subscripted items so that it can be unambiguously interpreted, and Kay seems to say in his pessimistic conclusion that a dictionary cannot be like that and hence cannot assist in lexicon construction. It should be noted here that, although his subscripting refers to a possible *lexicon*, it only makes sense in terms of subscripts that refer to sense numbering in some real dictionary, the point he started from but prefers to forget as the argument gathers speed. This is because mental lexicons, presumably, do not list and gloss sense-distinguished forms of the same symbol, as dictionaries normally do.

One of our own major empirical demonstrations in this book will be to show that a dictionary (e.g., LDOCE; see below chapter 7) can be so processed that the words in the defining vocabulary can be automatically sense-resolved within its definitions, thus producing forms like those Kay gives above for the concrete lexicon. If Kay's words mean anything precise and refutable at all, this is as clear a demonstration as one could wish for, that computations on a dictionary can produce forms that are like those he considers a lexicon. Doing that does not solve his other challenge, that of the large quantities of cultural and real-world information needed in the lexicon. But as we noted, it is an empirical sufficiency assumption that that can be mastered on the basis of what concrete dictionaries do provide, and that assumption will soon be tested in terms of the use made of the chief product of the researches described in this book: the machine-tractable lexicon.

Further Problems with Dictionaries

Dictionaries—at least until now—are passive entities: they wait almost all their useful lives on shelves waiting to be all too briefly consulted. And then, often, they fail for one reason or another when pressed into service. Sometimes dictionaries fail because they say too little. Definition by synonym can create this failure, as in the (possibly apocryphal) "furze" and "gorse" example where, so the story goes, a dictionary defined "furze" with its synonym, "gorse." The puzzled reader who looked to "gorse" found it too was defined by a synonym, "furze." A more realistic example is given by Sparck Jones (1986; see also chapter 6) where a dictionary mutually defines (at least in part) "good" and "excellent." As we shall see later, "dictionary circles" are inevitable, but one consisting of only two items could be considered a failure of a dictionary in its main purpose: to explain meaning.

Everyone has, at one time or another, known the frustration of following complex sequences where the words in a definition are still not simple enough, and must themselves be looked up. This regress can never be infinite, but can be annoying all the same. In the "furze" and "gorse" case, a persevering reader can learn about spiny, thickset shrubs with fragrant yellow leaves, but must go out and get a different, perhaps botanical, dictionary to learn that.

Sometimes dictionaries fail because they say too much. One example of this is when dictionary makers, in their zeal to outdo the competition, seemingly create new sense distinctions for the sake of it. Lexicographers are judged, in part, according to the new words they discover and to the refinements they can make to existing words. This is undoubtedly good for the science of lexicography, but it does not guarantee that dictionaries will be better, and certainly does not make them easier to use. If the problem at hand is to choose the correct sense for a polysemous word, this choice is always easier if there are fewer senses to choose from.

Dictionaries also say too much about closed-class words, in a way analogous to the problem with "give" that Kay discussed. One illustration of this is the dozens of definitions of the "be" verbs in the average dictionary. (LDOCE, e.g., has at least 21, depending on how you count). This is particularly odd when the general consensus in formal sciences is that there are really only two useful sense distinctions for "be": "is of identity" and "is of predication," as in "Mark Twain is Samuel Clemens," and "Mark Twain is a man," respectively.

Compounding the too much or too little failures of dictionaries is a problem of representational ergonomics. The sublanguage of dictionary definitions is inconsistent, and the vocabulary of that sublanguage is ill-defined. This is of little consequence when dictionaries are used as they are intended: as a resource for individuals who already understand the sublanguage of dictionary definitions. But when a dictionary is to become the foundation of a computational resource, our overarching aim in this book, a well-defined system for the semantics of definition is crucial.

Many other standard problems of dictionaries have been touched on already, such as the issue of what is a word; "riverrun" is a word used only by James Joyce and his commentators. Should dictionaries include it? What forms of a word should appear? Hanks (1986) points out that a survey of almost 18 million words of text showed that, in its rare occurrences, "hackle" almost always appears in the plural, so why is it normally introduced as a word that is singular unless otherwise specified? Again, dictionaries are not only wrong about instances of usage, as we noted already, but are probably also inconsistent, though that can only be shown by large-scale computation together with some analytic apparatus, a matter we turn to in later chapters. It is hard for a dictionary to be obviously and plainly inconsistent, since nothing prima facie demands that any word entry be consistent with any other, although, as we shall see, there *are* deeper forms of consistency lacking in dictionaries.

We have already touched on the justification of the very notion of sense division, but there is no uniform standard for the order of presentation of word senses. If we exempt dictionaries like the OED that give senses in an explicitly historical order, other dictionaries usually order senses by some intuition of degree of literalness or importance. Hanks (1986) has shown that intuitions of this kind have no connection at all with frequency of use, a matter that is certainly important if the intended user is a foreign learner. So, for example, "take" is rarely used in its literal or standard sense of a person taking an object from somewhere. It is used most often in forms such as "take place," "take care," "take part," and so on, and the subjects are often entities such as events and not persons, thus confounding the usual NLP system's definition of "take" as a verb requiring an animate agent as a subject. These are statistical facts gained from searching large bodies of text and we shall return to such work in later chapters. These observations are among many that have led to serious questioning of the notion of literal meaning in recent years (Searle 1979, Wilensky 1987).

In chapter 3 above we examined an argument of Searle's in connection with a discussion of truth conditions as a basis for meaning. He argued that 1–5 (see p. 31) have the same literal sense that and 6–8 have other senses. The context there was his claim that what he called the "semantic content" of 1–5 was far short of truth conditions and so, he seemed to say, short of what was required for understanding, since that seemed to require some additional world knowledge that he equated with truth conditions. Kay's argument discussed in this chapter had a great deal in common with this in its separation of dictionary sense from a deeper "understanding."

We countered that there is no reason to equate truth conditions with understanding and, more relevant, the examples he gave happen not to coincide with the sense assignments in these sentences to OED senses.

What follows is that authorities (in this case Searle and the OED) cannot agree on literal sense, which might be thought to give force to Hanks' arguments for dictionaries based solely on statistical frequency of use with no regard to literalness (Hanks 1990). However, our case here is that something can and must be saved from the wreck of the traditional notion of literal sense.

Literalness took a battering in the work of Wittgenstein, as it must in any work that contains a fundamental criticism of the notion of ostensive reference, for that is what gives literalness its appeal. There is an object to which a word points, and that is its literal meaning, a view which Ryle later called the fido-fido theory of meaning (1949). Wittgenstein (1953), like Cassirer before him and Quine later, held that even a single-word utterance can express a whole complex and indirect message, such as "bison" shouted by Early Person, and perhaps meaning that bison have been here, or that they will be, or how nice it would be to eat one right now. But that again does not question literalness, since any of those interpretations might be termed literal.

We shall continue here to discuss the literal meaning of individual words, thus avoiding the Fregean turn, which declined to discuss word meaning outside the compositional content of a sentence. Wilensky's arguments against literal meaning, for example, are all in terms of the literal meanings of sentences. If necessary, our arguments could be recast in sentence terms, but lexicographic discussion is essentially word-based, and we shall continue in that way.

In earlier chapters we argued that metaphorical use is widespread and normal but that there is a notion of preference (Wilks 1975c) by which words (especially the predicate-like terms, verbs and adjectives) take arguments of certain types preferentially to others. Both these positions seem to involve some lingering commitment to literal usage, for how can we call a use metaphorical unless we have a literal one with which to contrast it? If all usage is metaphorical, what meaning can we then assign to the word if, again, we have nothing to contrast it with? Preference for certain classes of arguments, if it exists, suggests a norm that one might identify with literal use.

We believe that a defensible notion of preferred, or main, use exists and that this can be established without regard to any theories of reference. It is simply a processing issue—whether preferences serve the purpose of ambiguity resolution when implemented in some process of the general sort set out by (Wilks 1975b). So, to return to Searle's examples, if we choose to set up a principal sense of "open" with a preferred object of "physical object," then that will select senses 1–5 as main, but not 8, since a restaurant is a location and only derivatively a physical object, a classification that happens to confirm Searle's sense taxonomy but not the OED's.

The argument for main senses is not statistical or merely conservative, but follows from the claim that one can seek to interpret metaphorical use (taken now as not conforming to the constraints explicit for the main sense) given the content of the main sense together with knowledge sources indexed by the arguments actually provided (i.e., what we know about meetings, restaurants, fire, etc. in the Searle examples 6–8). Sometimes this computation can be done (see, e.g., work on computational metaphor interpretation: Wilks 1975b, c, Fass 1988, Martin, 1992) and sometimes it cannot. If it cannot be done by such inferencing (and "open fire" might well be a case where it cannot), then the locution must be declared idiomatic and lexicalized. Such processes are intended to model the interpretation of novel locutions, whether or not they are already well known to dictionaries or other speakers.

In such a view it would be a proper empirical question to ask whether, were one to take a different sense as main and work from *its* constraints, it would then be possible, given the appropriate knowledge bases, to reach other senses, including the (former) main sense. Such a possibility is an experimental one, and if alternative routes were possible, these might well correspond to meaning shifts of the kind detected by the Hanks statistics, for example, one where "take place" has become the main or principal form of "take." This would give an empirical and defensible sense of literalness.

Let us turn, in conclusion, to one last issue: that of the systematic ambiguity of the defining items, or primitives, in dictionary definitions. Since they are themselves words, we must expect this phenomenon to be a necessary one. In the course of Kay's arguments above, he pointed out the need for the subscripting of definitional primitives, such as HAVE, without seeing that that assumption neither supported a concrete lexicon (which he believes to be "simple") nor undermines the value of an existing dictionary, given that one can now sense-tag such entities automatically.

One of the major pieces of empirical work to be described in this book is the sense tagging of LDOCE definitions at the Computing Research Laboratory at New Mexico State University (NMSU). The data were originally investigated by hand by Guo (1989), who showed that about half of LDOCE's 2000 defining words are always used in only one of the senses given for them in LDOCE itself (hence they are simple in Kay's sense) when used for defining that set of 2000, while the others (e.g., "state," which is sometimes used in definitions to mean country and sometimes chemical state) are used in definitions with very few of the senses given for them in their own entries. Our empirical, automatic, procedures have modeled Guo's hand-assignment of sense-taggings to the dictionary. If the whole dictionary is sense-tagged, no regressions of the sorts Kay seems to fear can occur.

There certainly do remain problems with defining primitives, as we admitted in chapter 4, and we have defended only a relativistic, pragmatic view of them here, with no objectivism or absolutism in it. As we noted earlier, Johnson-Laird and Quinn (1976) has shown that definitional primitives do have a reasonable psychological status with experimental subjects. Dailey (1986) has shown, however, that on reasonable assumptions about a defining vocabulary, the extraction of an absolutely minimum set of primitives is an NP-complete problem, implying that it is computationally insoluble. Again, this kind of result should worry no one, since it does not exclude a range of perfectly good pragmatic approximations, such as Guo's work where he showed that an iterative procedure would reduce the LDOCE defining vocabulary from about 2000 to about 1000, which could then be used to define the remaining 1000 and hence all the words in the dictionary itself. Nothing whatever requires that this be an absolute or provably minimum set, only that it be adequate for practical purposes, the only ones we have here. Note, finally, that by concentrating on the issue of sense definition within English, a single language, we have conflated what are, to some, quite different issues: the reduced language of definition for a single language vs. *universal* primitives of definition that function across all languages. This seems to us a non-issue, whatever its pedigree; if the *universal* set is to be found empirically, by some form of set union of the sets for different languages, then they must already, ex hypothesi, form *a* set in *a* primitive language and so the second issue reduces in practice to the first.

Chapter 6

Early Computational Approaches: Tasks and Tools

In this chapter we pay our debts to the past and cover the early work on dictionary analysis both as it was practiced in the early days of computing and as it related, and still relates, to efforts in thesaurus processing and information retrieval.

Computing over Whole Dictionaries: Olney and Revard at SDC

Johnson claimed that, in writing his dictionary, he had become one of "those who toil at the lower employments of life." Until quite recently that same description was thought by many in computational linguistics to apply to their colleagues working in what we now know as computational lexicology. It seemed to have neither the grand claims of syntax, nor the mystery of semantics and pragmatics, nor even the dull but precise satisfactions of phonetics and morphology. Yet now the value and interest of that early lexicological work is clear.

The earliest attempts to compute over a whole dictionary of substantial size were made by Olney and Revard (Olney 1967, Revard 1968) at Systems Development Corporation (SDC) in the late 1960s within the group headed by the late Bob Simmons. *Webster's Seventh New Collegiate Dictionary* (Gove 1969) was keypunched twice (to avoid errors) onto paper tape from paper text. These first efforts were therefore almost certainly the only ones for which the dictionary was put in machine-readable form primarily for the purpose of computational exploration, as opposed to the work being a mere byproduct of the existence of the printer's machine-readable form, as is now universally the case.

What they did with that vast amount of information was chiefly to explore word frequencies in definitions, itself an enormous computing task with the hardware resources then available. Their results, very broadly speaking, were that (discounting "a" and "the," the most frequent defining words in any dictionary) the most frequent words occurring in definitions, down to any rank order, were almost identical—give or take a synonym or two—to the names of the semantic primitives in the contemporary AI semantic coding theories (see chapter 3) or in linguistic semantic theories such as those of Fodor and Katz. They were items like SUBSTANCE, CAUSE, THING, KIND, POSSESS, BE, HAVE, and so on.

This was the first clear empirical link between semantic defining primitives, from whatever tradition, and the actual content of dictionary definitions, although it was not a link Olney and Revard themselves chose to emphasize.

At SDC, at the same time as these efforts, Givon (1967) and Gruber (1965) were developing the first lexically based linguistic theories within the Chomskyan paradigm, though any direct influence from the *Webster's* work is hard to document. Gruber was setting out the role of a lexicon as an active, or generative as the term then was, component in a linguistic system, an idea that is now commonplace but one with no antecedent in the Chomskyan world where a lexicon was a passive, derivative thing. Givon was exploring what have now come to be called "sense extension" rules (see chapter 8) using examples drawn from *Webster's*, such as the systematic extension of sense from common object names to mass terms, as in [grain (object) → grain (in the mass)].

Olney had also developed formal definitions of links, chains, and dictionary circles formed by words in the dictionary linking through their definitions, all notions central to the later work of Amsler (see below). Some of these dictionary circle methods were later automated by Calzolari (1977), but the main issues were explored at that time by Sparck Jones, then visiting the SDC group. She showed that although circles must in principle exist in dictionaries, since every defining word appears in the dictionary, some can be quite small and easily located, such as the mutual definitions of senses of "good" and "excellent." Sparck Jones defines a circle as existing when two words are linked by (at least) two different chains, a chain being composed of links such that A links to B if A is in the definition of B. However, she also showed that such good-excellent circles, easy to spot by inspection for a reader, are quite hard to locate formally if one takes certain exhaustive but empirical notions of circle derivation. As we shall see below with Amsler's work, circles are a diversion (though semantically important) in the overall establishment of whatever taxonomic hierarchy the dictionary allows.

At that same time at SDC, Wilks was exploring computational sense extension in newspaper texts, using AI-style but handcrafted semantic codings of the sort we illustrated earlier (chapter 3). When the semantic entries in his lexicon did not fit the constraints given by the neighboring text terms (what were later called agent, qualifier, and object preferences), the program would seek another semantically related word sense from the same text that did fit the constraints. That word sense was then attributed as a new or "extended" sense to the old, ill-fitting, word. This was a method that applied best to highly coherent text types, such as philosophy texts, and for which the newspaper texts were, in fact, only controls.

At that moment in SDC, then, in 1967, the three major ingredients of what is now a global style of work were actually all co-present: (1) empirical computation on dictionaries locating defining primitives, (2) linguistic work on lexicons and sense extension, and (3) AI-procedural work on lexical sense extension from texts. But the three components did not in fact interact at all within that building; the time was not then ripe.

Amsler's Thesis

The first structural work in computational lexicology was Amsler and White (1979) and Amsler's thesis (1980). It began as joint work with Simmons and hence has strong continuity with the work just described. What Amsler did was to establish, partly by hand but by potentially computable methods, a taxonomic structure (see chapter 10 for details on the construction of the taxonomy) for a representative subset of the *Merriam-Webster Pocket Dictionary* (MWPD 1964). He was the first to point out in a clear, procedural way, that dictionaries are ideally structured for taxonomic organization, since the defining words all appear in the headword list that is the dictionary itself (a fact that had long been noted for thesauri; see below).

Amsler showed the taxonomic development of both verb and noun primitives (to keep to our preferred term): MOVE was traced through the 171 definitions in which it occurs; similarly, VEHICLE was traced upward and downward (in the sense of a standard hierarchical tree of which VEHICLE is one level) and he showed how loops in the tree (identical to what Sparck Jones had called dictionary circles) could be collapsed by identifying the members as synonyms and flattening the tree at that point.

Amsler was the first to view a dictionary as a lexical database in a standard sense of that term, one to which standard Boolean techniques of information retrieval might be applied, at least in principle, for example, one could retrieve straightforwardly all the definitions containing a Boolean combination of words (and *not* containing certain words if desired). When he came to the key problem of dictionary definitions—the ambiguity of the defining terms, as we have put the matter—he made use of handcrafting; there was no alternative at that period. Teams of paid disambiguators manually disambiguated the core words of definitions and tagged the words with their appropriate senses, that is, in the context of the particular definition.

It was here that Amsler's key term emerged: the "tangled hierarchy." He showed that the taxonomy in a dictionary is not a simple hierarchy, but a forest of "tangled" trees. This meant that individual trees can be thought of as sharing nodes, so that a given node does not have a single parent, as in untangled/normal hierarchies, but rather many parents, although there is no reason to believe that any clean structure of another type (e.g., a lattice; see figure 6.1) is thus formed. A tangled hierarchy is

a formal data structure whose bottom is a set of terminal disambiguated words that are not used as kernel defining terms; these are the most specific elements in the structure. The tops of the structure are senses of words such as "cause," "thing," "class," "being," etc. These are the most general elements in the tangled hierarchy. If all the top terms are considered to be members of the meta-class "⟨word-sense⟩" then the tangled forest becomes a tangled tree. (Amsler 1980, pp. 133–134)

He then goes on to claim that this device of creating a single (vacuous) upper node ("word sense") does give stronger properties, that of the whole being a lattice or at least a semilattice, but there is no reason to believe this is so under any standard definitions (see Birkhoff 1961, and below). The importance of this work is not that the structures of definition Amsler found had any particular classic formal structure—they probably do not—but that he established the following empirically for the first time (1) dictionary-derived structures using sense-tagged words (developed by hand in his case); and (2) what the empirical linkages of definition between the topmost, or primitive, items in a real dictionary were.

These latter were highly interesting. Amsler showed that there were strong loops at the very top of the structure, of the kind Sparck-Jones had located long before, and that there was a fairly clear chain (NOT, note, a tangled hierarchy at all) formed by the defining terms with the highest numbers of total descendants—which makes them primitives in practice—but which had only one or very few *immediate* descendants. Moreover, at the very top, lexicographers had fallen back on defining the most

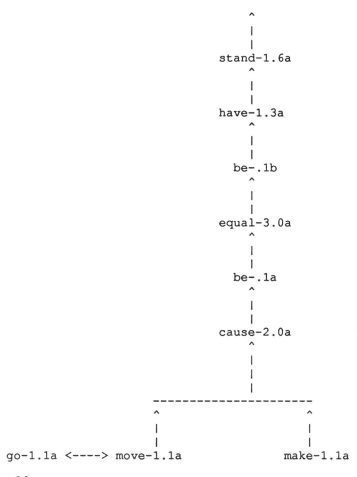

Figure 6.1
Relations between topmost tangled verb hierarchy nodes.

abstract words by more concrete ones (since their definitions had to contain something!) as in figure 6.1 where "have" and "stand" are ultimately defined by terms like "remain"—not something one would have expected from the abstract considerations of primitiveness of chapter 4:

Amsler also looked forward to many of the developments that others were to follow: the automatic disambiguation of definitions (he suggested metarules and co-occurrence techniques); a grammar of definition; and that morphological forms would have to be undone to achieve a full hierarchy of root or stem forms. In the end, one might say, the tangled hierarchy itself turned out to be one of the least interesting features of this work.

Michiel's Early Work on LDOCE

Soon after Amsler's thesis, Michiels' thesis (1982) at Liège began the first exploration of LDOCE, the machine-readable dictionary (MRD) that has been the one most used in the research described in this book. We shall delay till later (see chapter 7) a detailed description of LDOCE, a dictionary with a strong internal structure designed for foreign learners rather than native speakers of English. Michiels' interests were different from those of Amsler, but he, too, began a strain of work that has continued strongly. In a sense, Amsler was not concerened with the linear structure of individual entries in MWPD, which were treated as unordered strings of word atoms, much as Sparck Jones treated the lists of synonyms in Roget in an unordered way. That may have been reasonable in the case of dictionaries with no clear, well defined, internal format, though less so in LDOCE where the need to serve non-native readers led to formatted entries in a much stronger sense than was traditional.

Michiels, then, began to examine the structure of the LDOCE entries themselves, investigating the grammar of the definitions. He also gave descriptions of the grammatical codes in LDOCE, having seen early their relevance for NLP, and gave algorithms for transforming the codes (which were loosely based on a Firthian-style description) into forms that linguists could use to separate English verbs into classes closer to those of modern American linguistics (e.g., "equi" and "raising" verbs).

Lattices and Thesauri

Thesauri were investigated computationally somewhat earlier than dictionaries, and more definite claims were made about their formal structure, chiefly by Masterman (1957). She saw early on that a thesaurus could be a powerful tool for NLP, particularly for word sense disambiguation. Her belief was that a thesaurus could be seen as a lattice (in a technical sense; see Birkhoff 1961), namely, as a system of partially ordered sets, such that for any two sets (normally seen as nodes in a graph) there was a unique upper and lower bound.

Masterman was not a formalist herself, but believed passionately in the applicability of mathematical techniques to natural language and its processing. Without them, she believed, the subject would have nothing worth the name of theory, and she always contrasted what she saw as genuine structures, such as lattices about which theorems could be proved, with systems like Chomsky's transformational grammar, which she saw as simply formal NOTATION but with no mathematical content, a position not without some historical justification.

Her key notion was to link the concepts of "fan" (which she took from Brouwer 1952) as representing the way the senses of a word spread out indefinitely into the future as new spokes for the fan, together with that of lattice, which, in its classic form, can be seen as a fan and an inverted fan joined together at a set of "generator" nodes. It was these nodes she wished to identify with the heads, or main classifier typings, of Roget's *Thesaurus*.

The key hope was that every node in a full, complex, lattice for a thesaurus would be an interpretable Boolean join or meet of the sets of word senses covered by the 1000 main heads. The basic idea is thus simple: for the upper half of the lattice (INTERSECTION HEAD1 HEAD2) can be interpreted as the set of word senses that HEAD1 and HEAD2 share in common. Similarly, in the lower half (UNION HEAD1 HEAD2) will be the set of word senses appearing under either HEAD1 or HEAD2.

These sets are, in fact, of course, sets of word *names*. The additional assumption being made is that the appearance of a word under a particular head is an effective locator of a particular sense of the word; for example, "state" appearing under a head HUMAN ORGANIZATION will be taken to be the governmental sense of state, whereas the same word appearing under the head MATERIAL-FORM may be taken to be the chemical or physical state. A problem with the lattice model then appears: the intersection node (INTERSECTION MATERIAL-FORM HUMAN-ORGANIZATION) is non-empty, since it must contain "state," although it is unclear what interpretation we should assign to the word at that particular node.

Nonetheless, this methodology did have strong continuity with what became well-tested information retrieval techniques. And, as we shall see in a moment, it led directly to one of the earliest classic computational-semantic experiments. On the whole, fans and lattices have proved too specific as structures for the needs of NLP. Again, as we saw with Amsler's work above, once it is conceded that neither words nor things fall neatly under a single simple taxonomic tree, it is by no means clear they fall under anything as tidy as a lattice either, where every union and intersection node is guaranteed, but not guaranteed any interpretation. Harris (1957) did at one time toy with lattices as language structures and, more recently, Mellish (1983) has sought to link them again (cf. Parker-Rhodes 1978) to Halliday's categories of grammar and semantics. Nevertheless, more promising routes have been found through general applications of the theory of graphs, where the constraints on possible structure can be determined empirically rather than a priori.

Masterman and her colleagues did conduct one classic thesaurus experiment for word sense disambiguation, though it did not rest on there being any underlying lattice structure to Roget's *Thesaurus*. The experiment was a pilot machine translation scheme for a passage of Virgil's *Georgics*. A working coding was obtained for the Latin text by taking for each Latin word stem the words given for it in a Latin-English dictionary and looking them up in the word-to-head index in Roget. By this two-stage method, each Latin word stem was attached to a list of Roget head numbers.

The main procedure was then to compare the list of head numbers for each word with the lists for all the other words of the same sentence in turn, and to keep as a coding for the initial word only those heads that occurred at least twice for words elsewhere in the sentence. In the case of *Agricola incurvo in terram dimovit aratro*, for example, the heads still attached to the three noun stems after that procedure are as follows:

AGRICOLA: Region, Agriculture
TERRAM: Region, Land, Furrow
ARATRO: Agriculture, Furrow, Convolution

As one might expect, the lists have members in common, for the procedure adopted is causing the "coherence of sense" between the words of the sentence to show itself in a determinate way. If it were not for this, we might safely assume translation, like understanding itself, would be impossible unless words had only a single sense, a general hypothesis all observers reject. The final procedure was to take the list of the remaining words of the sentence in turn and find the English words occurring under all the heads listed above in the main body of the thesaurus. So, if one takes the heads REGION and AGRICULTURE in Roget, one finds that their only common words are "farmer" and "ploughman," either of which can be the final output for *agricola*. By the same method, the output for *terram* is "soil" or "ground," and that for *aratro* is "plough," "ploughman," or "rustic." It was then assumed syntactic considerations would filter out inappropriate parts of speech, although that alone would not select the correct "plough" from the other two noun alternatives.

The most important idea in this work is that of using the thesaurus heads as a set of semantic primitives for semantic coding and analysis; it was a set that had more empirical justification and grounding in some ways than the a priori sets of the AI-style codings, though, as we shall see below, it was a coding that could be indirectly linked back to them. The greater empirical grounding was not the system of Roget, for that was one man's classification, but the fact that the heads were linked to substantial empirical word distributions in the thesaurus itself.

This work was done on a form of Roget's *Thesaurus* that was hand-punched onto cards, and the computing was done in 1957 on a Hollerith card-sorting machine. It was all incredibly elementary by today's standards, but it was theoretically motivated: the set intersections and unions of the lattice were actually used even if that whole structure did not constrain the process. The results were satisfying, and, most interesting, the methodology has been rediscovered at regular intervals over the succeeding 35 years. That the method is inadequate at a deeper level has been no impediment to that; it has no notion of the role of syntax or of linear order on sense resolution in context. It has been a standard move since then to introduce semantically related words into sentences in such a way that this algorithm will not work, as in "our local policeman is a good sport; he plays for the village team," where "sport" does not mean "a recreational organization" even though any method like the one above will conclude (on the basis of semantic coherence with "team") that it does. The work described was highly original, and preceded similar computational work on dictionaries by many years.

Sparck Jones's Thesis and the Transition to Information Retrieval

In this section we illustrate the role of the traditional thesaurus in information retrieval by describing the work of Sparck Jones, and also use it to illustrate the (long forgotten but now resurfacing) continuities between work in NLP and information retrieval. Sparck Jones's work with the same thesaurus as used in the Masterman experiments above is a classic piece of research in statistical information retrieval techniques as well as in word sense semantics. Much more than the MT experiment just described, her work rested on the actual microstructure of Roget's *Thesaurus*.

Sparck Jones described a thesaurus as classifying word usages down to their appearance under main heads, of which there are about 1000, which were themselves hierarchically classified by Roget. As we noted, we can broadly identify a word's appearance under a head as pinning down a sense of it (though this can then become an initial definition of sense, not a description). Thus, "swelling" and "knob" can appear under a head AUGMENTATION. However, the latter can also appear under ROTUNDITY and therefore could be said to have two senses because of that fact. This cross-classification (often marked by explicit cross-reference in the printed text) is an important feature of a thesaurus. It is certainly a "tangled hierarchy" in Amsler's sense; indeed, it is an explicit one where Amsler's was discovered with great effort. This brings out a key difference between thesauri and dictionaries, one which made the former initially more attractive for NLP: the dictionary defines, but the thesaurus organizes individual words with respect to one another (cf. Scott 1987).

Sparck Jones then drew attention to a lower thesaurus level she called a "row" consisting of close semisynonyms, although these are sometimes organized by notions other than synonymy, such as agency with respect to one another, or by being agents of similar actions. The rows do not have explicit primitive names in the way that the heads themselves constitute a primitive coding of all the words falling under them. However, the row distinctions inside the same head do certainly distinguish usages and might be said to distinguish senses as well: "Thus the thesaurus at the same time distinguishes word senses through their thesaurus class allocations and defines or at least characterizes these senses in terms of explicitly or implicitly given class concepts" (Sparck-Jones thesaurus dictionary entry in the *Encyclopedia of Artificial Intelligence* edited by Shapiro 1992).

The basis of her empirical work was to set out and defend a notion of row that linked to both classic structural linguistic notions of substitution in a frame and to Quinean notions of synonymy (though it could be said that he was describing such possibilities only to reject them!). Rows based on substitutability in some frame might be as follows:

effort, exertion
effort, attempt

effort, manpower
effort, performance, achievement
conduct performance

These rows were actually handcrafted versions of context-based identity of just the kind that researchers now seek to find computationally by statistical means, a goal not possible with the text-computing resources of 1966. The core of Sparck Jones's thesis was then to treat the semisynonyms in a row exactly as if they were feature classifiers in the sense of information retrieval, where, say, a particular pot or jug in an archaeological classification task might be classified as

brown, handled, chipped, has-woman-painting, frieze-on-rim

A technique of automatic classification that had been contemporaneously developed was called the theory of clumps. It took feature descriptions like the one for the jug above and, given a large number of them, attempted to classify the jugs into classes based not on commondefining features—a relic of the old discredited notion of there being necessary and sufficient conditions for being in a class—but on commonneighborhood membership. To put it another way, a classifying feature was to be understood by the company it kept (cf. Firth "you shall know a word by the company it keeps"). Thus, two jugs might go into the same computed class because they had features that frequently occurred together on jugs. There is now a well-developed range of statistical algorithms for clumping, clustering, etc. on such principles. There was explicit linking at the time from this methodology to the Wittgensteinian "family resemblance" notion of a concept discussed earlier (see chapter 2).

Sparck Jones took these classic information retrieval techniques to apply to rows, as defined above, to see if rows could be classified on the basis of their common membership into thesaurus heads, which would then be explicated on an empirical basis for the first time. This was groundbreaking work in empirical semantics, even if it rested on an unempirical initial notion of synonymy (one that could now be remedied) and an abiding problem with all automatic classification techniques, that the clumps, when found, did not have *names*, a problem we shall return to later when describing an extension of these techniques to lexical work. Sparck Jones's work was the first explicit link from information retrieval to NLP, a link that was then buried for some 20 years (her thesis was finally published 20 years after it was written).

The relevance of this work for NLP is that it can be seen as establishing one empirical basis for the crucial notion of word sense, a matter that has remained highly disputable as we noted in an earlier chapter. The "clumpings" *in* a row (whose occurrences do not seem sufficient to establish a sense for a word) into clumps of rows (loosely to be identified with a head primitive) can be seen as fixing the sense of a word by the clump (or head), since we earlier took occurrence of a word under a head as being a working criterion of "being a sense of that word." Note again that, in this view, the thesaurus equivalent to a sense is then a structure of classification and not, as in a dictionary, a definition.

An interesting contrast here is with much more recent work of Plate and McDonald (Wilks et al. 1987) who established networks of words by means of large matrix inversions similar to those of Sparck Jones, based on occurrence and contiguity frequency within the 2000 "defining primitives" of LDOCE (see below). These structures, called Pathfinder networks (see in more detail below), are very intuitively appealing with, for example, the "financial" and "river" senses of "bank" separating out quite clearly as decomposable subnetworks.

The details of these algorithms need not detain us here, since we discuss co-occurrence algorithms in detail later in the book, but they are of the same class as the Sparck Jones algorithms, but carried out with much larger computational resources.

It might be objected that this demonstration is no proof at all of sense distinction by classification since the text analyzed for the associations is LDOCE, that is to say, not a normal text but a dictionary, one that assumes the very sense distinctions we are setting out to establish empirically! But this objection fails, and an empirical basis for word senses is preserved, because it is easy to show that most usages of any given word in the whole LDOCE (and the computation ranges over the whole dictionary) occur not in its own definition (where its senses are indeed distinguished a priori) but in the example sentences and in the definitions of *other* words. Hence, LDOCE is, in effect, just a text in these experiments, and the empirical separation of lexical senses by classification techniques is real evidence of their existence.

Information Retrieval and Thesauri

Sparck Jones' work had relevance not only for NLP but for information retrieval proper, because it was one of the first empirical attempts at thesaurus construction. The thesaurus already had a long history in information retrieval, initially as a structured system of descriptors drawn from a particular scientific literature (Luhn 1968), and given the normally unambiguous role of words in science it can be seen that the role of the thesaurus was not, as in the NLP work just discussed, to resolve ambiguity of sense but rather to widen the search space of texts or documents by using the thesaurus as a system of synonymous terms. A retrieval thesaurus is, in Sparck Jones' words (1964), "thus at once an indexing device designed to facilitate flexible topic characterization, and a searching device suited to mechanization through full or partial matching on term specifications ..."

However, the limitations on the use of an a priori thesaurus for information retrieval soon became apparent, and one way of looking at the Sparck Jones work just described is as one of the first systematic attempts to derive thesaurus classes empirically from data on the basis of co-ocurrences. The same methods she used could be, and now have been, applied directly to text rather than to the particular form of synonymous row data she chose to use, and part of that difference is one of greater computing resources; it is now possible to compute over vast text databases so as to identify co-occurrence between word sets (which would establish Sparck Jones rows) in a way that was then not possible. The Plate-MacDonald algorithm referred to above used one such method, essentially a variant on the clumps algorithm, though a substantial range of metrics were tried and compared (Wilks et al. 1987)

We now introduce a recent example of text-based information retrieval that links dictionary procedures to statistical methods to form a hybrid system, one that can also be thought of as growing directly from the Sparck Jones work described earlier. We emphasize its statistical aspects because its symbolic basis, LDOCE, is described elsewhere in this book (see chapter 7). Although the techniques described are information retrieval in a fairly classic sense, they are actually continuous with a range of specifically text-based NLP techniques of the kind we describe in this book. This closeness has often been ignored or obscured by writers on both sides of the NLP + AI-information retrieval divide and one of our aims in this book is to emphasize it.

Because text-based information retrieval (IR) deals with large bodies of natural language text, an efficient representation is a primary concern. This concern has often led to the use of representations based on statistical analyses of text, in contrast to the richer, semantic representations of text that characterize research in AI and NLP. Information retrieval systems have sought domain independence through the use of statistical measures for efficiency, rather than by incorporating domain knowledge that might increase retrieval effectiveness, but decrease efficiency. For information retrieval systems, the problem with any natural language approach, compared to traditional information retrieval techniques, is that NLP is computationally very expensive. Hybrid systems incorporating NLP techniques where possible, and relying on information retrieval techniques where efficiency in dealing with very large databases is necessary, provide an effective compromise (Croft 1986).

Up to Modern Times: Wilks on Thesauri and Frames

Another attempt to bring the thesaurus back into NLP was made by Wilks (1978) as part of a change in the semantic representational scheme used as a basis for preference semantics (see chapter 3). It was argued that the system of AI-style semantic formulas (as in chapter 3) could be enormously compacted if a thesaurus were used in addition. Thus the terms of a typical thesaurus row:

Vehicle: truck, car, train, wagon etc.

(where vehicle can be thought of as a notional name for the row, though as we saw in Sparck Jones's work above, rows do not generally have explicit names) are all terms with a strong overlap of meaning, in that they all contain the core notion of "vehicle." So two key shifts in notation were proposed (which could be incorporated into any detailed notation):

1. The semantic formulas for the terms truck, car, etc. could be compacted by inserting the atom VEHICLE into each formula, which would be a pointer to the formulas stored for VEHICLE.
2. This move has the side effect of allowing formulas to contain any word whatever, not just semantic primitives, provided that each word points in turn to its own formula.

In this way the set of formulas takes on more of the characteristics of a real dictionary in that they can be chained as far as needed, and the absolute distinction between primitives and nonprimitive words that many found objectionable (e.g., Bobrow and Winograd 1977) is abolished, while still allowing some crucial role to the original primitives (in that they point nowhere else).

An additional advantage of this method is that it brings to the semantic lexicon the levels of grain explicitly present in a thesaurus, but only to be found laboriously and with difficulty in a standard dictionary. A further move was to identify the primitives with the very highest levels of Roget's hierarchy (e.g., CAUSE, SUBSTANCE) so that the primitives then had no type distinction from symbols like "vehicle," but just a higher place in the hierarchy.

An additional representational move suggested in Wilks (1978) was that some of the "dynamic" benefits of frames or scripts in meaning representation could be obtained in a representationally uniform way by extending the notion of a thesaurus to include rows that were not unordered sequences of semisynonyms but *ordered* dynamic sequences. So, for example, it might be said that part of the very meaning of "smoking" was the sequence of actions that smoking consists in. These could be written as an ordered sequence:

smoke: take-out hold light suck blow etc. extinguish

The suggestion was not wholly serious, but it would have certain advantages if such structures were seen as "minimal cases" of frames or scripts. Since the words would now be pointers to formulas, those would contain the preferred agents and objects of the listed actions, so the compacted sequence above, in an extended thesaurus format, could contain all the information stored in more complex sequential frames or scripts.

Chapter 7

Text Analysis and Its Relationship to Dictionaries: Dictionaries as Texts

The relationships between dictionaries and lexicons, on the one hand, and texts, alias corpora, on the other, are many and complex. Calzolari (Wilks 1993) recently distinguished the following such relationships.

- Lexicon → corpus: lexical information is used for tagging;
- Corpus → lexicon: word frequency analysis is used for annotating lexical entries;
- Corpus → lexicon: lexical items unlikely to be found in dictionary sources are extracted (e.g., proper nouns);
- Corpus → lexicon: existing lexical entries are enriched by additional information extracted via corpus analysis;
- Corpus → lexicon: collocational information is collected, organized, and presented (e.g., studies could be performed on the basis of mutual information, idiom identification, grammatical pattern analysis, etc.);
- Corpus → lexicon: paradigmatic- and syntagmatic-driven semantic clustering is performed;
- Corpus → lexicon: (domain-specific) knowledge is extracted;
- Lexicon → corpus: existing taxonomies (e.g., from the ACQUILEX-I project) are used for semantic tagging of texts;
- Lexicon → corpus: the heavier use of lexical information for disambiguating naturally occurring texts;
- Lexicon + corpus: as used together in computational lexicography.

In this chapter we begin to explore some of these: firstly, considering the dictionary as a text itself; secondly, discussing the creation of dictionaries with the aid of text analysis; and thirdly, the text analysis of corpora with the aid of dictionaries as tools. These topics do not cover what is discussed at length in later chapters, namely, text analysis procedures applied to MRDs so as to extract meaning descriptions from them by a variety of methods, so as to produce what we are calling MTDs, or machine-tractable dictionaries.

The Dictionary as a Text: LDOCE and COBUILD

It is a trivial fact that dictionaries, in spite of their special status as source books on the language in which they are (normally) written are, nevertheless, themselves only texts with all the fallibility that implies. Johnson finally withdrew from his own great work with what he termed "frigid tranquillity," but more recently Atkins has shown in great detail the confusions and errors in an MRD like LDOCE (see below) and substantial error collections for that particular dictionary exist (Krovetz 1992). More generally, Wierzbicka has argued that dictionaries "say things that are untrue" and "waste precious space saying things which belong more properly in an encyclopedia" (quoted in Hanks 1994, p. 330). Such criticisms are, in part, of dictionaries as texts, as well as an assault on the *very idea* of a dictionary.

As we saw in chapter 6, the earliest computational work was done on dictionaries like Merriam-Webster's, large dictionaries compiled by what we might call traditional methods. More recently, there has been a group of new MRDs, largely from Britain and largely created for the TEFL (the teaching of English as a foreign language) market. They have been made subject to a much greater degree of internal formalization than previous dictionaries, and those formats have been computer-checked. Unsurprisingly, they have become the basis for much computational work using MRDs. The principal dictionaries have been the *Longman Dictionary of Contemporary English* (LDOCE), Procter 1978 the Collins COBUILD dictionary (Sinclair 1987a), and *The Oxford Advanced Learner's Dictionary* (OALD) (Hornby 1963), and we shall discuss the structure and production of the first two in some detail.

LDOCE: A Basic MRD
LDOCE is a full-sized dictionary designed for learners of English as a second language that contains over 55,000 entries in book form and 41,100 entries in machine-readable form (a typesetting tape). We define an **entry** as a collection of one or more sense definitions that ends at the next head. The **head** is the word, phrase, or hyphenated word defined by an entry. A **sense entry** is the sense definition, examples, and other text

Table 7.1
Head counts for words, entries, and sense entries in LDOCE

Heads	Words	Entries	Sense Entries
Controlled vocabulary	2,166	8,413	24,115
Noncontrolled vocabulary	25,592	32,687	49,998
Totals	27,758	41,100	74,113

associated with one sense of a head. If an entry includes more than one sense definition, then each sense definition will have a number.

The preparers of LDOCE claim that entries are defined using a "controlled" vocabulary of about 2000 words and that the entries have a simple and regular syntax. Table 7.1 shows some basic data derived from our analysis of the machine-readable tape of LDOCE. The true figure of 2,166 is arrived at as follows. The list of controlled vocabulary contains 2,219 words. We have removed 58 prefixes and suffixes that are listed as controlled vocabulary items and have also removed 35 items that did not have heads. Furthermore, the analysis shows that some words are not part of the controlled vocabulary, yet are used frequently in definitions; for example, the word "aircraft" is not part of the controlled vocabulary, yet it is used 267 times in sense definitions. About 40 such words have been added to the list of controlled vocabulary, giving 2,166 words.

The interesting thing to note from table 7.1 is the extremely high number of senses for words belonging to the controlled vocabulary. Although there are only about 2,166 words in the "controlled" vocabulary, over 24,000 of the 74,000 senses defined in LDOCE are senses of these words (including senses of phrases beginning with a word from the controlled vocabulary). To put this another way, controlled vocabulary items are roughly six times as ambiguous as noncontrolled items; words from the controlled vocabulary have an average of 12 senses, while other words have an average of 2.

The book and tape versions of LDOCE both use a system of grammatical codes (loosely based on Quirk et al. 1972, 1985) of about 110 syntactic categories which vary in generality from, for example, *noun* to *noun/count* to *noun/count/followed-by-infinitive-with-TO*.

The machine-readable version of LDOCE also contains "box" and "subject" codes that are not found in the book. The box codes use a set of primitives such as "abstract," "concrete," and "animate," organized into a type hierarchy. The primitives are used to assign type restrictions on nouns and adjectives, and type restrictions on the arguments of verbs.

The subject codes, referred to here as "pragmatic" codes to avoid confusion with grammatical subject, use another set of primitives organized into a hierarchy. This hierarchy consists of main headings such as "engineering" with subheadings like "electrical." These primitives are used to classify words by their subject; for example, one sense of "current" is classified as "geology-and-geography" while another sense is marked "engineering/electrical."

The LDOCE pragmatic coding system divides the world up into 124 major subject categories ranging from **aeronautics, aerospace,** and **agriculture,** through **geology-and-geography, glass,** and **golf,** to **vehicles, water-** and **winter-sports,** and **zoology.** Many of these subjects are further subcategorized (e.g., under **agriculture** is **soil-science** and **horticulture,** and under **zoology** is **entomology, ornithology,** and **ichthyology**), so there is a total of 369 different subject codes in the LDOCE pragmatic system. However, the LDOCE hierarchy is rather flat (only two layers deep), and the 124 major categories have equal and unrelated status; for example, **business** and **economics** are both at the top of the tree and are unconnected; the same is true of **science** and **zoology.**

The work we describe later (chapter 9) (Fowler and Slator 1989, Slator and Wilks 1987) to distinguish word senses use a text-specific lexicon to select the relevant portions of the flat LDOCE hierarchy, placing enumerated text elements at the leaves. Then, a deeper structure, relating pragmatic categories in a more natural way, is imposed onto the LDOCE pragmatic world in order to discover important relationships between concepts within text.

This particular restructuring is not one to be defended point by point; there has been, for instance, an arbitrary division made at the highest level. What can be defended is (1) the notion that, for example, words classified under **botany** have pragmatic connections to words classified as **plant-names,** as well as connections with other words classified under **science** (connections *not* made by the LDOCE pragmatic hierarchy as given), and (2) that these connections are useful to exploit when attempting to determine the subject matter of a text, or when attempting to choose the correct sense of polysemous words.

Later in this chapter we deal in detail with one particular analysis of the LDOCE controlled vocabulary. Substantial analyses have also been done by Jansen et al. (1985).

COBUILD

COBUILD is easy to describe in that its authoring has produced a very full account of what they did. The dictionary has strong similarities to LDOCE but, whereas LDOCE was wholly top-down in terms of its grammatical schemes, semantic and pragmatic codes, and even its definitions, COBUILD was tightly tied, at least as far as its examples and choice of lexical entries were concerned, to a large corpus of text (Sinclair 1987b).

The construction of the COBUILD dictionary broke the traditions of conventional lexicography by coupling the lexicographer's intuitions with computer tools for examining what was at that time probably the largest collection of spoken and written texts ever assembled.

The COBUILD corpus was made up of 20 million words taken from books, magazines, newspapers, pamphlets, leaflets, conversations, and radio and TV broadcasts, and although corpus researchers and lexicographers are likely to argue forever about what a balanced corpus is and whether or not one can be created, the COBUILD corpus certainly was a credible attempt in this direction, and constituted a large representative sample of English. The corpus provided the lexicographers with hard measurable evidence on a large scale about word usage. The sense divisions of a word were determined from large samples of concordance lines containing that word and examples in the dictionary are taken from the corpus.

Certainly the practice of using citations from actual texts follows the old lexicographic tradition of Dr. Johnson's 1755 dictionary and the OED begun in 1878, but this practice differs from the recent one used in the construction of learners' dictionaries which relies on artificial examples of usage.

COBUILD also breaks the long-established traditions of style in which dictionary definitions are written. In COBUILD, the definitions are complete sentences using the headword, thus serving as an extra example of usage. For example, the definition of one of the senses of the adjective "clear" is:

If you are **clear** about something you understand it completely.

In many cases, the complete sentence definitions also serve to indicate syntactic or semantic features of the word being defined. For example, the definitions of count nouns begin with an indefinite article (An **encyclopedia** is ..., and, A **messenger** takes a message ...).

Verb definitions often indicate typical subjects and objects (To **sink** a ship is to ...), or give information about the semantic class of verb arguments. The definition of "conceal," for example, indicates a human subject and many possibilities for the direct object (If you **conceal** something you ...). Metaphorical, figurative, and other nonliteral usages are often signaled by the phrase "If you say that ... "

In addition to the definitions given in an entry, column notes indicate other aspects of usage such as syntactic patterns, synonyms, antonyms, and superordinates.

As for the corpus being used to decide how to partition a word into senses, it should be noted that although the corpus helps the lexicographer to partition a word into senses, the process is still a subjective one. The corpus allows the lexicographer to get an idea of which senses are used most frequently and ensures that the senses defined in the dictionary cover the usage of that word, but it does not determine *which* senses are defined. The number of word senses that correspond to a given set of sentences is still based on the lexicographer's intuition. A general definition of one lexicographer may cover several more specific senses defined by another.

Nonetheless, the decisions made in the design of the COBUILD dictionary were based on extensive consultation with a large corpus and the dictionary provides us with a principled and unique account of English usage.

Dictionaries as Texts

Although their entries are normally in a fixed syntax, explicit or implicit, and even though they may contain substantial structural features and constraints like the two dictionaries just described, nonetheless dictionaries are real texts, and the clearest demonstration of that is that their defining words are ambiguous, just like those they define. Or, rather, as Guo showed (see below) they are, in LDOCE at least, substantially less ambiguous in fact than one might expect from the table given earlier, but still ambiguous.

Cheng-Ming Guo: Deriving Semantic Primitives from MRD

Guo (1989) tackles the problem of deriving a "natural set of semantic primitives" from LDOCE. The aim was to develop an approach that could exploit a very specialized process of bootstrapping. The ultimate goal of this research is "the construction of the machine lexicon," but this has not been completed. Four types of words and word senses were searched for in LDOCE, each type being a subset of the next set:

1. "Seed senses" are senses of the semantic primitives used to define in the dictionary. The words that the seed senses are senses of are called the "seed words"; finding these seeds is the aim of the second step in the procedure described below. Seed words and seed senses are a subset of the "defining words" and "defining senses."

2. Defining words are the words used to define the meanings of all the "controlled words" in their sense definitions in LDOCE. Not every controlled word is used in definitions of the meanings of controlled words. "Defining senses" are individual word senses of the defining words that are actually found used in the definitions of the meanings of the controlled words. Defining words and defining senses are a subset of the "controlled words" and "controlled senses."

3. Controlled words are words from the list of the "controlled vocabulary" given at the back of the LDOCE. LDOCE uses the controlled vocabulary words in all its word sense definitions and usage examples. All the word senses of the controlled words defined in LDOCE are controlled senses. Controlled words and controlled senses are a subset of the "LDOCE words" and "LDOCE senses."

4. Any word contained in LDOCE is an LDOCE word. Any word sense of any LDOCE word is an LDOCE sense.

The first step of the procedure was the derivation of the defining senses. LDOCE has a list of 2,139 controlled words (after affixes and other morphs and removed), 137 of which do not participate in defining the word senses of any of the controlled words; therefore, there is a reduced set of 2,002 controlled words. This reduced set is called the defining words of LDOCE; these are used in the definition of the meanings of the 2,139 controlled words. Choosing which senses of the defining words are the defining sense of LDOCE is done by hand (with computer-aided editing assistance). Those word senses that are found to be used in defining the meanings of at least one of the controlled words are recorded as the defining senses of that word. Below are all the occurrences of the word "father" in the definitions of the 2,139 controlled words.

aunt(0,1): the sister of one's father or mother, the wife of one's uncle, or a woman whose brother or sister has a child
by (1,16): having (the stated male animal, esp. a horse) as a father

get(0,17): to become the father of | BEGET
grandfather(0,0): the father of someone's father or mother
grandmother(0,0): the mother of someone's father or mother
parent(0,1): the father or mother of a person
uncle(0,1): the brother of one's father or mother, the husband of one's
aunt, or a man whose brother or sister has a child
uncle(0,3): a man who takes the place of a father, esp. in relation to the
children of a woman who is or was married to someone else

The word "father" can either be a noun or a verb, and LDOCE provides eight senses for "father" as a noun. Among them are "father" as a male parent and "father" as a priest. In the above example, only the male parent sense of "father" is used to define the word senses of other controlled words. Hence "a male parent" is recorded as the defining sense of the word "father" in LDOCE. This process, which is a machine-aided human editing task, was repeated until a total of 3,860 word senses of the 2002 defining words had been determined as the defining senses of LDOCE. One thousand fifty-one defining words have single defining senses; 526 words have two defining senses; and 425 words have three or more defining senses.

Once the defining senses are chosen, it remains to derive the seed words for LDOCE. To do this, a "hunch set" for the seed words is chosen by using frequency of occurrence criteria; the words of the initial hunch set are the intersection of three basic lexicons: the 4000 most frequently used words in all sense definitions in LDOCE as found in a word frequency study of LDOCE (Wilks et al. 1988); the 850 words of Basic English used in *The General Basic English Dictionary* (Ogden 1942); and the 500 most common words in Kucera and Francis (1967). The assumption is that a large portion of the seed words will appear in all the above-mentioned word lists. This operation yielded a preliminary hunch set of approximately 400 words.

The empirical procedure to find the seed sense in LDOCE then becomes a matter of testing whether the hunch set accounts for the controlled words within three or four defining cycles (where a "defining cycle" is the ability of one group of words to define a larger group). Those words whose own defining senses have been defined join the words that define *their* meanings to define yet more words at the next defining cycle. Either this process starts with a hunch set and a small number of cycles yields the "LDOCE words," in which case the hunch set is a set of seed words, or the LDOCE words are not found at the end of the sequence, in which case the hunch set must be revised.

According to this study, the first defining cycle in LDOCE starts with a set of some 1200 seed words. At the end of the first defining cycle, around 700 more controlled words join the seed words to define more words at the next defining cycle. The second defining cycle has another 200 or so controlled words defined. By the end of the third defining cycle, all the controlled words are defined. It takes another one or two defining cycles for all the LDOCE words to be defined.

Testing the hunch set means finding whether it accounts for the 3,860 defining senses within two or three defining cycles. This testing can be carried out by a computer program in a fairly straightforward way. Note the implicit assumption that there is no one, true, correct set of seed senses. These "naturally occurring semantic primitives" are derived empirically, and different hunches about what the initial set should be will result in different sets at the end of the procedure. In other words, there could be any number of hunch sets that survive this procedure, and that is in accordance with our intuitions about the nature of primitive meanings, and conforms to the arguments in chapter 2 as to why this must be so.

Dictionaries as Knowledge Structures

A considerable amount of the work described in this book is devoted precisely to resolving this ambiguity of defining words in MRDs, so as to convert them to MTDs. Some of the newer dictionary construction projects (see the CUP dictionary in chapter 14) aim to go directly to a machine-"tractable" dictionary and avoid this phase. When human readers see ambiguous words used in the definitions of real dictionaries, they appear to recognize those words as used in a particular sense, understand the intended senses of the words, and hence disambiguate the words in the dictionary definitions. For those concerned to "convert" dictionary definitions to tractable forms, the first strategy is to mimic what humans appear to do and run a program on dictionary definitions and disambiguate those definitions when using them. The second possibility is to remove beforehand the lexical ambiguity from the dictionary definitions and thus have definitions which contain only word senses, a solution proposed by Quillian (1967) and Amsler (1980) among others. The third solution is to not attend to the problem until it becomes essential that it be dealt with.

At various places in this book, we have taken up a position that might be called the inseparability of knowledge and language (chapter 2) and this has implications for the point under discussion. We argue that particular language structures, text structures, are in fact a paradigm for knowledge structures (Wilks 1978) or, to put it very crudely, knowledge for certain purposes should be stored in textlike forms (as opposed to, say, predicate calculus-like ones). Examples of knowledge structures in such forms include the planes of Quillian's memory model (1967), pseudotexts from preference semantics, and sense frames from collative semantics (Fass 1988). Our position is far deeper than the superficial claim that we, as people, normally store information as pieces of paper with writing on them, but rather that common principles underlie the semantic structure of text and of knowledge representations.

Given that the purpose of dictionaries is to provide definitions of words and their senses, it might well be expected that, of all forms of text, it would be in dictionaries that the semantic structure of language would be the most explicit and hence most accessible for examination and comparison with the semantic structure of knowledge representations. And indeed, the semantic structure of dictionaries has been analyzed, compared to the underlying organization of knowledge representations, and similarities have been observed. Dictionary entries commonly contain a genus word and its differentia and the genus terms of dictionary entries can be assembled into hierarchies (Amsler 1980, Chodorow, Byrd, and Heidorn 1985).

Likewise, in the study of knowledge representation, a frame (Minsky 1975) can be viewed as containing genus and differentia pairs, as can semantic networks. The key point here is that its ineluctably textlike features should not be thought of as disqualifying a dictionary from being a knowledge structure in the stronger AI sense: sense-tagging the defining words of a dictionary only does what is implicitly claimed to have been performed by those (like the researchers involved in Cyc, Kl-one, or any framelike representation) who present knowledge representation (KR) formalisms containing recognizable *words* in them.

Text Analysis on a Large Scale

We turn now to a very brief review of large-scale text computational analysis projects—of which there are far fewer than one might think— before asking how they might bear on the construction of new dictionaries from corpora by methods more radical than those of the MRDs just discussed. As we noted earlier, Pat Suppes used to say 20 years ago that he would pay attention to AI-based NLP only when it could "do something book length." That day is now pretty close, though old-fashioned machine translation systems like SYSTRAN (Toma 1976) met his criterion at a low level a good while ago. The present period could seem like a rerun (in NLP) of the struggles within machine vision in the late 1970s; the high-level, top-down, paradigm of scene analysis (Guzman, Brady, Waltz, etc.) was crumbling in the face of low-level, bottom-up, arguments posed by Marr. NLP has been told for some time that it should be more scientific, like machine vision, so perhaps the current emergence of connectionist, statistical, and associationist techniques in NLP is a form of progress in virtue of that fact alone.

One of us (Y.A.W.) has a personal interest in this matter in that his own first major program ran on texts, using a coherence-based approach that was later called preference semantics (Wilks 1975a). The program ran on philosophical argument texts with newspaper editorials as controls. None of that was on a very large scale, although it was probably pretty big for LISP programs in the mid-1960s. Its aim was to locate coherent text structures that were more revealing and information-providing than those coming from the information retrieval and associationist methods of the period. It was obvious to many in AI then that such methods had been totally discredited, at least as far as text content was concerned. Wilks's own efforts continued to be to find an appropriate level of structure, lying above those, yet without going impossibly deeply into what later came to be called knowledge-based text understanding. Although, as Augustine used to point out, truth may not be in the middle at all, but at both extremes.

The autobiographical note of the last paragraph was to make the point, if it still needs making, that the current statistical/connectionist, etc. approaches are not essentially novel or revolutionary, as their proponents tend to claim; their techniques are, by and large, well-known and long-rejected. The interesting question now is: Can those techniques now be optimized in some way, by software or hardware methods, so as to produce more plausible results than before? Another very important issue is whether the benefits of "higher"- and "lower"- level methods can be combined to scale up NLP in the way we all now accept as necessary.

Before examing several large scale text processing projects which rely on the use of dictionaries, we give a brief and cursory taxonomy of other large-scale text-processing efforts to set the stage. One could distinguish at least the following components or phases:

1. The SYSTRAN machine translation system has a core 25 years old but still processes whole books in a few minutes every day at the Federal Translation Division at Dayton Ohio. It is massive text processing by any standard, and gets a rate of something like a 75% of Russian sentences acceptably translated into English. SYSTRAN is very efficiently programmed, but the core consists of routines no one fully understands any more in linguistic terms, and which cannot be edited; it certainly has no high-level semantics or knowledge-based capacity.

2. The FRUMP system by DeJong (1979) at Yale analyzed Associated Press (AP) newswires with "sketchy scripts." Its final hit rate was about 38% of the stories it should have got (as judged by human readers). It was an analysis system based on structured keywords, although it claimed derivation from a higher-level system (conceptual dependency, Schank 1975). Its performance was never compared with standard information retrieval techniques over similar material.

3. Leech's (Garside and Leech 1982) automatic tagging system for parts of speech in the LOB text corpus used low-level probabilistic procedures. AI workers mocked it for years but it turned out to have a success rate on the order of 95% and has been reimplemented by Marcus with the addition of intonational tagging.

4. Waltz's (Mott et al. 1986) implementation of keyword information retrieval on a connection machine embodies a range of interesting string-matching techniques. This work is not connectionism (albeit Waltz's [1987] simultaneous interest in connectionist methods) but is large-scale text analysis precisely because it is not hamstrung by the scale-up problems of connectionism (including connectionist information retrieval, Belew 1986). Waltz's proposals are much more like a combination of "weak" methods that combine to produce a strong effect.

5. Church's (Church and Hanks 1990) recent work computes digrams in large texts to give probable successor information in such a way as to partition occurrences of a word in text in a way that corresponds closely to plausible sense groupings in many cases. Related work is reported by Brown et al. (1988, 1991), and this work should be compared to the McDonald and Plate computations of sense clusters described in chapter 8. Related work is reported over dictionaries and texts by Boguraev et al. (1989). This is undoubtedly large-scale computation but the relationship to "meaning" that Church and Hanks claim is unclear, since no individ-

ual (who presumably knows the "meanings of words") has such information, unless we postulate a very large corpus base for reading skills. However, one could reply that an individual may indeed have had access early in life to the 100 million or so words of text (spoken and written) required for such algorithms. Hanks's efforts to construct a new dictionary, based in part at least on such information measures, is described in chapter 14.

6. Jelinek (Brown et al. 1988) and his colleagues at IBM are doing machine translation based on hidden Markov models of redundancy in text, applied to parallel text in two languages (French and English). This may turn out to have the flaw that it relies on similar orders of "related" words in the source and target languages, a condition not normally met. Even between two languages that have some such relationship (English and French in their case) the success rate of correctly parsed sentences is low, even when compared with SYSTRAN. They are, however, at the time of writing, importing higher-level grammatical structures, also obtained from corpora, into their system and it is as yet unclear at what level of percentages-of-sentences-correctly-translated the system will top out.

What can one say generally about such massive text-processing methods? They are a very mixed bag: *1*, for example, relies on hand-coding like almost all machine translation, whereas the IBM approach *6* is wholly automatic, all its information being derived from the text with no hand-coding. One could rate the systems on whether or not they do achieve their (even if limited) goals; *3* clearly does. Or one could ask whether one can be fairly certain that no amount of optimization could allow the chosen method to reach the goal (as in *1* and *6*, we suspect), whereas other systems do not have goals clear enough to be sure (e.g., *5*).

These are almost certainly not the fundamental questions to ask, however much fun they may be to answer. The better way ahead is to ask whether such different types of method can be combined, "higher" and "lower" ones, to give a strong combination of what Newell (1973) called inherently weak methods. We now consider several examples of large scale text processing in which dictionaries play an essential part.

TIPSTER

One of the largest-scale projects to date in the area of text analysis is the ARPA (*A*dvanced *R*esearch *P*rojects *A*gency)-funded TIPSTER project in the United States. The 2-year first stage of the TIPSTER project was initiated in September 1991 to fund research in two areas: very large-scale information retrieval and information extraction. It is the intention of the funders that the second stage of the project will support the combination of some of the best methods produced by the participating research groups (University of Massachusetts at Amherst, Syracuse University, and Hecht Nielson Corp. for the information retrieval portion; and General Electric and Carnegic-Mellon University; New Mexico State University [NMSU] and Brandeis; and University of Massachusetts at Amherst, Hughes Aircraft, and Bolt-Beranek Newman Corp. for the information extraction portion) to produce an actual working system for document classification, analysis, and retrieval.

In this section we describe the information extraction portion of the current TIPSTER project as well as our own work in incorporating information from an MRD into a working text analysis system, work which to a large extent distinguishes our system from the other TIPSTER systems. Descriptions of each of the TIPSTER systems are given in Workshops (1992a, 1992b, 1993).

Information extraction is the name being used in the TIPSTER project for an automatic process which performs a task similar to one that a human would in reading a document and filling out a predefined form (which is referred to as a "template" in the TIPSTER world) corresponding to that document. It is interesting to note that this automatic process is intended to aid human analysts to sift through the huge number of documents that are now available to them electronically, but it does not attempt to automate a task that human analysts actually do. It might replace the task a human analyst performs by reading a document and making notes on an index card, or the automatically filled templates might be used to indicate the potential importance of particular documents and signal a careful reading by the human analyst.

As part of the TIPSTER project, information extraction systems were created for two domains (broadly, business and microelectronics) and for two languages (English and Japanese). It should be noted that this is not a translation task. For the Japanese systems, Japanese articles give rise to a completed template in Japanese.

One thousand texts with their corresponding human-filled templates have been supplied to the researchers in each of the domains and languages for training, development, and testing purposes. In addition, for each domain and language, a complex set of rules describes the information to be extracted from the specification of the project. This specification of the requirements for TIPSTER is, in a way, an attempt to pose a restricted set of NLP problems. The two languages and two domains have been required to encourage system development, which is language-independent and domain-independent.

THE NMSU-Brandeis system

Each of the research groups participating in the information extraction task has relied on methods of part-of-speech tagging, partial parsing (parsing certain segments of the texts for crucial information), and programs to recognize and mark the semantic class of proper names (i.e., programs to identify people, places, and organizations). The NMSU-Brandeis system is to a large extent distinguished by its use of an MRD in several aspects of the project, and by its commitment to construct system lexicons based on sound linguistic principles.

LDOCE has been used in two parts of the system: the semantic tagging of proper names and in the construction of the lexicon. In the first, the main use of the dictionary was used to aid in the recognition of unknown words that are potentially part of a novel organization or human name. In order to accomplish this, an algorithm was written to determine if a word appeared in the dictionary as a headword, if it could be generated as an inflected form of a headword, or if it could be generated from the dictionary indications of a derived form (for example "-ly" is indicated in the definition of "frequent"). All the words in the text were marked whenever they were not a headword or an inflected or derived form of a headword.

The lexical knowledge base in the system consists of lexical items called generative lexical structures (GLSs), after Pustejovsky (1991; see also chapter 8). This model of semantic knowledge associated with words is based on a system of generative devices which is able to recursively define new word senses for lexical items in the language. For this reason, the algorithm and associated dictionary is called a *generative lexicon*. The lexical structures contain conventional syntactic and morphological information along with detailed typing information about arguments.

The creation of the GLS lexicon begins with the machine-tractable version of LDOCE called LEXBASE (Stein et al. 1993) which contains syntactic codes, inflectional variants, and box codes as well as selectional information for verbs and nouns indicating what kind of arguments are well-formed with that lexical item. A GLS entry is automatically derived from LEXBASE (Pustejovsky 1991). The most novel aspect of this conversion involves parsing the example sentences as well as parenthetical texts in the definition. This gives a much better indication of argument selection for an item than do the the the box codes alone. For example, the verb *establish* is converted into the GLS entry shown in figure 7.1 as a result of this initial mapping. The two arguments to the verb *establish* are minimally typed as a result of the conversion from LDOCE, this information being represented as a *type-path* for each argument (Pustejovsky and Boguraev 1993). For example, the subject is typed as a *human* and the object as a type-path relating *solid* and the specific type encountered in the definition, *shop*.

The syntactic and collocational behavior of a word is represented in the *cospec* (cospecification) field of the entry. The *cospec* of a lexical item can be seen as the paradigmatic syntactic behavior of a word, involving both abstract types as well as lexical collocations. This field is created automatically by reference to the syntactic codes of the verb, as represented in LDOCE, in this case T1 (i.e., basic transitive). That is, the *cospec* encodes explicit information regarding the linear positioning of arguments, as well as semantic constraints on the arguments as imposed by the typing information in the qualia.

Tuning GLS Entries Against a Corpus
It is often the case that the lexical structures derived from MRDs do not reflect the behavior of the actual words in a given corpus. There are two major ways in which the lexical structure may differ from its actual corpus use: (1) syntactic mismatches, and (2) selectional mismatches. For example, in the joint venture domain, there is a sense of *establish* as a three-argument verb, when the second argument is a relational noun such as *joint venture* or *consortium*, as in

IBM will establish a joint venture with a local company.

Using statistical techniques described in Pustejovsky (1992), and similar to those in Grishman and Sterling (1992), the contexts and type restrictions for this use of the verb in the corpus are automatically identified.

An example of a selectional mismatch comes with cases of *type coercion*, where the verb expects one type but an apparently inconsistent type appears, as in:

Mannheim Industries announced a joint venture with Maykoe Inc.

Here, the verb *announce* is typed from LDOCE as taking a sentence as object, but it appears in the corpus with an noun phrase. The acquisition

```
gls(establish,
  syn([type(v),
    code(gcode_t1),
    eventstr([]),
    ldoce_id(establish_0_1),
    caseinfo([subcat1(a1),
        subcat2(a2),
        case(a1,np),
        case(a2,np)]),
    inflection([ing(establishing),
        pastp(established),
        plpast(established),
        singpast1(established),
        singpast2(established),
        singpast3(established),
        past(established),
        pl(establish),
        sing1(establish),
        sing2(establish),
        sing3(establishes)])]),
  qualia([formal(['set up']),
      telic([]),
      const([]),
      agent([])]),
  args([arg1(a1,
      syn([type(np)]),
      qualia([formal([code_h]),
          telic([]),
          const([]),
          agent([])])),
    arg2(a2,
      syn([type(np)]),
      qualia([formal([code_2,shop]),
          telic([],
          const([]),
          agent([])])))]),
  cospec([[A1,*,self,*,A2],
      [A2,*,past(self),*,by,A1]]),
  types([]),
  template_semantics([]).
```

Figure 7.1
A GLS entry for the verb *establish*.

technique presented in Pustejovsky (1992) shows how coercive contexts can be identified automatically from corpus analysis. This is an adaptation of the techniques of preference semantics (see chapter 3 and Wilks 1978) where the arguments of verbs were adapted to *preferred* ones. In general, the lexical structures described here can be thought of as providing for the shallowest possible semantic decomposition while still capturing significant generalizations about how words relate conceptually to one another. The lexical entries for Japanese follow exactly the same specifications, with the same degree of flexibility.

Walker and Amsler

Walker and Amsler (1986) used the LDOCE pragmatic (subject) coding system to do "content assessment" on wire service stories from the *The New York Times* News Service. Using the LDOCE subject coding system, they collected codes and counted the number of times each appeared in a story by keeping counters for each subject code, looking up each word in a story, and incrementing counters for every word sense definition that included a subject code.

For example, if the word "current" occurred in a story, the subject code counters for "geography-and-geology" (as in the "current" in a stream), and for "engineering/electrical" (as in electrical "current") would be incremented. If, later in the story, the word "river" occurred, then the subject code counter for "geography-and-geology" would be incremented again. The focus was to arrive at a list of codes that, taken together, would reflect the subject matter of each story. This was an ingenious early application of the LDOCE coding systems to approximate the automatic classification power of a thesaurus resource.

Pathtrieve

Pathtrieve is a hybrid information retrieval system developed at NMSU that has served as a testbed to explore the application of Pathfinder networks (PFNETs) in solutions to problems of document indexing and retrieval (Fowler and Dearholt 1989, 1990).

PFNETs provide graph structures to represent statistical associations among concepts, and are automatically derived for bodies of natural language text used in the information retrieval process. Pathtrieve has been extended to use a contextually organized lexical semantic structure derived from LDOCE (Fowler and Slator 1989).

Like many information retrieval systems, Pathtrieve operates over lexemes; the PFNETs used by the system, both for retrieval and user interaction, do not currently distinguish among word senses. However, as the system is extended to deal simultaneously with text from a number of domains, deeper analysis must be provided. Yet it is also necessary to retain the efficiency required by an interactive system operating on a very large database. The synthesis of the PFNET network representation with an efficient lexical semantic analysis is an attempt to meet both these requirements.

At present, document retrieval is the only practical means for accessing knowledge in very large databases of natural language text. Users' information needs are met indirectly by providing documents, or references to documents, likely to contain relevant information. The basic retrieval strategy matches conceptual representations, and the nature of these representations is central to the performance of a system. Most document retrieval system representations are based on the assignment of indexing terms to documents. The goal of indexing is to provide a set of terms describing the subject domain of each document. Unfortunately, indexing documents with high reliability and validity is not possible in practice. In fact, remarkably low consistency both between and within indexers has long been evident (Cooper 1969). Furnas et al. (1983) show that human object naming behavior is marked by lack of agreement among individuals, even in restricted domains with subjects with similar experiences. This lack of agreement has important implications for the design of information systems. One means of dealing with problems inherent in indexing is to provide associational structures that reflect not only semantic relations but other types of relations as well. This is the approach taken by Pathtrieve.

Practical information retrieval systems present a paradox: the user's information need is to know the subject area, but to supply the index terms necessary to use the system to meet the information need, the subject area must be known. One way to resolve this paradox is provided by iterative query techniques such as relevance feedback (Robertson and Sparck Jones 1976). Another approach is to develop an expert system to aid in formulating searches (Fidel 1986). The most widely used aid is a thesaurus of index terms that gives subject information by presenting the vocabulary of terms used in classifying documents in a domain. Most thesauri specify a limited number of relations (e.g., synonym, super-ordinate) among terms and group-related terms together to facilitate browsing and searches in a particular subject area.

Graph-based representations have been a cornerstone of AI research, but most cannot be used in large-scale information retrieval systems for two reasons. Firstly, producing knowledge bases for most AI applications is not done automatically. Virtually all AI knowledge bases are produced by extensive human encoding, that is, knowledge engineering. The size of the bodies of natural language text accessed by information retrieval systems, and the need to have documents made available in a timely fashion, argue against deep manual encoding of documents. Secondly, the time complexity of procedures for manipulating these representations is not acceptable for the very large databases that information retrieval systems access.

Pathfinder Networks

Pathfinder is a method for deriving network structures from estimates of distance (McDonald and Schvaneveldt 1988, Schvaneveldt, Durso, and Dearholt 1985). The algorithm derives a family of minimum-cost graphs for a data set and is in that way similar to other path analysis techniques (e.g., Doreian 1974). However, the particular types of minimum-cost graphs derived are closely related to models of semantic memory in humans (Collins and Loftus 1975) and have proved useful as a means of elucidating conceptual structure.

Pathfinder requires as input a measure of distance between each pair of concepts in the target domain. Conceptually the algorithm is quite simple. Concepts in a domain are represented by nodes, and links are assigned weights (from distances in the data matrix) according to their strengths. The link membership rule assures that links that are a part of some minimum-distance path are preserved between each pair of nodes. To derive a PFNET the direct distances between each pair of nodes in the data matrix are compared with indirect distances. A direct link between two nodes is included in the derived PFNET unless the data contain a shorter path of two or more links.

The resulting, least complex, network displays only the most salient relationships among nodes and can be thought of as the union of all minimum-cost spanning trees.

Pathfinder provides an alternative procedure for automatically deriving network representations for information retrieval systems. Statistically based graph construction techniques used in information retrieval and Pathfinder can both utilize proximity measures in deriving link structure, yet there are important differences. One difference is that statistically based graph representations used in information retrieval have seldom been concerned with providing a psychologically salient representation, whereas the PFNET representation has been developed from the outset as a representational scheme for human conceptual structure. Only a few information retrieval systems, such as Jones's (1986) Memory Extender system using spreading activation retrieval, have explicitly applied models of human cognition in the retrieval process. Another difference is that most statistically based graph derivation techniques in information retrieval systems are based on link membership determined by similarity thresholds between node pairs; links are included in a graph if the association between two nodes is above some criterion. In contrast, Pathfinder considers similarity over a wider range of nodes in deriving networks. The two approaches lead to quite different link structures.

The representations of documents used in retrieval are constructed from the texts of document abstracts. The statistical text analyses Pathtrieve uses for PFNET derivations essentially rely on recovering conceptual information from lexemes (strings). This shallow analysis has advantages in that it can be performed sufficiently quickly for use in interactive query formulation. The proximities used in constructing the different natural language PFNETs are derived from term co-occurrence in different textual units.

The problem with this method, and one shared by all information retrieval systems, is word sense ambiguity in index keys. As a trivial example, suppose the goal is to find physics documents concerned with the concept of "mass" in a scientific database (i.e., mass as weight). Further, suppose a biology document exists in the same database, and this document's abstract refers to some "mass of data" (i.e., mass as a large collection). Information retrieval systems, working only over lexemes, have no method of distinguishing these different senses of "mass," and errors are inevitable.

An efficient method for extracting knowledge structure from text has been developed (Slator 1988a, 1988b). The method relies on a notion of contextual coherence in text and employs the subject codings of LDOCE (see The NMSU Lexicon Provider, chapter 9).

The first step in analyzing each document and query is to use the dictionary to look up all of the word senses for all parts of speech for the words in the text. This procedure gives a "text-specific" lexicon reflecting all word senses and parts of speech. Along the way, an ordered list of pragmatic (LDOCE, subject) codes is collected for the text to be used in "content assessment" (cf. Walker and Amsler 1986), where lists of frequently occurring LDOCE pragmatic codes are compiled by simply counting up the instances found in the various senses of the words in the text.

The scheme implemented here to distinguish word senses uses the text-specific lexicon to select the relevant portions of the flat LDOCE hierarchy, described above, placing enumerated text elements at the leaves. Then, a deeper structure, relating pragmatic categories in a natural way, is imposed onto the LDOCE pragmatic world in order to discover important relationships between concepts within text.

The pragmatic and part-of-speech codes are related through the restructured hierarchy making **communication, economics, entertainment, household, politics, science,** and **transportation** the fundamental categories. Every word sense defined with a pragmatic code therefore has a position in the new hierarchy that is attached below the node for its pragmatic code. At this point every node in the hierarchy is assigned a value according to the number of words in the original text that bear that code, and then values lower in the structure are propagated by summing upward toward the root. At the end of this process a single pragmatic code for one of the seven fundamental categories, high in the hierarchy and therefore general in nature, asserts itself as the domain description term for the text. One could compare here Fontenelle's (1990a) critique of the pragmatic code system of LDOCE and his suggestions for revision.

The result is a knowledge structure capturing the subject domain of the text (and coherent in the sense that a set of, say, engineering terms are coherent with respect to engineering). The implication of discovering a global domain description term for a text is that this term carries an entire subhierarchy of more specific pragmatic codes with it. Every word sense defined with a pragmatic code therefore has a position in the hierarchy, attached to the node for its pragmatic code, with the scores computed at every relevant node. The flat LDOCE hierarchy is clearly an overcompartmentalized view of the world. The deeper hierarchy gives a far better intuitive ordering of the important concepts in each text than the given LDOCE hierarchy.

The contextual knowledge scheme described above can be applied in a number of ways in information retrieval. In extending the PFNET-based system, it can provide a mechanism to discriminate among senses of a concept through the domain description term, and so provide a refinement to the basic strategies the system implements. Moreover, it might be incorporated directly in retrieval systems, for example, deriving document and query representations from the restructured pragmatic hierarchy.

The cluster-based retrieval used by the Pathtrieve system is an example of document retrieval based on the relationships of documents, here as a PFNET of documents. More generally, any ordering or classification of documents can be used to guide retrieval, such as hierarchical clustering based on common index terms. Just as the contextually organized lexical semantic knowledge can be used to provide a domain description term for selecting word senses, that domain description term might be used to assign a class for the document that has been analyzed. Further, the lower levels in the pragmatic hierarchy might be used to provide index terms for a document automatically, to be used in other forms of retrieval. Finally, the pragmatic hierarchy structure for an item can itself be considered an encoded summary of that item. In this representation a hierarchy of subject terms is derived with values at each node. The values represent the relative importance of each subject term in the overall subject matter of the article. This is essentially a weighted term vector representation derived making use of the knowledge in the pragmatic hierarchy and the value propagation mechanism. Query-document comparisons can then be made efficiently using any of the well-known vector similarity functions in information retrieval (Jones and Furnas 1987).

Chapter 8
The Construction of Modern Lexicons

From a practical point of view, the first citizen of natural language understanding is the word. Over the years, there have been countless individual efforts devoted to collecting small populations of these, which has resulted in a great diversity of practice. From the words, every system requires its own collection of lexical facts, and each collection is informed by its own (competing) theory of language and meaning.

This history of competition and individual effort has had several practical implications. The most obvious is the difficulty, and notable lack, of cooperation and sharing of lexical resources among researchers (the Consortium for Lexical Research [see chapter 14] was founded to address exactly this problem). Not only do resource formats differ substantially, but central issues of content and meaning are treated so differently that, in the main, sharing is often more trouble than it is worth. Similarly, there is an historical difficulty with comparing and reconciling systems that arise from different theoretical foundations, and just as competing systems differ, so do their lexical representations, so much so that it is difficult to separate the lexical issues from the theoretical ones addressed by the systems themselves. This is compounded by the differing origins of these theories: linguistic, psychological, and even philosophical.

In the case of language understanding systems where the underlying theory has a component with lexical implications, the task of creating theoretically appropriate lexicons can take on particular strategic importance. If words and their properties are to be in the front line, so to speak, they carry the weight of theoretical support with them. But when there is some high-powered theory of linguistics or psychology in play, this tends, quite naturally, to dominate the scene. For this reason, lexicon construction has often been held to a subsidiary role within many parts of the language-understanding business, the expectation being that lexical matters will simply fall out. While this priority ordering may have changed a bit in recent years, it remains the case that with these systems (discussed below) the theories are most often linguistic or psychological, and not lexical, which in turn means the lexical representations are forced to conform to the preexisting theories, and not the other way around.

Lexicons vs. Wordbooks

Wordbooks are dictionaries for human readers and we now need to contrast these with lexicons: formalized, or computer-readable, entities for use in systems to process texts. Wordbooks can be the basis for these, as we discuss in chapter 5. In the linguistic systems of chapter 4, the lexicons were not computational. Kay's use of a mental "abstract lexicon" in chapter 5 referred only to a psychological entity, and not a linguistic one.

The lexicon in its "ultimate" sense might involve problems of word meaning that will go forever unsolved. Words fall from use, and experts disagree on the number of, or meanings of, the surviving senses. One giant lexical resource, created from the union of all others, and recording every sense ever assigned to any word, will fail because the key concept, conflation, is ill-defined. But hope persists because this conflation is part of what we call lexical acquisition: the process of assimilating new word senses when they are encountered in the world. The lexicon in its ultimate sense must do the same thing.

While a 2-year-old might know a single sense of the word "play," a college sophomore might know several, and a lexicographer might know dozens, and yet somehow, a percentage of 2-year-olds grow up to be lexicographers. Further, each can converse with the other, at least on some level, even though their respective knowledge of the language is incomplete, idiosyncratic, idiolectic, and in a way incompatible. Should computational language understanders be any different?

It has been suggested by some that word senses are social artifacts that arise from dictionaries in the first place. Words unambiguously denote entities in the world, so the argument goes, and lexical disambiguation is only a problem because lexicographers have made it so. Whatever truth this suggestion carries, the standard answer is that it does not help to know this; dictionaries and texts are what we have to work with and on, so dictionary research is something that must be tried. But this nondefense leads to another charge from another quarter, namely, that dictionary research lacks theoretical grounding. It is sometimes claimed that the driving force behind dictionary analysis is nothing more than "because it's there."

We shall show that dictionaries hold considerable theoretical interest both in terms of empirical evidence for semantic relations and as a way to test computational linguistics theories against large-scale problems (where the typical methodology has been implementing so-called toy systems). In terms of theory building it is surprising, and perhaps a little disturbing, to discover how little of the literature in the recent lexical renaissance concerns itself with fundamental questions of meaning.

The distinctions to be made in this chapter hinge on the nature of the theoretical requirements of diverse language-understanding systems, and on how these differences are related to lexical matters. Not all theoretical disputes are reflected in the lexical representations of the various systems, and there are plenty of computational linguistic paradigms that are indistinguishable at the lexical level. Insofar as the lexicon is not at issue, these disputes are of little interest here. For example, the years have seen several systems for language processing that depended on formally equivalent variations of context-free grammar; the interesting theoretical issues concerned the grammatical structure of surface level strings, while the lexical issues ranged from trivial to nonexistent. From a lexical point of view, these historical mileposts matter not at all.

On the other hand, there is a plethora of competing systems whose unique claims are either principally lexical in nature, or whose foundations, while lying in some other theoretical bedrock, have direct lexical implications.

AI and Linguistic Principles of Lexicon (Re)construction

Systems for lexical representation that spring from linguistic theories are quite naturally motivated from, and highly constrained by, the theories themselves. Sometimes this gives the impression that decisions about the lexical items, what they should contain and how they should interrelate, are made somewhat blindly in order to conform with the theory. It is certainly true that linguistically motivated theories of the lexicon almost universally demand components in the lexicon that are not usually found, either explicitly or implicitly (see chapter 7), in the dictionaries that people use. Sometimes, too, it is a challenge to the uninitiated to discover what the underlying theoretical assumptions actually are.

What follows is a brief survey of some of the better-known linguistically motivated lexical representation schemes. It is intended to be a representative tour, not an exhaustive one.

Dorr (1991): UNITRAN Machine Translation

The UNITRAN machine translation system uses lexical entries that are part of a "lexical conceptual structure" and also part of a mapping to syntactic structure. This two-level lexical description is specifically intended to resolve "divergences" between languages: those frequent cases where target (output) language expressions are in different syntactic order from the source (input) language, or where the lexical items are realized in different ways from one language to the other, for example, when the English "to stab" becomes Spanish words directly equivalent to "to give knife wounds."

The underlying linguistic theory for the lexical part of this system originates with Jackendoff (1983). The lexical conceptual structure is described as both a hierarchical and a compositional artifact, and this is only confusing until it becomes clear that this "structure" is a method for forming lexical-semantic formulas composed of primitive elements like CAUSE, AT-POSS, and WITH-INSTR. That is, the CAUSE primitive takes two "arguments," a THING (or an EVENT) and an EVENT. The conceptual structure, it turns out, is not a knowledge representation device that enables inference, but rather a graphical notation for displaying well-formed logical expressions.

Normally, a hierarchy is included in a representation scheme to enable inheritance *operations*, which in turn serve the purposes of inference. However, when the notion of inheritance is addressed in UNITRAN, it simply means that argument formats are inherited by logical predicates, so, in the lexical representations of, say, the GO-EVENT, it is an expression that includes optional modifiers taking intentional, instrumental, temporal, and locational arguments. The lexicon in this system is a collection of logical formulas whose argument structure is determined by the theoretical demands of the formalism. As with most systems that owe intellectual debts to linguistic theory, the bulk of the semantic load is carried by representational components that are required by the linguistic theory, are not found in dictionaries, and are probably not derived from them in any straightforward way. When the lexical system is made to conform to a particular linguistic theory, there are bound to be demands on the lexicon that cannot be served easily by an existing dictionary. This is just to say that many linguistic theories are not well represented in dictionaries printed for people.

Using the Grammar Coding System of LDOCE

Boguraev and Briscoe (1987) implemented a transduction algorithm that takes the grammar codings of LDOCE and produces codings suitable to other grammatical formalisms. The LDOCE grammar codes (described in detail in chapter 7) comprise a relatively finely grained system of approximately 110 grammatical codings that range from "[C] countable" to "[C3] countable and followed by the infinitive with to" for nouns and from "[T] transitive" to "[T5a] transitive and followed by a sentential complement using that, where the that is optional" for verbs. It is usual for verb entries to have more than one of these codes. The codings are based on the grammar of English developed by Quirk et al. (1972, 1985).

The purpose of the project, conducted at Cambridge University, was to convert the LDOCE codings for complement-taking verbs into the format accomodated by a PATR-II parser (Shieber 1984). This entailed classifying the verbs into classes like "Subject Raising," "Object Equi," "Object Raising," and so on. The method for making this classification was implemented with a fairly small set of rules like "if the verb contains a [V] or [X] and a [T5] or a [T5a] but none of the [D] codes, then classify it as Object Raising." These rules are based on suggestions in Michiels' (1982) thesis.

Boguraev and Briscoe's study contained an appendix with the so-called semantic type classification for the 719 LDOCE verb senses that are coded as having the potential for predicate complementation (LDOCE defines a total of nearly 8000 verbs). The claim is that not only does LDOCE provide sufficiently detailed codings for this transduction but that the information in LDOCE's "comparatively theory neutral lexical entries" (Boguraev and Briscoe 1987) would support a transduction of this sort into any of several formalisms, including GPSG, FUG, or LFG.

AI and Psychological Principles of Lexicon (Re)construction

In contrast to systems for lexical representation that spring from linguistic theories, systems founded on psychological theories are often rooted in an experimental model of how people think about and use words.

WordNet

The WordNet system of lexical organization is a network representation that arranges lexical items into sets of synonyms (synsets, which are intended to represent a single concept) and then associates these sets with one another through links whose labels are chosen from a small set of relations (Beckwith et al. 1989). The psychological underpinnings are of two sorts. First, word association experiments show that certain words (and usually nouns are used in these experiments) are associated in conventional ways with other words by a significant number of people. Secondly, reaction time experiments show that semantic networks (Quillian 1967, 1968), are a reasonable model for human memory. The combination of these results has led to a lexical model that conforms in many ways to common intuition.

The WordNet scheme distinguishes between what the authors call "lexical items," by which they mean spelling forms, and "senses," by which they mean the different occurences of a particular spelling form in different synsets. For example, the lexical item "check" would appear in one WordNet sense because it is found in a synset with other lexical items like "plaid" and "tartan," and would appear in another sense found with synonyms like "audit." Sense distinctions in WordNet are explicit, but they are not numbered in the convention of the usual dictionaries. On the contrary, the WordNet notion of sense distinction is as an indirect by-product of network connectivity. As in a classic thesaurus, a word has as many senses as it has synsets to belong to, and synsets are distinguished by the relations that connect them to other synsets.

The senses in a synset are related to the senses in other synsets with one or more of the following lexical relations: hyponomy/hypernymy (superordinate/subordinate relations), meronymy/holonymy (part-whole relations), troponymy (manner relations for verbs), antonymy (opposition relations), and pertainymy (relating nonpredicate adjectives with the particular nouns they pertain to). This constitutes a fairly perspicuous set of relations with which to encode a lexicon, but the authors make no claim that this set of relations is in any way exhaustive; rather, the relations in WordNet capture a fairly conventional set of lexical relations, the base set that usually appears in the lexical semantics literature (Cruse 1986). This set of relations is a useful reduction device, and allows the WordNet representation to encode the standard conception of genus, while giving a very limited account of differentia. That is to say, the relations between synsets, aside from the hyponomy/hypernymy relations, are all that survive of differentia, and these are in quite conventional forms.

At this point, WordNet has seen little by way of practical applications, though these are growing. Software can be obtained, in the form of tools for building and browsing WordNet itself. This is bound to change before long. Various researchers have started building applications using Word-Net, and the Consortium for Lexical Research (see chapter 14) has, as of this writing, acquired a copy for distribution to members.

The CyC Project

Perhaps the most famous, large-scale, hand-coding initiative ever undertaken is the CyC project at MCC Corporation (Lenat et al. 1986; Lenat and Feigenbaum 1987). This project has been allotted 10 years to encode a million entries from a desk encyclopedia, an estimated 2 person-centuries of work, into a large, general-purpose, knowledge base. The original intention, never published but widely rumored, was carefully to encode a sufficiently rich and robust ontology by hand, using highly trained AI researchers, and then, at some point, turn the work over to an army of high-school students who could complete the job with a minimum of specialized training. This point has not yet arrived.

However, Lenat has claimed (Leibowitz and Fjermedal 1988) to have achieved "semantic convergence" where new concepts are being, at last, defined in terms of other, previously encoded, conceptual structures. The principal criticism of this approach has been the sheer volume of effort that it presupposes: 1 million entries from an encyclopedia and 2 person-centuries of work is a major investment of time and effort. Many believe it is a mistaken approach because of the great potential for wasting precious human resources, and of the difficulty of retaining consistency across the huge database. Of course, this prediction is easy to make, and almost certain to come true, of any sufficiently large-scale software project. False starts and changing requirements inevitably occur and lead to a certain amount of waste. This has happened with CyC, as the developers freely admit in the midterm progress report (Guha and Lenat 1990). Behind all this, of course, is the renewed "nuclear ALPAC dark age Lighthill" fear—that the failure of a project of this magnitude, if indeed it should fail, will engender unparalleled hostility toward AI, and the consequent end of funding for AI research.

Other critics believe the CyC project makes dubious theoretical assumptions, despite Lenat's early claims that the work is theory-free. There are, indeed, theoretical assumptions in play here, and this is nowhere more obvious than in the fact that the representation is coded as purely symbolic conceptual structures, and entertains no explicit statistical or associational encoding of lexical co-occurence data (see chapter 11). Another perspective on the notion of theory-freeness is that it equates somehow to "theory-full," which is just to say that the CyC project now seems to want to cover all bets by making every representational choice available in one way or another. Where the early CyC descriptions concentrated on a frame representation for knowledge, later work has moved toward a more eclectic and formal approach. The CyC scheme now combines elements of framelike slot, role, filler constructions, with first order predicate calculus, with nested propositional attitudes, and with nonmonotonic logic.

In any case, the CyC project of handcrafting an encyclopedia in a "knowledge representation" raises the lexicon/dictionary vs. encylopedia problem in a new form. It is interesting to note that the notion of CyC encoding an encyclopedia is now fashioned as an "unfortunate myth." Rather, Guha and Lenat (1990) "hope [to lay] this misconception to rest. If anything, CyC is the complement of an encylopedia. The aim is that one day CyC ought to contain enough commonsense knowledge to support natural language understanding capabilities that enable it to read through and assimilate any encyclopedia article" (p. 34).

Lexical Acquisition from Human Subjects

The WordNet project is a long-term effort directed at hand-coding a lexicon for natural language. WordNet was constructed by hand, but by reference to a variety of lexical resources: dictionaries, thesauri, and specialized lists. Added to this, of course, are the intuitions of the "lexicographers" who work on the project. Recently, the Princeton team under the direction of George Miller has begun a project to tag the million-word Brown corpus with WordNet concepts. As this project evolves, WordNet is being amended to increase its coverage of the corpus.

In this sense, the WordNet project is more than usually eclectic; most projects of this sort concentrate on source material of a single type (often a single source text).

NMSU's Pathfinder

Various approaches to lexical acquisition have been explored by the New Mexico State University (NMSU) Computing Research Laboratory

(CRL), including a project that creates Pathfinder associational networks from co-occurrence data in LDOCE (but that uses experimental data from human subjects to verify the associations). The Pathfinder algorithm (Schvaneveldt and Durso 1981, Schvaneveldt, Durso and Dearholt 1985, Schvaneveldt 1990; see chapter 7), was developed to discover the network structure implicit in psychological data. Pathfinder takes a completely connected network as input and removes most of the links. The networks have an interesting structure, and the links remaining correspond quite well to intuitive ideas of which nodes should have relationships between them. Related studies use Pathfinder networks to do lexical disambiguation, as a means to judge whether any *useful* information is discarded when reducing the number of links using the Pathfinder algorithm.

The Pathfinder experiments explore the co-occurrence of words in LDOCE. The claim is that co-occurrence data can provide an automatically obtainable measure of the "semantic relatedness" of words. The hypothesis is that statistics of co-occurrence of words in LDOCE can (1) give some empirical evidence for word sense distinctions, and (2) be used in conjunction with sense definitions to perform lexical disambiguation within LDOCE (McDonald, Plate, and Schvaneveldt 1990; see chapter 7). The lexical disambiguation task represents a test of whether the statistical information is useful, which is necessary because of its unconventional form.

In these experiments, statistics of co-occurrence of words are collected and psychological tests show high correlation of human judgments of relatedness with values derived from these co-occurrence statistics, which supports the claim that co-occurrence data can provide indications of the relatedness of words. A reduced network representation of the co-occurrence data is shown to provide empirical evidence for word sense distinctions. The assumption at play here is that two word senses occurring in the same sentence will be semantically related. This follows from the assumption that sentences are coherent wholes, which implies that every item is involved in some relationship and every pair of items is linked by some chain of relationships.

The Pathfinder experiments attempt to make a stronger claim: first, that the probability of a relationship between two word senses occurring in the same sentence is high enough to make it possible to extract useful information from statistics of co-occurrence; second, that the extent to which this probability is above the probability of chance co-occurrence provides an indicator of the strength of the relationship; and, third, that if there are more and stronger relationships among the word senses in one assignment of word senses to words in a sentence than in another, then the first assignment is more likely to be more correct. Sparck Jones (1964, 1986) makes a similar claim and likewise bases a method of sense disambiguation on it. Lesk (1986) also presents a method of sense disambiguation that relies on the same assumptions. (See chapter 11 for an overview of the disambiguation techniques.)

The NMSU experiments involve developing a suite of relatedness functions for assigning a value to the association strength between a word being defined in LDOCE and the words in its definition. The values assigned by the various relatedness functions are compared with the judgments of relatedness made by human subjects. The results of these experiments validate the notion that measures derived from statistics of co-occurrence can be used to indicate the relatedness of words automatically. For N words, human subjects were asked to "indicate the relatedness" of each of the $N(N - 1)/2$ pairs of words. The subjects were not given any explanation of what "relatedness" was. They indicated the degree of relatedness by positioning a mark on a scale. Several experiments were conducted; for further details of these, see McDonald et al. (1988). All had similar results.

In one experiment five human judges rated the relatedness of all pairs of words from a set of 20 words. The intersubject correlation ranged from .70 to .83 (where 1.0 would be identical, 0.0 would be no relation, and −1.0 would be opposite.) The correlation between the mean of the human judgments and a straightforward conditional probability statistic was .66. This is a reasonably high correlation and indicates that these statistical measures are strongly related to human judgments of semantic relatedness.

Lexical Acquisition from Texts

The theme of this section is to review systems for lexical acquisition where the majority of the work is done by human analysis, with only some interactive, computer-assisted support tools (as opposed to those systems where the majority of the work is done by machine analysis, reviewed in chapter 13). The present section concerns the construction of a dictionary-independent lexical database where the goal is not so much to address formatting issues, but one of trying to identify a large set of facts from which lexicons for NLP systems might be constructed, possibly by combination with material extracted from MRDs.

The task of actually identifying this information for NLP in general is an extremely difficult one for several reasons. First, the range of projects classified as "natural language processing" is enormous; for example, machine translation systems; natural language query systems; all parsing programs; systems attempting to process discourse and recognize metaphor and metonomy; generation systems; systems that do inferencing and planning; and systems that summarize articles or extract bits of important information. Second, the existing systems that are potential sources for identifying lexical information applicable to this wide range of projects are often very small and therefore likely to be underspecified as far as the lexical knowledge necessary to scale up their work. It is probably the case that to make any progress in this area, the scope of projects that this lexical database will serve must be narrowed.

Of course, NLP projects have often drawn their lexicons, formally or informally, from texts; a less obvious development in that history would be Becker's (1975; see also Zernik and Dyer 1986) "phrasal lexicon": his demonstration that stereotypical multiword phrases covered a larger portion of a text's lexicon than might have been thought. What follows are more recent developments in lexical aquisition from texts.

Lexical Workbenches: Carnegie Mellon's ONTOS and MCC's LUKE

ONTOS (Nirenburg 1989) is a knowledge and lexical acquisition tool developed at Carnegie Mellon University in support of their KBMT (*k*nowledge-*b*ased *m*achine *t*ranslation) system. ONTOS is used to construct a multiply interconnected network of concepts implemented as frame structures in the Framekit knowledge representation language (Nyberg 1988).

This "concept lexicon" has higher, more abstract, nodes (general ontological postulates) that contain inherited properties and constraints used to define domain concepts. Elements of the ontology and the domain concepts are associated there, and are used to define lexical elements. The lexical elements are also connected to language-dependent structures that encode syntactic features and structural mapping rules. ONTOS allows new concepts to be created and integrated into the existing model. Graphical decision aids help the user find the appropriate way to describe the new concept, and help identify potential problems and inconsistencies.

The problem, as the authors freely admit, is that it takes 5 personmonths to create 1000 concepts, which is far too long. If we equate concepts to content words (nouns, verbs, etc.), it will take 20 years to encode the equivalent of a medium-sized dictionary like LDOCE (which defines 50,000 of these). This is no particular criticism of the ONTOS system. Rather, it comes from the essential conflict between book and demo (see chapter 1), or horizontal and vertical approaches to lexicon construction. The entry-by-entry approaches face fundamental scaling problems and have no particular advantage over traditional lexicography (albeit the modern version of the craft with computer-assisted support). This approach takes little advantage of previous lexicographic work.

The LUKE knowledge and lexical acquisition system (Knight 1989, Barnett, Rich, and Wroblewski 1991) attempts to automate the acquisition task further. In order to do this, an unknown word is injected into various contexts and the user is asked to rate it as good or bad. The idea, that users are better able to rate lexical usage than generate lexical entries, is a plausible one, although this procedure is sorely limited by LUKE's ability to generate useful test cases, that is, those where grammatical decisions are not confounded by semantics. Similarly, LUKE requires that the user make decisions about all manner of morphological variation, which appears to require considerable effort for marginal return, that is, for the user to define "eat" requires selecting or rejecting "uneat," "deeat," "miseat," "maleat," and so on.

Apart from this, the critical factors affecting both ONTOS and LUKE are the constraints and limitations of their environment. Both systems only allow new items to be defined in terms of preexisting items (in the case of LUKE, these are the items defined in CyC; see above). This simply means that high-level, abstract decisions about meaning are crucial to the success of the representation. Because everything is built top-down, it is possible to enforce consistency across lexical entries. LUKE accomplishes this with a "truth maintenance system" that keeps track of the slots and fillers in the lexical entries. If a new item is defined that somehow contradicts existing structure, this can be noted and attended to through human intervention.

Extended-Aspect Calculus

Pustejovsky (1987, Pustejovsky and Bergler 1987) has designed an interactive lexicon construction system that builds verb entries from LDOCE definitions. The theoretical assumptions are inherited from Jackendoff (1972, 1976) as revised by Dowty (1979). Essentially, this means that verbs are defined to have a certain fixed polyadicity (the number of arguments each takes), which includes a record of the syntactic role of the arguments as well as whether they are optional or obligatory, and what selectional restriction each has. Further, verbs are marked by aspect (as state, process, or event), the crucial point to aspectual coding being that it interacts with tense information during syntactic analysis.

As has often been the case in building knowledge bases throughout the history of AI, the acquisition process begins with the lexicon builder selecting a set of lexical primitives from the dictionary's definition vocabulary: words like cause, move, etc. Each of these is assigned a thematic mapping index, which is a template composed from elements from the aspect calculus. For example, if a verb definition contains some reference to "cause," then a two-place predicate (with arguments for causer and causee) will become part of the lexical representation for the verb. Once this preliminary coding is accomplished, the lexicon builder can set about creating lexical entries. This entails an interactive procedure to assign case roles and aspect labels to each lexical item.

The interactive procedures begin with the lexicon builder picking a candidate to define. This is done by composing primitives (e.g., CAUSE and MOVE) and then picking a lexical item that contains both in its definition, (e.g., one of turn, shake, propel, etc.). The templates for CAUSE and MOVE are composed, and a series of questions are posed to the user, in order to elicit particular facts about the lexical item. These particular facts include whether the agent is animate, whether the action is sustained or momentary, and so forth. These questions are apparently attached to the primitives in the first phases of acquisition, and this appears to perform a certain labor-saving function.

The acquisition process makes weak claims to psychological plausibility in that general terms are acquired before more specific ones, and lexical items acquired earlier are used to define those that come later. Like other theoretically motivated systems for lexical acquisition, the representation is predicated on the demands of the theory. This means ignoring, inventing, or redoing a great deal of the lexicography for the sake of the theory. Further, this particular system takes no account of word sense distinctions in definition text. When "propel," say, is used in the definition of "throw," there is no recognition that "propel" might be intended in one of its particular senses. This is just the difference between assuming primitive words and primitive senses in dictionary definitions.

Again, as with other systems described in this chapter, the principal drawback is the failure to fully exploit the professional lexicography that goes into MRDs. The time to construct a lexicon through these methods can hardly be less than that required to build the dictionary in the first place. This is basically a system for interactive lexicon transduction that, although claiming to facilitate MRD analysis while modeling human language acquisition, focuses on translating definitions into complex formulas of first order logic with argument typing, selection restrictions, case roles, and aspectual type (i.e., state, process, or event). The transduction is almost completely interactive (and not automatic), and is a system of tools for hand-coding a lexicon using an MRD as a database.

The "Neutral Lexicon"?

Could there be a lexicon that was linguistically and computationally *neutral*? It has been a much-discussed research idea, whose possibility is supported by the strong intuition that different dictionaries and lexicons all express roughly the same semantic facts. Like many aphorisms and idiomatic expressions, terms like the "neutral" and, more recently, the "poly-theoretic" lexicon are traded in the research community, but often without any specific agreement as to what they mean. This sometimes makes the resulting debates seem unfocused, since the central notions are ill-defined.

There are several competing threads in this discussion. The earliest attempts at MRD analysis (in the "modern" era, dating from Amsler and White 1979), were straightforward AI projects; the point of the exercise was "knowledge," broadly construed. That meant treating the dictionary as a text to be converted into a semantic network which, in the absence of any particular application, would represent the relationships between the content words of the language. Without prejudice, it is fair to say these studies were not "theory-driven" in any real sense, or even in the sense outlined in the introduction to this chapter. Rather, they were hunting expeditions or, if that sounds too ad hoc, they were data-driven and pre-theoretic.

Later MRD work was often undertaken with a similar orientation: to explore the dictionary and see what was there, and then use it in whatever way possible. The motivation was often defended on purely pragmatic grounds. Lexicons for NLP systems are a time-consuming proposition, and nobody wants to do it by hand if it can be avoided.

This pragmatic attitude led to the criticisms mentioned earlier, that people were undertaking MRD research simply because "it was there." As discussed above, these criticisms erred in focusing on the engineering components of the MRD research program. One thing that has kept these criticisms alive is that the intellectual motivations for MRD research are grounded in common sense rather than in formal linguistic, or semantic, theory. Simply stated, a single dictionary, sitting on a shelf somewhere, serves the many different needs of users. Therefore, so the thinking goes, these same resources should be able to serve the needs of many different systems for NLP. How could it be otherwise?

Another source of confusion and confused debate has been the unfortunate genesis of the terms "neutral lexicon" and "theory-free lexicon," and the later idea of the "poly-theoretic lexicon," which is sometimes loosely spoken of as synonymous with the first two. There are problems that arise here and, consonant with a lexical dispute, they revolve around pedestrian matters of definition: what is meant by "neutral" and what is meant by "theory." For example, in his essay on the impossibility of the neutral lexicon, to which we return later, Ramsay (1992) concentrates on lexicons servicing the competing needs of all the different theoretical approaches to NLP. In his view, "neutral" applies to a lexicon that could be nothing other than a "least common denominator," since, according to Ramsay, only that could serve all the (theory-driven) users equally well. A lexicon of this sort would be very pale indeed, and, under Ramsay's interpretation, practically useless.

Connected with this is a devaluation of the term "theory." The notion of science and the role of theory in science have been thoroughly explored over the millenia. A scientific theory is traditionally composed of a vocabulary of entities in a model, a calculus for describing the entities in the model and their relationships to one another, and a mapping between the model and the world. This is the textbook formulation of "theory" that has evolved within the scientific community, and that has been formally described by philosophers of science at least since Braithwaite.

This fundamental misunderstanding about science has, for decades now, led to mischief in the field of linguistics and continues now to create problems in computational lexicology and in the work surveyed here. As Wilks (1974) points out, there are several ways to use the word "theory" in a debate, and they're all fine so long as the declarer and the rebutter have the same sense of "theory" in mind. This clarity has not, unfortunately, always been the case in this field.

This chapter has reviewed recent theory-driven lexical research, where the driving theories are linguistic or psychological, and we have seen how these theories can fail to be served by MRD research to some degree or another. By contrast, in chapters 2 and 3 we reviewed competing theories of meaning and showed how one in particular, which we have called Theory K, "Meaning as equivalent to symbolic structures," arises naturally from the intersection of lexicographic tradition and AI theories of meaning. It is our thesis that what we have called "contextualist-proceduralist assumptions" and the "coherence" view of meaning (see chapter 3) forms the basis for a theoretically motivated and lexically driven research program. In the next chapters we described lexical research and applications that we claim are both more natural and more sensible than the others, in that they preserve an unbroken line from the lexical facts from which they arise.

Chapter 9
Automatic Techniques for Analyzing Machine-Readable Dictionaries

It is, by now, a well-documented fact (and it has been a popular trend in the recent literature to emphasize it) that there has been renewed emphasis on scale in computational linguistics, and a corresponding disillusionment with the so-called toy systems of linguistic and AI models. Recent years have also seen rising interest in computational analysis of MRDs as a lexical resource for various purposes. These two trends are neither accidental nor independent of each other; an obvious place to look for large-scale linguistic information is in existing dictionaries.

The use of MRDs for semantic analysis is a straightforward attempt at exploiting the work-years of effort by professional lexicographers. The assumption of that work is that a wealth of implicit information lies within dictionaries, and that that information can be made explicit for use by programs. In lexicography, words are defined in terms of other words, which themselves have definitions elsewhere in the dictionary. From a computational linguistics point of view, the trick is to "unpack" the meanings that have been encoded in text by lexicographers, converting them into a computationally tractable form. The research described in the following chapters can be distinguished from the preceding chapters by emphasis on the automatic analysis of machine-readable texts, rather than hand-coding, as the best method for building computational lexicons.

Pattern Matching and Parsing

The effort to parse, or otherwise automatically process dictionary entries (e.g., by pattern matching, etc.), is made for a variety of reasons. The general idea is to construct a "lexical database" of some sort from the contents of the dictionary. This essentially means the transduction of a dictionary text into some other form, with the intention of transforming the contents into a structured format that, thereafter, can be accessed in some algorithmically consistent way. This notion of automatically converting an MRD into a "machine-tractable" one (Wilks et al. 1987, 1988, 1990) is the central theme of this chapter.

The motivation for creating lexical databases in this way is to take advantage of the extensive lexicographic work that goes into creating the dictionary in the first place. The systems discussed in this chapter stand in contrast to those systems for constructing semantic networks or hierarchies. In general, the network/hierarchy efforts are more narrowly devoted to detailing hypernymic and hyponymic relations (at other times referred to as IS-A relations, or AKO [a-kind-of] relations) between words and word senses defined in the dictionary. These are meaningful (semantic) relations explicitly intended to support inheritance (see chapter 10).

There are two basic approaches to, and two essential motivations for, the automatic processing of dictionaries. One is to manipulate the codings and strings of the definitions into a regular format in order to allow efficient random access to the various fields of the individual entries. This is an approach to the explicit information in the dictionary. The other is to attempt to process definitions in some way, in order to identify unambiguously the elements within definitions, and to identify relations between them. This is an approach to the implicit information in the dictionary.

Explicit and Implicit Dictionary Information

Much of the data needed for NLP lexicons can be found (explicitly or implicitly) in a dictionary. Research investigating the kind of information needed for NLP (Nirenburg 1989, Pustejovsky and Bergler 1987, Boguraev and Pustejovsky 1990) plausibly supports this claim.

The problem, of course, is that none of this comes without great effort. Every dictionary is printed in a different format, and every format is designed to be both information-bearing and pleasing to the eye. This combination makes it very difficult to remove or reformat the strings and symbols in the dictionary automatically, to decide, by program, what is intended by the lexicographer, what to keep, and what to leave out.

Creating lexicons for NLP often involves solving many intellectually trivial but ergonomically vexing problems of data format and data transduction (see the next section for an outline of these). The next section is a discussion of three kinds of information (for monolingual dictionaries) for which uniform formats and tags would be useful to the NLP community and to dictionary publishers.

1. A format for MRDs that would preserve the content and the form of the published page. The goal here is to define a set of tags to be used in the electronic version of any dictionary that would reflect both the content and the formatting of the corresponding printed version. Each piece of information given in an entry, such as example sentences, sense definitions, cross-references, pronunciation, etc. would be tagged. This type of format would aid in language processing, but its main advantage is that it would provide a standard form from which to start.

2. A format for MRDs (possibly similar to the IBM format for MRDs; see the next section for a description) that allows other software to access the various parts of an entry easily. In particular,

a. It separates the portions of an entry, such as definitions, examples, cross-references, grammatical information, proununciation, etc.

b. It makes explicit any subsenses of a sense.

c. It makes explicit any elided information.

The format should include a tag for each of the fields in an entry, and the set of all formatted entries would make up a database for which search and accessing software would be written. The intention is that this format could be used for any MRD, and any software written to access or search a particular MRD would work on any MRD that had been transduced in this way. An example should make this more clear. In LDOCE, the word "abrade" appears on the page much like this:

abrade, v [I0;T1], (*tech*) **a** (esp of skin) to wear away by hard rubbing **b** to cause (esp skin) to wear away by hard rubbing

By contrast, the LISP version of the LDOCE entry for "abrade" is as follows (LDOCE was "lispified" at Cambridge University; see section 9.3.1, below):

```
((abrade)
  (1 A0008100 a *80 brade)
  (3 E
  (5 v )
  (6 I0 *DE T1 tech)
  (7 0  ——  ——Z—5)
  (8 *45 a *44 (esp of skin) to wear away by hard
     rubbing *45 b *44 to cause (esp skin) to wear
     away by hard rubbing))
```

Although this format is available from Longman and is an improvement on the actual printer's tape, considerable processing must be done to extract information from this entry. Below is a form that captures the essential features of this entry.

HEADWORD: abrade
SENSE NUMBER: 1
PART of SPEECH: verb
GRAMMAR CODES: [I; T1]
SEMANTIC CATEGORY OF THE SUBJECT: Z (no restriction)
SEMANTIC CATEGORY OF THE OBJECT: 5 (organic materials)
DEFINITION: (especially of skin) to wear away by hard rubbing
DEFINITION: to cause (especially skin) to wear away by hard rubbing

Note that this differs from the formatting described in the "lispified" item, in that it does not attempt to preserve type fonts, or abbreviations, but rather to interpret them. This format represents a first attempt to attach semantics to the various font forms in printed output.

As another example, in COBUILD, the words in boldface following the pronunciation give the spelling for each form of the word, for example, in the definition of "echo," we find:

echo/pronunciation/echoes, echoing, echoed

The database format could have a field for DERIVED FORMS and one for INFLECTED FORMS since there are special symbols on the tape that would allow these to be identified by inference (and a separate entry might be created for each of these special forms, but neither the type font nor the position of the words in the entry would be preserved). Note that this format does not attempt to preserve the published page and that the printed version could not be recovered from the transduced version. As discussed above, it is important for NLP to be able to look up any derived or inflected form. This format has the advantage of allowing a table of those forms, linked to their citations, to be easily generated.

It should be noted here that this is still not the ideal format of an MRD for NLP. The format suggested above would contain example sentences and definitions, whereas a more useful format should contain the implicit relations extracted from definitions (rather than the definition) and possible typical arguments of verbs and adjectives extracted from the example sentences (rather than the example sentences themselves). As an example, consider the following modification of a format (Slator 1988a,b) for the LDOCE entry of "ammeter":

ammeter—an intrument for measuring, in amperes, the strength of an electric current.

ammeter
genus—instrument (so ammeter IS-A instrument)
purpose—measuring
units—amperes
measures—electric current
part of speech—noun
subject category—electrical engineering
semantic category—movable solid
grammar code—count noun

In a perfect situation, the words "instrument" and "measuring" would be disambiguated. If MRDs are transduced in one of these ways, research using richer representations will be made much easier.

Methodological Issues in the Analysis of Machine-Readable Dictionaries

Extraction of semantic information from dictionaries entails certain assumptions about the extent of knowledge in a dictionary, about where that knowledge is located, and how that knowledge can be extracted from the language of dictionary definitions. These are not assumptions about semantics, but are about the extraction of semantic information from text. These assumptions are methodological assumptions because they underlie the decisions made in choosing one method for semantic analysis rather than another. These assumptions are about sufficiency, extricability, and bootstrapping (Wilks et al. 1990).

Sufficiency addresses the issue of whether a dictionary is a strong enough knowledge base for English, specifically as regards linguistic knowledge and, above all, the knowledge of the real world needed for subsequent text analysis. Sufficiency is of general concern, even for hand-coding projects like Cyc, where they attempt to make explicit the facts and heuristics one needs in order to understand language, the generalizations of those facts and heuristics, and the inferences that fill intersentential gaps (Lenat and Feigenbaum 1987).

Different positions have been taken toward sufficiency within computational lexicography. Some researchers believe that there is not enough knowledge in dictionaries in principle (Hobbs 1987); in other words, that certain specific semantic information is not available anywhere in a dictionary and hence must be derived from another, outside, source. Atkins, Kegl, and Levin (1986) maintain that these sources should be linguistically motivated and theory-driven. Other researchers believe that dictionaries may indeed contain sufficient knowledge, although that knowledge may be implicit, because that knowledge can be made explicit by using information from entries in other parts of a dictionary (e.g., Slocum and Morgan 1986, Boguraev 1987, Kegl 1987).

Extricability is concerned with whether it is possible to specify a set of computational procedures that operate on an MRD and extract, through their operation alone and without any human intervention, general and reliable semantic information on a large scale, and in a general format suitable for, though independent of, a range of subsequent NLP tasks.

Bootstrapping refers to the process of collecting the initial information that is required by a set of computational procedures that are able to extract semantic information from the sense definitions in an MRD. The initial information needed is commonly linguistic, normally syntactic and case information, which is used during the processing of dictionary sense definitions into an underlying representation from which semantic information is then extracted.

Bootstrapping methods can be internal or external. Internal bootstrapping methods obtain the initial information needed for their procedures from the dictionary itself and use procedures to extract that information. This is not as circular as it may seem. A process may require information for the analysis of some sense definition (e.g., some knowledge of the words used in the definition) and may be able to find that information elsewhere in the dictionary. By contrast, external bootstrapping methods obtain the initial information for their procedures by some method other than the use of those procedures themselves. The initial information may be from some source external to the dictionary or may be in the dictionary but impossible to extract without the use of the very same information. For example, the word "noun" may have a definition in a dictionary, but the semantic information in that definition might not be extractable without prior knowledge of a sentence grammar that contains knowledge of syntactic categories, including what a noun is.

There are differences of opinion in computational lexicology regarding extricability and bootstrapping. Slocum and Morgan (1986) are generally pessimistic about the use of MRDs in machine translation. Others (Boguraev 1987, Kegl 1987) appear to believe that the semantic information in dictionaries can be extricated, but only with some external bootstrapping, that is, only if at least some prior knowledge is hand-coded into an analysis program.

The straightforward approach to creating an MTD is to segment the dictionary into a collection of records, one for each word sense, composed of a set of labeled constituent fields, where each field is roughly equivalent to a single meaningful element in a sense definition (similar to 2, above). This procedure makes the contents of the dictionary explicit, and is the so-called lexical database approach to forming an MTD. The more difficult approach is to process the labeled constituent fields in some way, in order to retrieve the implicit knowledge that lies buried there. This is the semantic approach to creating an MTD. Note that it is practically impossible to do the second until the first is complete.

Database Approaches to the Machine-Tractable Dictionary

By some accounts, the first serious reports on lexical databases were the papers by Michiels, Mullenders, and Noel (1980) and Michiels and Noel (1982), which were followed by a special session on the lexicon held at the Tenth International Conference on Computational Linguistics (COL-ING-84); the papers presented by Calzolari (1984) and Kay (1984) are the most widely cited. The following year, a paper appeared by Alshawi, Boguraev, and Briscoe (1985) that described work done to permit on-line access to a machine-readable copy of the LDOCE (Procter 1978). Between that time and the eventual publication of the first edited collection in the field (Boguraev and Briscoe 1989), much of the seminal work in the field was accomplished. Lexical databases have also been implemented by Nakamura and Nagao (1988) and Evens (1988).

The computer laboratory of Cambridge University was among the first places to recognize the special potential of the LDOCE.

A large number of research sites have benefited from the Cambridge initiative. It was here that the widely distributed "lispified" version of LDOCE was first created (as of early 1992, at least 100 copies had been distributed worldwide). Later work at Cambridge (Boguraev et al. 1987) extended the grammatical processing of LDOCE with the addition of a morphological generator and an interactive workbench-like system (see chapter 8) for human intervention in the encoding and translating process.

IBM: Dictionary Entry Parsing

Extensive study of the structure of MRD entries was carried out at IBM (Neff and Borguraev 1989, Borguraev et al. 1989), resulting recently in the DEP (the dictionary entry parser). The purpose of this device is to transduce MRD entries into a lexical database without loss of information, which is not as easy as it sounds. Dictionary publishers release data tapes intended to drive printing devices. These tapes include all of the lexicographic conventions and diacritics necessary to achieve eye-appealing layout, but they make no concessions to computational processing. Dictionary entries are full of content-sensitive conventions, and breaking them into their constituent fields requires a nontrivial structural grammar. One special problem concerns restoring elided information in multisense definitions, for example, when the first sense of a "grate" is defined as "a framework of parallel or latticed bars for blocking an opening; a grill," and some later sense is defined as "such a framework of metal, used to hold the fuel in a stove, furnace, or fireplace." The later sense clearly refers to an earlier one and some facility for deciding *which* one is required. This means defining an extragrammatical set of rules for the sake of special cases: another complication to the algorithm.

But this is a practical device: to allow retrieval and browsing for the purpose of discovering relationships among words. To retrieve a pronunciation field for a voice synthesizer, or to check syllabification for text processing, devices of this sort have usually concentrated on individual lexical items. The DEP approach takes a different tack: to enable the selection of entries sharing some attribute so as to make generalizations about classes of lexical entries. This capability for querying the dictionary permits a great deal of flexibility and enables studies that would otherwise be quite difficult. IBM has undertaken several other interesting projects: dealing with dictionary comparisons, bilingual cross-studies, and corpora analysis (Guo 1989).

Byrd et al. (1987) describe a large inventory of tools for manipulating MRDs, and give an impressive list of MRDs over which these tools are to work. These include a database management scheme for handling lexical data, a menu-driven query interface to the databases, several tools to build network structure from definitions (through "sprouting," "filtering," etc.; see chapter 10), utilities for finding recurring phrases in text, and morphological analyzers for definition text.

IBM research was among the first in suggesting that a useful database for NLP might store information from multiple sources, multiple dictionaries or other large corpora (Klavans et al. 1990; Byrd et al. 1987), but there are drawbacks to such an eclectic body of sources. First of all, it introduces the problem of sorting out differences of opinion among lexicographers as to, for instance, the possible senses of a given word. Furthermore, constructing a database from multiple sources forces one to resolve which is indeed the "correct division" of word senses; all this is in addition to solving the usual problems of extracting information from a single machine-readable source. There are good reasons to pursue this line of inquiry, but the problem of combining input from multiple sources has not yet been solved conceptually, let alone practically.

Semantic Approaches to the Machine-Tractable Dictionary

In addition to research into constructing networks of genus terms from MRDs discussed in chapter 10, various proposals in the past have suggested that different specialized link types should be added to the network. Nakamura and Nagao (1988) identified 41 function nouns and replaced their IS-A taxonomic link with other links (except in the definitions "kind of," "type of," etc.), while Amsler (1980) suggested incorporating an IS-PART-OF link in addition to the IS-A links into the earlier taxonomy of Amsler and White (1979). Klavans, Chodorow, and Wacholder (1990), do an in-depth study of other possibilities.

Other approaches to forming semantic networks from dictionary text using hand-coding have also been tried. The Princeton group (Beckwith et al. 1989; discussed in chapter 8) is now in the process of creating a network of nouns, verbs, and adjectives in accordance with psycholinguistic guidelines. The nodes in their network are synonym sets and its links are of many types. Within the category of nouns there are both hypernym, hyponym, meronym (is-part), and holonym (reverse of meronym) links. Within the verb category are troponym (manner-of) and entailment (implication) links. Aside from these various individual efforts at extracting semantics from MRDs (and others discussed in chapter 8), there are several longstanding, ongoing efforts or "schools" of thought. These sites each represent a history of thematically related research into the lexicon.

Boguraev and Levin
Several researchers, including Byrd (1989) and Wilks et al. (1988), have described what an idealized lexical storehouse can and would look like. The usual characterization is one where static lexical structures, either tables or trees, are referred to as lexical databases (LDBs); and lexical knowledge bases (LKBs) are LDBs augmented with other machinery, typically rules for inference or sense extension.

Boguraev and Levin (1990) start from approximately the same place, and argue for a particular flavor of LKB—one where there are rules for "certain types of linguistic generalizations which are an essential component of lexical knowledge" (p. 65). In particular, they claim that rules such as the "causative/inchoative alternation rule" is necessary for classifying verbs related to "change of state," for example, "melt," "thicken," etc. Without this, they argue, the LKB will be unable to assist in the processing of words used in unexpected ways, what they call the "productivity problem."

Their claim is actually tied to, and motivated by, a particular linguistic theory, and, as a consequence, reduces to an explication of the extralexical knowledge required to process language within their chosen theoretical framework. Other frameworks would solve the problem differently, and indeed, the work on metaphor processing and sense extension of Wilks (1975b, 1975c, 1977), Fass (1988), Wilks et al. (1988), and Martin (1992) directly addresses these issues.

Defining Formulas and the Relational Lexicon: Illinois and Liège

The Illinois school has concentrated on analysis of *Webster's Seventh New Collegiate Dictionary* (W7) (Gove 1969), originally parsing it with the linguistic string parser (Sager 1981) and then with analysis programs of their own design. Their most widely cited paper is probably Markowitz, Ahlswede, and Evens (1986) and their edited collection (Evens 1988). Aside from "taxonomy and set-membership relations," which is another way of talking about the IS-A or AKO hierarchies discussed earlier, the Illinois school has been characterized by the study of "defining formulae" and with the construction of what they call the "relational lexicon." Ahlswede and Evens (1988) describe the design and implementation of their project to convert MRD into an LDB in relational database form. In 1990 their LDB contained syntactic and semantic information for about 50,000 words (Evens and Conlon 1990), and was implemented using commercial database software (the Oracle Relational Database Management System).

Defining formulas are recurring patterns found in dictionary definitions. Probably the simplest defining formula is "any NP [noun phrase]" which turns out to be fairly reliable for indicating a taxonomic relation between the word being defined and the grammatical head of the NP. For example, in W7 the definition of "nectar" is "any delicious drink," which is used to infer that an IS-A link exists between "nectar" and "drink." Describing taxonomic relations is the most straightforward application of the defining formula idea; they are very useful for creating IS-A hierarchies.

Defining formulas are also used by procedures for the automatic recognition of nouns that represent human beings, and the recognition of active and stative verbs and adjectives. Markowitz et al. (1986) suggest that MEMBER-OF links, to represent part-whole relations, be created from noun definitions that use the phrase "a member of." For example, one definition of "hand" is "a member of a ship's crew," and they propose a defining formula that associates the headword "hand" with "crew," the head of the NP of the "of" PP (prepositional phrase). Further, they observe, the headword almost always refers with this pattern in definitions to a human, which is a useful thing to know when parsing verbs that take human subjects, or generating pronouns in text and deciding between using "who" and "which."

Verbs can also be distinguished with defining formulas as active or stative when they appear in noun definitions. Predictably, the pattern "the act of" can be used to identify active verbs, as in "plumbing" defined as "the act of using a plumb"; interestingly, the pattern "the state of being" does not identify stative verbs, but nonstative verbs being used in a stative way, as in "displacement" defined as "the state of being displaced." Other patterns are used for discovering collocations of adjectives (the nouns they typically modify), and patterns containing parentheses can be used to gather selectional information about verbs; for example, "mount" is defined as "to put or have (as artillery) in position," which indicates that mount can take artillery as an object.

The defect of this method of analysis is centrally connected to the problem of word sense distinctions. As discussed in great detail elsewhere in this book, it is one thing to find a relationship between two words; it is another to distinguish which sense of these words is intended. For example, when we learn that "nectar" is a "drink" and that a "hand" is a part of a "crew" we still need to find out what senses of "drink" and "crew" are intended; this is exactly what is needed if the relationships we need are to be made explicit.

Defining formulas applied to LDOCE definitions have been used also at Liège (Fontenelle and Vanandroye, 1989) to retrieve potentially (causative/ inchoative) verbs by taking patterns such as "to (cause to)" in conjunction with LDOCE codes for transitive and intransitive verbs. The Liège work uses symbols not as dictionary elements needing disambiguation, but with the claim that they are primitives (e.g., cause) already, as having a single sense, as in chapter 2.

Categories for Prepositions

Slator et al. (1990) have developed a methodology for deriving a consistent and well-motivated set of semantic relations for the most commonly used prepositions of English. The result is a set of relations characterized by the prepositions of English that express them and, further, one that characterizes the linguistic structures they participate in, and the semantic environments that they prefer.

The definitions of prepositions in LDOCE contain none of the special codes that the content words have for grammatical subcategorization, semantic restrictions, or pragmatic classification. The only information associated with prepositions in LDOCE is (1) definition text (usually made up of synonyms or short phrases, as opposed to the definitions for the content words, which are generally more expressive); and (2) example text (sentences or phrases showing the preposition being used).

If a preposition is defined by synonymy with another preposition (e.g., one sense of "off" and one sense of "from" are defined in terms of each other as in: Take the matches from/off the child), they carry, or mark, the same semantic relation. By the same token, each of the example sentences shows the preposition in a context. That context includes at least a prepositional object, and often also includes a verb or noun attachment, as well as verb subject and object. These contextual items are content words (nouns and verbs), and these have grammatical subcategorization, semantic restrictions, and pragmatic classification codes in LDOCE. Therefore, the examples not only show what words a preposition can appear with, but they also show what *kinds* of words they appear with.

The initial analysis of the prepositions was carried out in three phases: (1) data acquisition, (2) similarity analysis, and (3) cluster analysis. The results of the data acquisition yielded a collection of preposition senses in which each sense encoded a feature vector of 15 elements. Each element within a vector contained a set (possibly empty) of LDOCE codes or other information taken from the sense definitions. One element is the set of box codes associated with the prepositional objects, another is the set of subject codes associated with the verbs, and so on. In addition, one vector element contained a set (again, possibly empty) of strings in the definition text judged to be semantically relevant, such as "by means of," "because of," "as a result of," "the direction of," etc. The inventory of potentially meaningful definition phrases or "defining formulae" was constructed by finding all word sequences that occurred at least twice and choosing the most plausible ones (e.g., "by means of" is found in 10 preposition definitions, whereas "the possession of" occurs only twice). Another vector element encoded whether the example texts showed a preposition attached to a verb, modifying a noun phrase, or both.

Similarity evaluation was conducted by comparing pairs of senses. Because each feature vector is made up of diverse elements (grammar codes, semantic codes, etc.), different metrics were applied to those elements. The resulting similarity matrix was then submitted to cluster analysis using graph-theoretic techniques.

The results of this study revealed between 40 and 50 common semantic relations of varying specificity and granularity as well as dozens of prepositions that exist in a class of their own. Many of the clusters were quite reasonable, as we expected, while others were more finely distinguished.

The next phase of this study will attempt to predict the kinds of verbs that a given semantic class of prepositions prefers, the kinds of objects a class may relate to, and the strength of these preferences. The first two are revealed by collective assessment of the feature vectors of the members of a class. The third is a function of the strength of association between a preposition and the cluster it belongs to. All together, these results provide us with an empirically motivated semantic foundation for capturing lexical facts about prepositions.

The NMSU School

The New Mexico State University lexical research program combines a system for creating a Pathfinder network of clustered word senses (described in chapter 7), in which the clusters are based on co-occurrence statistics, with a hand-coding initiative (described in chapter 7), to find the defining senses of the dictionary with a dictionary parsing system, described immediately below, that processes definitions as well as using the semantic and pragmatic codes of LDOCE to disambiguate the genus terms of definitions.

NMSU: The Defining Spiral

The parallel efforts pursued at the NMSU school all take as input the forms of information given on the LDOCE tape (English definitions, syntax codes, subject and pragmatic codes, etc.) and provide any one of:

1. A clustered network of LDOCE words whose clusters correspond to empirically derived senses (McDonald et al. 1990; see chapter 7). These

are transduced to a network of senses (the SPIRAL procedure; see below) on the way to a yet further transduction to a labeled network, with either predicate labels (the ARC procedure; see below) or as a connectionist network with numerical weights on the arcs.

2. A formalized set of definitions of sense entries in a nested predicate form, where the predicates are a "seed set" of senses, half the size of the existing controlled vocabulary of LDOCE (Guo 1989, 1992; see chapter 7). This would be a Fregean "compositional" formalization of LDOCE.

3. Framelike structures containing (as well as the given LDOCE syntactic codes) a formalization of the English definitions using predicates that are English words (not senses) from the controlled vocabulary (Slator and Wilks 1987, Slator 1988b).

The SPIRAL Procedure

The chief problem in making LDOCE tractable is explicitly to tag the senses of the English words in LDOCE definitions. The SPIRAL procedure cycles information between Slator's (method 3) LDOCE parser (augmented with data gathered from Guo's [method 2] analysis of the LDOCE vocabulary), and McDonald, Plate, and Schvaneveldt's (1990) (method 1) distributional network so as to yield a sense-tagging of the words in the frames Slator outputs from parsing LDOCE, while at the same time providing a filter for the networks so as to cut down the search space required. It also gives senses (rather than words) at the network nodes. This passing of material between the modules is not circular but a spiral that yields, from a combination of weak sources, a stronger semantic database.

The SPIRAL procedure is a method for synthesizing different methods into a coherent procedure for constructing a lexical database. Each of the individual techniques concentrates on different sources of semantic knowledge. The SPIRAL procedure is a way to integrate these. The procedure is as follows:

1. Consider only the words in the control vocabulary.

2. For a given word sense:

a. Look up the words that appear in the Guo (method 2) list of 1051 seed senses. These word are used in only one sense in the definitions of control vocabulary words (see chapter 7). Sense-tag these words.

b. Parse the definition text using a syntactic parser (Slator 1988b) for the LDOCE definitions as part of method 3. Refinements to this parser have been made by replacing words in the definitions of the control vocabulary with a list of their possible defining senses developed in method 2. Other refinements are made to identify relationships that are closely related to the genus word.

c. Look up the part-of-speech–tagged words in the Guo list of "used in 2 senses" or "used in 3 or more senses" to see if the part-of-speech tag resolves the ambiguity.

d. Identify the genus word. For nouns and verbs, identify the genus word (IS-A relation to the headword), if one exists. We also identify words that have a special relation to the headword (such as part of, member of, set of, etc.). This work was begun as part of the lexicon provider system of Slator (Slator 1988a,b, Slator and Wilks 1987, 1990) and has been augmented to recognize new semantic relations.

e. Disambiguate the genus words using a system called the genus disambiguator (Guthrie et al. 1990). This system both identifies and disambiguates the genus word in noun definitions based on pragmatic coherence and semantic distance. Several refinements of this system have been developed and empirical evidence suggests that these refinements give a very high success rate (more than 90%) on identification of the correct sense of the genus word. Another module is under development to display the derived ontology in a windowed, hypertext environment.

f. Use a range of disambiguation techniques, including the McDonald-Plate techniques, with a new notion of relative neighborhoods (Guthrie et al. 1991) and a technique using simulated annealing (Cowie et al. 1992) for disambiguation of the remaining content words in the definition (see chapter 10).

3. Where possible, use selection restrictions given in LDOCE to refine the ratings.

The ARC Procedure

This procedure refers to methods by which the arcs of Plate and McDonald's networks are labeled automatically with either predicates, yielding a conventional semantic net, or with numerical values, yielding a connectionist network (Rumelhart, McClelland, and the PDP Research Group, 1986). The latter follows fairly directly from Pathfinder techniques, but the former presents a great challenge. ARC can be thought of as a fourth stage of the SPIRAL procedure, described above.

The first phase of ARC is driven from the already obtained frames (based on Slator's work in method 3); for each appropriate predicate in a frame that has two word senses s1 and s2 as its arguments, ARC seeks nodes n1 and n2 in a Plate and McDonald network corresponding to those senses. When found, ARC labels the connecting arc with the predicate from the frame. This method simply transfers information from the frames to the networks.

A second phase now begins from the networks: for any two nodes in a network n1 and n2, both representing English word senses, and not already connected by a labeled arc, ARC seeks their occurrence in LDOCE entries, immediately linked by plausible predicate and case forms (e.g., IS-A, ON, USED-FOR, PART-OF, etc.) and in senses that Slator's LDOCE parser asserts are the appropriate ones. If the occurrences in the whole dictionary are consistent, as in:

hand (=bodyhand) IS-A-PART-OF body (=human body)

with no other predicate appearing where PART-OF does in any LDOCE entry, then that label could be attached, at that point, to an arc of the network.

The SPIRAL and the ARC procedures are part of a range of empirical possibilities to explore. For example, many of the co-occurrences of the two word senses in the body of LDOCE will be in forms for which Slator's parser may not provide a predicate unless augmented with inferential techniques; for example, if we seek co-ocurrences of "bridge" and "tower" in the text, a form like "tower bridge" will not, without deeper analysis of the kind developed within NP analysis systems, provide any linking predicate, showing the type of linkage of the two concepts.

An interesting empirical question, after the application of the SPIRAL and ARC techniques, is whether the sense-tagged frames (from method 3, augmented by methods 1 and 2) and the labeled network (of method 1 augmented by method 3) will then be equivalent, consistent, or even contradictory, "strengthened" semantic databases, each formed from a different combination of the same weak methods. Note that, in the two phases of ARC, as described above, since the second (but not the first) phase ranges over the examples in the dictionary text, the two sorts of information may be expected to be different, though, it is hoped, consistent.

The NMSU Lexicon Provider

The NMSU lexicon provider (Slator and Wilks 1987, Slator 1988a,b) is a subsystem to provide text-specific lexicons from selected MRD definitions from LDOCE. The input to this subsystem is unconstrained text; the output is a collection of lexical semantic objects, one for every sense of every word in the text. By building a lexicon on a text-by-text basis, the lexicon provider achieves two distinct goals: firstly, there are computational advantages, in terms of time and space, in keeping things small; secondly and more important, the text-specific lexicon can itself reveal properties of the text. In particular, an analysis of the lexicon can reveal facts about the content of the text.

The lexical semantic objects in the lexicon contain grammatical and subcategorization information, often with general (and sometimes specific) grammatical predictions; most of these objects also have semantic selection codes, organized into a type hierarchy, and many have encoded contextual (pragmatic and LDOCE subject code) knowledge as well.

In order to reveal various facts about the content of the text, and as a natural byproduct of the lexicon construction, a relative contextual score is computed for each object that bears an LDOCE pragmatic code. These scores provide a simple metric for comparing competing word senses for text-specific contextual coherence, and this provides a way to address directly the problem of resolving lexical ambiguity in the text.

Besides exploiting those special encodings supplied with the machine-readable version of the dictionary entries, the text of selected dictionary definitions is analyzed, to enrich the frame representation further. The lexicon-providing subsystem uses LDOCE as a database and produces a structured (and much smaller) knowledge base of lexical semantic objects, specific to the text, and organized by pragmatic context.

Constructing the Lexicon

The lexicon-providing subsystem produces lexical semantic objects that are further manipulated in two ways: (1) they are organized into a hierarchical contextual structure and (2) they are enriched by means of further processing over the text of the dictionary definitions themselves, as described below. Consider, for example, the following short text:

Current can be measured. The technician measures alternating current with an ammeter.

The basic lexicon for this text contains 30 frames for content words (not counting 18 senses of the infinitive "be" and 10 senses of the auxiliary "can"). These 30 frames are: alternate (three adjective senses, one verb sense), ammeter (one noun sense), can (two nouns, two verbs), current (three adjectives, four nouns), measure (eight nouns, three verbs, one adjective), technician (one noun sense), and the phrase "alternating current" (one noun sense). LDOCE defines about 7,000 phrases.

Each basic frame has five slots: GRAMMAR, POS, SENSE-NUM, PRAGMATIC, and TYPE. The GRAMMAR slots are filled with category information and predictions from the LDOCE grammar for English with its 110-odd members (Quirk et al. 1972, 1985) ; POS is *part of speech*, the top level of the GRAMMAR hierarchy; and SENSE-NUM is the *sense number*. PRAGMATIC slots are filled with contextual domain terms, such as engineering or religion. TYPE slots are filled, in the case of nouns and adjectives, with selection restrictions like solid, human, or abstract, and, in the case of verbs, with selection restrictions on the functional arguments to the verb such as human subject and abstract direct object (figure 9.1).

Contextual Structure

The subsystem for constructing the lexicon also establishes the conceptual domain of texts. In the basic lexicon construction process, all of the word senses for words in the text are converted to a lexicon and, along the way, an ordered list of pragmatic (subject) codes is collected. Walker and Amsler (1986) did something similar for "content assessment," using wire service stories from *The New York Times* News Service (see chapter 7). These codes are applied to a hierarchical structure representing the pragmatic content of the text. This structure is extremely useful for word sense disambiguation and parsers (see chapters 7 and 13).

Enriching Frames

The basic frames constructed directly from dictionary entries are a large step toward the knowledge required for word sense selection and parsing by some lexicon-consuming program operating over other, nondictionary text. However, there is a hidden wealth of further information implicit within the text of the definitions themselves, namely, in the genus and differentia.

When resolving lexical ambiguity or making nontrivial phrase attachment decisions, the needs of a knowledge-based parser extend beyond the initial frame representation and they are enriched by appeal to parse trees constructed from the dictionary entries. The text of the definition entries is analyzed to further enrich the semantic structures.

A chart parser was developed that accepts LDOCE definitions as LISP lists and produces phrase-structure trees. A context-free grammar covers

(measure

(POS . v)

(SENSE-NUM . 1)

(GRAMMAR

(or

((I) . V/Intransitive)

((T1) . V/Transitive/N+-or-PRON+-Follows)))

(PRAGMATIC nil)

(TYPE

((H T -)

(SUBJECT . Human/Sex-Unspecified)

(OBJECT1 . Abstract)

(OBJECT2))))

(ammeter

(POS . n)

(SENSE-NUM . 0)

(GRAMMAR

((C) . N/Count)))

(PRAGMATIC

(EGZE (Engineering/Electrical)))

(TYPE

((J) (RESTRICTION . Solid/Movable)))

Figure 9.1
Some basic lexical semantic objects (frames).

the language of content word definitions in LDOCE at a success rate exceeding 90% for the sublanguage of LDOCE definitions (but only the open class [content word] portions of that language). The LDOCE content word definitions are typically one or more complex phrases composed of zero or more PPs, NPs, or relative clauses singly or severally. The syntax of sense definitions is relatively uniform, and developing a grammar for the bulk of LDOCE has not proved to be an intractable problem.

Chart parsing was selected for this system because of its utility as a grammar testing and development tool. The chart parser is driven by a context-free grammar of 100-plus rules and has a lexicon derived from the 2219 words in the LDOCE core vocabulary. The parser is left-corner and bottom-up, with top-down filtering (Slocum 1985b), producing phrase-structure trees. The context-free grammar driving the chart parser is virtually unaugmented and, with certain minor exceptions, no procedure associates constituents with what they modify. Hence, there is little or no motivation for assigning elaborate or competing syntactic structures, since the choice of one over the other has no semantic consequence (Pulman 1983a,b). Therefore, the trees are constructed to be as "flat" as possible. The parser also has a "longest string" (fewest constituents) syntactic preference. A tree interpreter extracts semantic knowledge from these phrase-structure definition trees (Slator and Wilks 1987).

The Tree Interpreter
The output of the chart parser, a phrase-structure tree, is passed to an interpreter for pattern matching and inferencing. The first step of the interpreter picks off the dominating phrase from the tree and, after restructuring it into GENUS and FEATURE components, inserts it into the frame for that word sense under a GENUS slot.

More detailed differentia information, beyond the GENUS and its FEATURE modifiers, is also extracted from definitions. The relationship between a word and its definition can trivially be viewed as an "IS-A" relation; for example, an "ammeter" is "an instrument for measuring . . . electric current." The frame created for each word sense from its definition, then, represents the intension of that word sense. This observation motivates the assumption that portions of this intensional material can be isolated and given a label. For example, by noting that an "ammeter" is "for measuring" it becomes reasonable to create a slot in the "ammeter" frame that is labeled PURPOSE and filled with "measuring." This kind of knowledge is precisely what is needed to compute case roles and preferences.

For example, the pattern "for ⟨verb⟩-ing" in the differentia of a noun strongly predicts the PURPOSE case role for that noun. By the same token, the preposition "with" in English predicts various case roles for its NP object, principally ACCOMPANIMENT, POSSESSION, and INSTRUMENT (e.g., see Jensen and Binot 1987, Binot and Jensen 1987):

ACCOMPANIMENT ("a man ate a meal with a friend")
POSSESSION ("a man ate a fish with many bones")
INSTRUMENT ("a man ate a fish with a fork")

See chapter 13 for a further discussion of case roles and related issues. Consider this sentence again:

The technician measures alternating current with an ammeter.

The definition for ammeter contains a pattern indicating it is a constituent that prefers to fill a PURPOSE and, in particular, prefers to be "for measuring." In cases like this a parser should prefer the INSTRUMENT reading over both the ACCOMPANIMENT case relation and the POSSESSION NP complement alternatives because the object of the "with" preposition (ammeter) has a PURPOSE case role marker (filled with measuring) that suggests an INSTRUMENT attachment. What is needed to achieve this is a set of general inference rules to associate these things together. For example, this case could be handled with a rule like the following:

```
(if    (and (case-role verb? (case INSTRUMENT x?))
            (case-role noun? (case PURPOSE y?))
            (equal verb? y?))
(then (assign x? <=noun?))
```

Other case roles that appear extractable from LDOCE differentia in this way, but still subject to further investigation, are PART-OF, MEMBER-OF, MEANS-OF, and MEASURE-OF, among others. Again, it is important to distinguish this prior chart parser of dictionary texts from the knowledge-based parser of general texts. The output of the former (the lexicon provider) is the knowledge base for the latter (the lexicon consumer). The output of the dictionary parsing program described here is a lexicon of word sense frames, with each frame explicitly or implicitly positioned in multiple preexisting hierarchies.

Alshawi

Alshawi (1987) describes a system for locating meaningful patterns in definition text. Using LDOCE, definitions are analyzed by passing them through a hierarchy of phrasal patterns. When a higher-level pattern matches a substring in a definition, the children of that pattern are recursively tested in order to find the most refined possible pattern. This top-down approach contrasts with the more usual parsing algorithms, where a parsing attempt that does not succeed can be attempted again with relaxed rules.

The output of the system is described as "structures carrying information enabling the classification of the new word sense with respect to an existing classification of entities in a discourse domain." The classification of entities in the domain is expected to be part of whatever domain the eventual consuming system is applied toward. In other words, this dictionary analysis system assumes there will be a lexicon consumer that needs this kind of lexical representation and also has a domain model within which to interpret the entities in the lexical representation.

A word like "mug" has definitions that are both nouns and verbs. For example, one noun sense of "mug" is the following (Alshawi 1987):

mug: (noun), a foolish person who is easily deceived

which is converted to:

((class person)
    (properties (foolish))
    (predication (object-of ((class deceive)))))

and one verb sense of "mug" is the following:

mug: (verb), to rob with violence, as in a dark street

which is converted to:

((class rob)
    (adverbial ((case with)) (filler (class violence))))

The system has most success finding the genus terms in definitions, which Alshawi calls the "semantic heads of the definitions" (Alshawi 1987), and which usually appear in semantic formulas under a "CLASS" slot label. As the two "mug" examples show, other semantic labels, such as PROPERTIES and PURPOSE, are also used.

The principal difficulty is that none of the fillers in these structures are sense-tagged, so it is not possible to tell, for example, what sense of "person" is intended in the noun definition of "mug"; that is, a human being, a place adjacent to a human being "he had a banana on his person," or a grammatical device to mark inflection on verbs. Nor is it possible to distinguish the intended sense of the prepositions in definitions, and so the "with" argument identified as a "case" is not further elaborated, and the earlier discussion applies: Is this an ACCOMPANIMENT relation or an INSTRUMENT relation? It is certainly not a "with" relation, since there is no such thing in this system. The notion of a hierarchy of phrasal patterns is an appealing one that, as an approach to the analysis of structure, has the computational advantage of limiting search. However, this approach appears to depend on a strong domain model that will fill the many missing details in the representation.

The Dutch School: Tagging the LDOCE "Corpus"

Several dictionary-related projects have been undertaken in the Netherlands in recent years, originally under the auspices of the ASCOT project (automatic scanning system for *c*orpus *o*riented *t*asks) at the University of Amsterdam. Akkerman (1989) initially made a very thorough and revealing comparison between the grammar-coding schemes of LDOCE and OALD. These two MRDs are recognized as having the most elaborate grammatical information of any on-line resource, and it turns out that the bulk of their codings can be mutually translated back and forth. As a consequence of this analysis, the LDOCE coding scheme was chosen. Other projects that make use of the ASCOT lexicon include TOSCA (ASCOT spelled backward), which is working toward building a grammar of English using the extended affix grammar formalism, and the PARSCOT project which aims to reimplement the linguistic string project grammar (Sager 1981).

Chapter 10

Genus Hierarchies and Networks

In chapter 9 we gave an overview of the work on extracting semantic information from MRDs. We devote this chapter to one aspect of that work: constructing semantic networks from MRDs.

Many researchers believe that in order to process language effectively, it is necessary to build a knowledge base that includes hierarchical information. It is not difficult to argue that the knowledge base should "know" facts like a poodle IS-A dog, a dog IS-A mammal, a mammal IS-A animal. Most researchers would further argue that in the knowledge base, poodles will have all the properties of dogs, and dogs will have all the properties of mammals, etc. and although there are differing opinions about whether this knowledge is inferred at the time of processing or inferred earlier and stored in the knowledge base, this is nonetheless crucial information which must be available for language processing.

Dictionaries provide a rich source from which we can extract this kind of information automatically on a large scale. Beginning with the original work of Amsler and White in the late 1970s and early 1980s, the problem of automatically extracting semantic hierarchies from MRDs has been investigated by many researchers.

The Basic Technique

Dictionary definitions of nouns are normally written in such a way that one can identify for each headword (the word being defined), a "genus term" (a word more general than the headword), and these are related via an IS-A relation. The information following the genus term, the differentia, serves to differentiate the headword from other headwords with the same genus. For example, from the LDOCE (Procter et al. 1978):

knife—a blade fixed in a handle, used for cutting as a tool or weapon.

Here "blade" is the genus term of the headword "knife" and "fixed in a handle, used for cutting as a tool or weapon" yields the differentia. In other words, a "knife" IS-A "blade" (genus) distinguished from other blades by the features of its differentia. The standard technique for creating a semantic network from noun definitions is to identify the IS-A relationships of this type. Note, however, that for this information to be useful, it is necessary to distinguish the sense of "blade" used in the network from other possible senses (ruling out blade of grass, propeller blade, and an amusing fellow). If this is not done, we could use any sense of "blade" from LDOCE including:

blade—a gay sharp amusing fellow.

to construct a piece of the network with the relationships knife IS-A blade IS-A fellow, and inheritance of properties would allow "knife" to inherit the properties of "fellow"! If the words in the network are disambiguated, the network contains more desirable information like:

knife_sense1 IS-A blade_sense1

and

blade_sense4 IS-A fellow_sense1

Therefore we can view the process of building a semantic hierarcy of IS-A links from noun definitions as twofold: (1) to find the genus term (or terms) in the defintions and (2) to disambiguate them. Several researchers have attempted one of these, and others have attempted both, using different dictionaries and varying degrees of automation. In this chapter we give a brief overview of the research projects in this area, with an indication of whether (1) or (2) or both were attempted, the dictionary used in the work, and the degree of human intervention required. Then follow two sections which give details of the techniques used for (1) and (2).

Overview of the Work

Amsler and White pioneered the work in this area in the late 1970s and early 1980s using the *Merriam-Webster Pocket Dictionary* (MWPD 1964, Amsler 1980, Amsler and White 1979). Beginning with the concordances of Olney and an implementation of a tree-growing algorithm by Amsler, they worked with computers much less powerful than the desktops of today to create a semantic network of noun senses (Reichert, Olney, and Paris 1969). Their techniques were somewhat automated, but required a great deal of human intervention for the disambiguation process. Nonetheless, their work was among the most dilligent and complete in the field, and descriptions of their work provide the backbone of all that has followed. Unfortunately, the actual network of word senses never became publicly available for further research. A range of other researchers in NLP began to replicate their work for other dictionaries, using better computers, and more automation. Amsler (1989) coined the term "computational lexicology" for this new generation of research, and showed the research community that information potentially useful to NLP could be extracted from MRDs.

Michiels, Fontenelle, and Noel, together with their group from the University of Liège, have done extensive studies of the structure of LDOCE (Michiels et al. 1980, Michiels and Noel 1982, Michiels 1982, Jansen et al. 1985, Fontenelle and Vanandroye 1989, Fontenelle 1990a,b). Michiels's 1982 thesis was the first large-scale exploration of the LDOCE database. As part of this work he derived taxonomies of vehicles, a grammar of definitions, and gave a detailed description of grammatical codes. Michiels and Noel applied Amsler's tree-growing algorithm to LDOCE definitions and observed that the controlled defining vocabulary of LDOCE gave rise to shallower hierarchies than those produced by Amsler for MPD. Later work by Fontenelle (1990a) describes a lexical-semantic study of ergative verbs and color verbs in LDOCE.

In 1985 Chodorow et al. proposed a new algorithm and constructed noun and verb networks of spelling forms automatically from the *Webster's Seventh New Collegiate Dictionary* (Gove 1969). In addition, they developed interactive processes for disambiguation.

The late 1980s had a flurry of work which automated the construction of semantic networks using the machine-readable version of LDOCE. LDOCE was a very appealing source of information for researchers, and this, in addition to the cooperation of the publisher with the research community, has certainly made it the most widely used English dictionary for language processing. Parsers have been developed which parse the definition text of LDOCE (Slator 1987, Vossen 1989). There have been successful efforts, with various dictionaries, to create networks from the genus terms of noun definitions in an automatic way, but LDOCE is the only English dictionary that has been used for disambiguating the terms of the network automatically.

Extracting Semantic Networks from LDOCE

Nakamura and Nagao (1988) constructed a network of spelling forms
from LDOCE automatically and created a database of LDOCE definitions. Although they did not attempt automatic disambiguation of the
terms, they identified patterns of words in the definitions and created links
corresponding to them (see also Fontenelle 1990a).

Using the semantic category markings in the machine-readable version of LDOCE, both the NMSU group (Guthrie et al. 1990, Bruce and
Guthrie 1992, Bruce, Wilks, and Guthrie 1992, Bruce 1992) and the
Cambridge group (Copestake 1990) developed similar, but not identical,
heuristic procedures that, to a great extent, automate the task of developing a hierarchy of word senses.

The ACQUILEX project (Calzolari and Bindi 1990, Calzolari and
Zampolli 1989; see chapter 12) in Europe is developing disambiguated
networks for a range of dictionaries and has provided extensive studies on
the structure of LDOCE. Vossen (1990, 1991a) has created complete networks of noun senses for both LDOCE and the Dutch Van Dale
dictionary (*Groot Woordenboek van Hedendaags Nederlands*, Van Sterkenburg and Pijnenburg 1984) using a technique for disambiguation that
combines information from both dictionaries with information from the
Van Dale bilingual Dutch-English dictionary. Copestake and Briscoe at
Cambridge University use heuristics based on the structure of LDOCE
together with information from the *Longman Lexicon of Contemporary
English* (McArthur 1981) in their disambiguation algorithm.

Finding the Genus Term

It is estimated that about 90% of the noun definitions in dictionaries have
a genus term, which is the head of the first noun phrase (NP) (as is the
case in the knife blade example above), and for these cases the standard
method for identifying the genus term is to parse (or partially parse) the
definitions and extract the head of the first NP. This method has been
usefully applied by all researchers in this area. However, all dictionaries
seem to have a set of noun definitions that do not conform to this rule.
Constructing taxonomies from the genus terms of definitions thus forces
one to take a stand on how to treat a rather large class of noun definitions
which are not as "standard" as the definition given above for **knife**. The
characteristic property of many of these definitions is that the head of the

first NP (the usual place to find a genus term) seems vacuous, and another easily identifiable noun in the definition gives information about the headword. Nakamura and Nagao (1988), identify this group of non-standard definitions syntactically as:

{det.} {adj.}* ⟨Function Noun⟩ of ⟨Key Noun⟩ {adj. phrase}*

For example, the following definitions have the property that the head of the NP following the "of" is more semantically relevant to the headword than the head of the first NP.

arum [LDOCE]—a tall, white type of lily
cyclamate [LDOCE]—any of various manmade sweeteners ...
deuterium [MWPD]—a form of hydrogen that is twice the mass of ordinary hydrogen
academic [LDOCE]—a member of a college or university

The form of this type of definition is predictable whenever certain words are used as the head of the first NP. Amsler and White (1979) kept a list of these words, calling them partives and collectives. Nakamura and Nagao (1988) call them function nouns. Chodorow et al. (1985) refer to a subset of these as "empty heads." Guthrie et al. (1990) disagree with certain elements of these characterizations, and use the term "disturbed heads." Vossen (1991a) subdivides this group into what he calls *complex kernels* (candy: a type of sweet), *derivations* (the genus is the derived form of a verb or the genus is very general and followed by a verb phrase, in a definition such as gasp: an act of gasping), and into five *relators* such as member vs. group (e.g., band—a group of musicians) or instance vs. concept (e.g., classic—a piece of art.). In addition, he identifies an additional kind of nonstandard definition as definition by enumeration

color—red, blue, green, black, brown, yellow, white, etc.

Vossen, like Klavans (Klavans et al. 1990) separates out what we have referred to as the standard case into hyponomy (IS-A) and synonymy relations. Vossen (1990) views the dictionary as a source of empirical evidence for relations between nominal predicates. He does a thorough study of the *kernels* (Amsler's word for the genuslike word in a definition) of noun definitions. He distinguishes two kinds of relations in what he call complex kernels: hyponomy (or IS-A) as in the definition of:

sheepdog: a dog trained ...

and synonomy as in the LDOCE:

abattoir: slaughterhouse

He defines a topology for what he calls complex kernels: type vs. class, quantity vs. mass, etc., and his treatment of these in the LINKS project is to create different links for each of what we would call the "disturbed heads." The question remains: what is to be done with these exceptional cases?

In the original work of Amsler and White (1979) with the *Merriam-Webster Pocket Dictionary* (MWPD 1964), human "disambiguators" were asked to sense-tag the head of the first NP in the definition and in the disturbed head cases. They were also asked to sense-tag any other noun in the definition which "made a significant semantic contribution to an IS-A link" (Amsler and White 1979) with the headword being defined. So, for the **deuterium** definition above, "hydrogen" was sense-tagged as well as "form." The taxonomy actually contained both a link from **deuterium** to "form" and a link from **deuterium** to "hydrogen," although the hydrogen sense was marked in a special way to indicate it is not the syntactic head of the definition.

In cases like the "hydrogen" example just given, the marked "semantic contributors" were never given ancestors, since the link often represented a more loosely defined relation than the strictly transitive "is a subset of" definition of IS-A, which ideally relates the headword and its genus sense. This degenerate form of IS-A precludes inheritance in the network. It is included in the taxonomy in order to form links to words which may not be related in a strict IS-A sense, but which convey useful information about the word being defined.

There have been various proposals over the years suggesting that different specialized link types be added to the taxonomy (besides the degenerate IS-A). Markowitz et al. (1986) suggest HAS_MEMBER links be created in definitions which use the phrase "member of" (i.e., "college" HAS_MEMBER "academic" in the definition of **academic** above). Nakamura and Nagao (1988) identify 41 different function nouns and replace the IS-A link in their taxonomy with various other links (except in the "kind of," "type of," etc., definitions). Amsler (1980) suggests the incorporation of an IS_PART_OF link in addition to the IS-A links in the earlier taxonomy of Amsler and White (1979).

Chodorow et al. (1985) were the first to automate the genus finding process for nouns and verbs in *Webster's Seventh New Collegiate Dic-*

tionary. However, in their work, only the spelling form of the genus is identified automatically; the sense selections are made by humans. The disambiguation is not to attach a sense number, but rather to perform a function called "sprouting," which interactively selects among all words that have a given word sense as a genus. Their taxonomy contains only IS-A links, and they partially attack the "disturbed head" problem by identifying automatically a small class of what they call "empty heads." The effect of their method is to skip over seemingly vacuous terms (located where a genus is usually expected), and treat the more semantically relevant term as the actual genus.

The Empty Head Heuristic

The identification of a satisfactory genus term is not straightforward in all cases, and the problems associated with classifying the relationships expressed are difficult and numerous. A thorough study of this shadowy area is necessary in order to make optimal use of the semantic information available in MRDs. (Chodorow et al. 1985) examined a phenomenon that they described as follows: "If the word found belongs to a small class of "empty heads" (words like *one, any, kind, class, manner, family, race, group, complex,* etc.) and is followed by *of*, then the string following *of* is reprocessed in an effort to locate additional heads." (p. 301).

Although the empty head rule seems to be a reasonable one in certain situations, one must be careful about its use. The empty head rule produces undesirable effects in an IS-A hierarchy for some of the collective words (which Chodorow et al. [1985] treat as empty): set, group, class etc. A response (Guthrie et al. 1990) to the empty head phenomenon is to process the heads in the same way, but to limit this processing to a much smaller set, that is, to those heads that are truly empty: the set containing {one, any, kind, type}. Consider the LDOCE definition:

canteen—(British English) a set of knives, forks and spoons, usu. for 6 or 12 people

Since "set" is one of the empty heads in the Chodorow et al. procedure, they would create IS-A links from "canteen" to "knives," "forks," and "spoons," and this again would violate the inheritance properties that should be preserved by IS-A links. Guthrie et al. (1990) treated the collective heads, {set, group, collection, class of, family of} (which we maintain are not truly empty, simply disturbed), to form a taxonomic link to the correct sense of "set," "group," or "class," etc. and to form a HAS_MEMBER link to the noun or nouns which describe the elements of the collective, as found in the differentia of the headword definition. Further, definitions in which the genus term is plural are treated in the same way as those which begin with "a set of." In general, our view is that the disturbed heads should be grouped in the sense of Nakamura and Nagao (1988), and that additional links (like HAS_MEMBER, IS_PART_OF, etc.) should be created whenever they are appropriate. However, it is our position that IS-A links should also be created for every word sense given in the dictionary. Moreover, in order to maintain inheritance and transitivity in the IS-A network, a strict "subset of" definition of IS-A should be maintained. But, unlike Nakamura and Nagao (1988), we propose that "member of" definitions should not be grouped with the "set of," or "group of" definitions. All but one "member of" definition in LDOCE (see below) uses "member of" to mean "person who is a member of." We recommend that, in this case, a link be created from the headword to "person," and that the appropriate MEMBER_OF link be constructed.

The exceptional case, where "member of" does not refer to a person, is in the definition of **feline**: "a member of the cat family." This case must be treated separately, since it is impossible to identify the correct sense of the word "member" here, given that all its senses in LDOCE are marked as referring to a human or a part of the human body. The difficulty of these many varieties of special case (and they are not that special, since there are hundreds of them in the dictionary) is that they call into question certain of the long-held assumptions about the taxonomic structure of dictionaries. The conventional wisdom has always been that dictionary definitions contained a genus term (a term more general than the one being defined), and that this term could almost invariably be found in the first phrase of the definition text. Further, the exceptions to this convention, the "empty heads" like "one of" or "any of," have been viewed as being similarly well-behaved. Our investigations lead us to conclude that things are not as simple as they once appeared, and the question of what to do with these troublesome cases is far from resolved.

A heuristic procedure has been developed at NMSU which automatically disambiguates the genus terms of noun definitions. This procedure, together with a procedure for locating the genus word, is called the genus processor (see figure 10.1). The genus term is identified by the lexicon provider (denoted as LP in figure 10.1) (Slator 1988a, 1988b, Slator and

Genus Processor (GP)

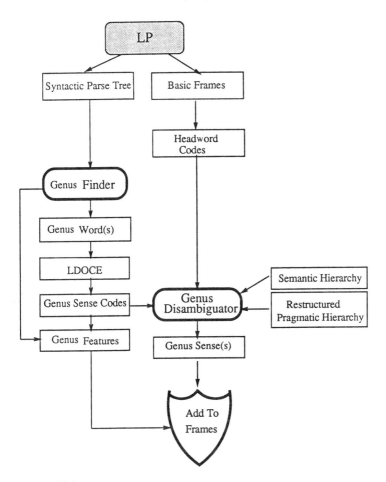

Figure 10.1
Overview of the genus processor.

Wilks 1987) as the head of the first NP in the definition. As discussed above, this simple rule for locating the genus term succeeds with over 90% of noun definitions, and a more complicated algorithm is necessary in the general case (Guthrie et al. 1990) which is implemented as the "genus finder" portion of the process.

The second phase of the process is to find the correct sense of the genus term. A program called the genus disambiguator, which takes as input the subject codes (pragmatic codes) and box codes (semantic category codes) of the headword, taken from the machine-readable version of LDOCE, and the spelling form of the genus word, identified by the genus finder, is used to select a sense of the genus word.

In Guthrie et al. (1990), an algorithm is suggested for disambiguating the genus terms of noun definitions in LDOCE. The procedure used was based on the assumption that the semantic relationship between the headword and its genus should be reflected by the relation of their semantic categories. In other words, the semantic category of the genus word should be identical to, or an ancestor of, the semantic category of the headword (an ancestor is a superordinate term in the hierarchy of se-mantic codes). These codes (there are 34 in all) were defined by the LDOCE lexicographers, who placed 16 of the basic categories in a hier-archy. The hierarchy for the genus disambiguator was restructured to include the remaining 18 semantic category codes. In addition, a similar relationship was postulated for the pragmatic codes. The pragmatic codes of the genera of noun definitions were required to be identical to, or an-cestors of, the pragmatic code of the headword, where "ancestor" referred to the pragmatic code hierarchy that Slator implemented in the Lexicon Provider and which imposed deeper structure onto the original LDOCE subject hierarchy (see chapter 7). A random sample of 500 noun word senses from LDOCE was used to test this assumption. The algorithm was as follows:

1. Choose the genus sense whose semantic code matches the headword.
2. If this is not possible, choose the sense whose semantic category is the closest ancestor of the headword's semantic category.
3. In the case of a tie, the subject (pragmatic) codes are used to determine a winner.
4. If the subject codes cannot be used to break the tie, the first of the tied senses appearing in the dictionary is chosen (frequently used senses are ostensibly listed first in LDOCE, but see discussion, chapter 5).

The following example illustrates the most straightforward application of the algorithm. In it, the ordered pair following the headword consists of the box code and subject code as found in the dictionary (the English gloss for these particular codes follows them). Definitions that are not given a subject code in LDOCE are indicated with a dash (—).

flute (J: movable-solid; MU: Music): a pipe-like wooden or metal musical instrument with finger holes, played by blowing across a hole in the side ...

The genus of **flute** is the word "instrument." Therefore, the input to the genus disambiguator would be

(flute J MU instrument)

The following are the LDOCE definitions for instrument:

instrument-1 (J: movable-solid; HWZT: Hardware/Tools): an object used to help in work; *medical instruments*
instrument-2 (J: movable-solid; MU: **Music**): ... an object which is played to give musical sounds (a piano, horn, etc.) ...
instrument-3 (Z: unmarked; —): someone or something which seems to be acted on by an outside force to cause something to happen; *an instrument of fate*

In this example, the first two senses of **instrument** are marked "J: movable-solid," which matches the selection restriction for **flute**. The tie is broken, however, by an appeal to the subject code Music, which selects the second sense of **instrument** as the genus of **flute**, giving us "instrument-2" as the output. The algorithm did not require the semantic category to match exactly (as in the above example), but only to be compatible (having an ancestor in its semantic category hierarchy) to disambiguate the definition. The algorithm was successful about 80% of the time.

In an effort to improve the algorithm, three factors that contributed to the determination of the genus sense (the semantic code relationship, the pragmatic code relationship, and the usage frequency information) were considered and a series of experiments were designed to improve the contribution of each factor and to weight its contribution appropriately (Bruce and Guthrie 1992). As a result of the tests run on isolated sense selection mechanisms, the disambiguation algorithm was reformulated as follows:

1. Choose the most frequently used genus sense unless an alternative sense choice is indicated by a strong relationship between headword and genus codes, either semantic or pragmatic.

2. If the sense selection based on semantic codes differs from that inferred by the pragmatic codes, base the sense selection on the pragmatic codes.
3. Select among competing genus senses with identical code markings by choosing the most frequently used sense.

A final set of tests was performed to evaluate the algorithm above, which considered all three factors in combination. Review of the output data from the disambiguation trials using the three-parameter algorithm revealed that the majority of the failures were on a very small number of frequently occurring genus words. For each of these words, the pragmatic and semantic classifications of the senses were either deficient (lacking in code information), or redundant (more than one word sense having the same markings). Such situations frequently arise with very abstract words (e.g., "part," "quality," "piece," and "number") where there are numerous word senses, and most senses have identical semantic codes and no pragmatic codes. The final modification to the genus sense selection algorithm was introduced to solve this problem: sense selection for words with errors in their code information, as well as certain words which convey very abstract concepts, were preselected and assumed to be constant. Fewer than 10 words required hand-coding of the correct sense and almost all were abstract words such as "part" or "quality." This final modification to the sense selection algorithm increased performance by 10%, resulting in a success rate of 90%.

The Disambiguated Network of Noun Senses—NounSense

NounSense is the hierarchy of concepts automatically constructed from the noun definitions provided in LDOCE. Formally it is a database of triples, where a triple consists of a headword sense, a genus sense, and a relation descriptor (e.g., "IS-A"). The word senses in the triples are actually implemented as pointers to the frame representations of the designated word senses, thereby creating a network of concepts, not terms. The database of triples contains roughly 39,000 entries, including entries for noun phrasals, and the added tokens correspond to the Longman's semantic categories for nouns. It should be noted that in the case of a headword with multiple genus terms, each genus is designated by a separate entry. The database contains entries for all noun senses in LDOCE with the exception of idiom definitions.

The *tangled* hierarchy (see next section) we have constructed is a strict IS-A network in which all nouns senses in LDOCE are linked to the syntactic head of the first NP. It should be noted that the head of the first NP can be a disjunctive structure which will produce multiple genus terms; this includes the case of "definition by enumeration." There are four exceptions:

1. The head of the first NP is a word on the list of "empty heads" (type, kind, any, one, etc.).
2. The head of the first NP is a disturbed head that is not an empty head.
3. The head of the first NP is a pronoun, or a word that is not defined as a noun in LDOCE (and its base form is not defined as a noun in LDOCE). This second situation arises when the definition is "derivational" in structure.
4. The genus is one of a small set of circularly defined words.

The definition structure corresponding to each of the exceptions cited above yields a problem genus term. A problem genus term is a word that fulfills the requirements of the genus relationship but is lacking some semantic quality considered essential in the noun hierarchy; either the potential genus provides no substantive information about the word being defined (i.e., the headword) and is considered empty (exception 1), or the concept it expresses is so general and abstract as to be considered nearly vacuous (exception 2), or it is not itself a noun (exception 3), or it is directly or indirectly defined in terms of itself (exception 4). The treatment of the above exceptions are designed to enhance the semantic information provided by problem genus terms.

In the case of the first exception, the empty head is passed over and the next noun in the definition, not used as a modifier, is selected as the genus term in a fashion similar to that described by Chodorow et al. (1985). In the case of the last three exceptions we augment the information conveyed by the problem genus term through the introduction of semantic categories used to classify the noun sense in LDOCE. We consider these a set of semantic primitives.

The introduction of semantic primitives in a dictionary-derived hierarchy has been previously discussed (Vossen 1990, Amsler 1980, Wilks 1978), but not implemented owing to the difficulty of identifying and characterizing an appropriate set of primitives, and determining the correct placement of those primitives in the hierarchy. Our approach to both concerns is based on a combination of theoretical and practical considerations.

The choice of primitives is suggested by viewing the genus term as "an upward pointing reference that distinguishes between members of a primitive type (Slator 1988a,b). Within LDOCE, all nouns are positioned in a primitive-type hierarchy by virtue of being assigned a semantic code (alternatively referred to as the box code). Our approach is to view the genus terms as differentiating headwords with the same "type" code, or, stated another way, if the semantic code is viewed as a concept, then the genus serves as the differentia. Within this framework, the LDOCE semantic codes serve as semantic primitives, and the appropriate formulation and assignment of those semantic categories are provided by LDOCE.

The placement of the semantic primitives within the noun hierarchy is again a somewhat straightforward implementation based on practical considerations. The semantic primitives form the top level of the Noun-Sense network and are connected to the remainder of the network through their association with problem genus terms. Our objective in introducing these associations is to augment semantically deficient genus terms. We want to preserve the information conveyed by the problem genus while assuring that the headword is embodied with an adequate set of properties. To accomplish this goal, the headword defined by the problem genus is linked to a special token (as opposed to the appropriate sense of the semantically deficient genus term). The token is constructed by joining the spelling form of the unsuitable genus to the semantic code of the headword. This token is then linked directly to the semantic category of the headword. This treatment not only retains the information conveyed by the genus but also prevents the hierarchical expansion of the semantically less relevant genus term, and assures that the properties of the semantic category of the headword are directly attributed to that word. In the remainder of this section we clarify this procedure with examples of its implementation for the definition structures corresponding to exceptions 2 through 4.

Exception 2 occurs when the function noun (using Nakamura and Nagao's [1988] terminology) associated with the complex genus structure is of a nearly vacuous type. Genus terms receiving this treatment are referred to as "disturbed heads." As our example we will take the definition of **island**. In this example, and all examples that follow, we contrast the hierarchy constructed by the procedure defined above with the hierarchy as it would exist if constructed using the default rule for genus selection.

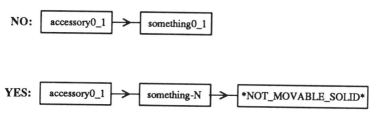

Figure 10.2
Hierarchies from the two methods ("island" example).

Figure 10.3
Hierarchies from the two methods ("accessory" example).

In all examples the semantic category of the headword is shown in parenthesis immediately preceding the text of the definition.

island—(S:solid) a piece of land surrounded by water [see figure 10.2]

When the genus term of a noun definition is not defined as a noun in LDOCE (exception 3), the genus is typically either a pronoun or a derived form of a verb or adjective. For example, consider a noun definition with the pronoun genus "something."

accessory—(N: non-movable solid) something which is not a necessary part of something larger but which makes it more beautiful, useful, effective, etc. [see figure 10.3]

The fourth and final exception to the rule for straightforward treatment of genus terms deals with the phenomena of circularly defined word sets, or loops. In NounSense all loops are broken by selecting the most general genus sense in the loop and linking that word to the semantic category of its headword. In this way, we produce a hierarchy that is acyclic. The hierarchical structure for every word originates from a semantic primitive thereby assuring the inheritance of a minimum set of appropriate properties. Consider, for example, the words "disorder," "illness," and "disease" (figure 10.4).

WITH CYCLES:

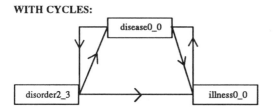

WITHOUT CYCLES:

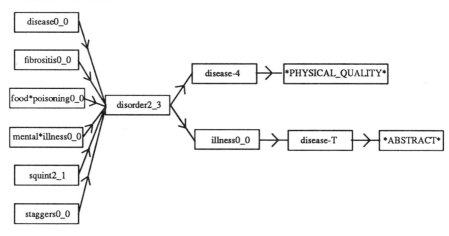

Figure 10.4
Hierarchies with and without cycles.

disorder—(4:physical quality) slight disease or illness
illness—(T:abstract) disease; unhealthy state of the body
disease—(4:physical quality) illness or disorder caused by infection or unnatural growth

In this discussion, we have made no mention of any attempt to capture the information contained in genus phrases with "disturbed heads" by introducing additional links in the network, links such as "part-of" or "member-of." Although this information is being expressed by the disturbed head, we are not attempting to capture it in the network at this time. Our reasons are multifold. Firstly, defining a minimum consistent set of link types that captures all relationships expressed by the "disturbed heads" is by no means a trivial task. Consider the diversity of meaning conveyed by the word **part** in the following three examples:

anode—the **part** of an electrical instrument (such as a battery) . . .
frontage—a **part** of a building or of land that stretches along a road, river, etc.
arc—**part** of a curved line or circle: . . .

Even if it were possible to define such a set of links, or perhaps just process a subset of links that could be concisely defined, it is not clear that our approach to disambiguation is applicable to these types of relationships. Without disambiguation, inheritance of properties is not possible.

Secondly, the frequency with which this type of definition occurs in LDOCE is not great. We estimate that not more than 11% of the noun definitions contain a disturbed head in the first NP. Which brings up another point, and that is that these types of relationships are often expressed in the differentia of the definition as well (Vossen 1990). Therefore any attempt to capture this information in a consistent manner must look beyond the first NP in the definition.

Evaluation

From a practical point of view, the question about the value of Noun-Sense is: Is the information automatically extracted from LDOCE by the procedures described above complete and consistent enough to be useful to an NLP system, and is it sufficient for such tasks? The most straightforward concern is that the information in the network be error-free.

The usefulness of NounSense is application-dependent, but the fact that this is a network representation forces certain requirements. For example: Is the information at each node of the network sufficiently complete to specify or distinguish a concept? Are the relationships between nodes at each level consistent, that is, is the level of specificity or generality approximately equivalent for all nodes on a given level of the network? Are similar concepts connected or closely associated? Are the divisions between concepts appropriately motivated? Does each path through the hierarchy result in an adequate set of properties for the concept being defined? Each of these questions is very difficult to answer even for a small number of nodes, and perhaps impossible to answer for a network the size of NounSense. In the following sections we analyze the structure of the NounSense network in a way that addresses these concerns.

We begin with a description of the structure of semantic networks derived from MRDs in general, and then focus on the aspects of LDOCE that are somewhat unusual. Finally, we describe some details of the

NounSense network and the attempts to enhance the representation of information provided there.

General Topology

The genus of every definition also occurs as a main entry in the dictionary. There are exceptions to this statement, but for the bulk of dictionary definitions the statement holds, and indeed it is this property of (near) closure that forms the basis for construction of taxonomies from MRDs. Because one definition can have multiple genus terms (linked by disjunctives), a taxonomy can have more than one upward path, a property described as being "tangled."

The tangled hierarchy derived from the *Merriam-Webster Pocket Dictionary* was described by Amsler (1980) (see discussion earlier and in Chapter 6). Amsler's statement should serve to describe any IS-A hierarchy derived from an MRD, as it mirrors the underlying premise of the construction.

Many interesting observations have been made regarding the top level of the hierarchy (Amsler 1980, Vossen 1990). As noted earlier, the words forming this level are typically not very informative, expressing the most general of concepts. Another property typical of top-level words is a high degree of polysemy (i.e., a high measure of ambiguity). Perhaps the most interesting property of these words is that they are often defined in terms of one another; their definitions are circular, forming loops which indicate something akin to synonym sets.

Amsler (1980) suggested that each circular set of definitions comprised a primitive concept, essentially equivalent to sets in mathematics. The relevance of these circular definitions has intrigued many researchers, but the top-level words are important for other reasons as well. What is stated at the top level is inherited by all nouns on more specific levels, and what is omitted is lost to a entire category of word senses. It is exactly this concern that has motivated our treatment of the top level of the hierarchy.

The remainder of the network consists of word senses that serve both as a genus and that have a genus, and the bottom-level word senses, which are not further subcategorized. Hypothetically, the terms on the bottom level are the most highly specified concepts defined in the dictionary, concepts so specific they are not further differentiated in normal usage. In actuality, the choice of genus terms is based on a lexicographer's intuition and custom, and cannot be viewed as a complete measure of the generality of a word sense. There are roughly 30,000 word senses on the bottom level of the NounSense network.

The middle of the network is the most difficult to study because of its magnitude and, for the same reason, the middle level contains the most information. In attempting to characterize the information found there, statistics on word usage have been gathered from a limited number of traces through the network.

Statistics

The following statistics have been compiled from the NounSense network:

• The frequency with which each word sense is used as a genus. This is the number of direct children of a word sense.
• The total number of descendants each word sense possesses (i.e., both direct and indirect children).
• The network level of each word sense.

Figure 10.5 provides examples of the formulation of each of these statistics based on a small segment of the NounSense network. These statistics were gathered for every entry in the network, and are summarized in terms of maximums, medians, and averages. Similar statistics are not available for other MRD-derived networks. As discussed above, all cycles inherent in the dictionary definitions were identified, analyzed, and removed from the network structure.

A major concern regarding a taxonomy, particularly one derived from an MRD, is that it have enough depth to adequately define the interrelationships between the concepts. In the NounSense network, the median depth of a word is two levels down from the semantic primitives (level 1). This indicates that the majority of the words in the network are a subcategorization of a more general concept (subcategorization has occurred at least once below the primitives). The average level of a word in the network is 4.6, and this is more than the median, indicating a substantial number of words at the deeper levels of the network. Bruce et al. (1992) provides a count of the words at each level (excluding level 1, which contains the semantic primitives), as well as a listing of the words on each level, for levels 13 through 9. Bruce et al. (1992) analyze the number of children stemming from each of the 200 most frequently used genus terms (including semantic primitives), and tabulate a summary of the frequency of all genus terms in the network. Considering only the

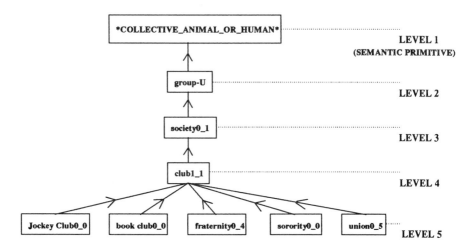

Example Statistics Based on the Above Segment of the Network:

club1_1:	fraternity0_4:	society0_1:
No. of children: 5	No. of children: 0	No. of children: 1
No. of descendants: 5	No. of descendants: 0	No. of descendants: 6
Network Level: 4	Network Level: 5	Network Level: 3

Figure 10.5
NounSense results

class of word senses used as genus terms, the median for that class is one child, while the average number of children is 7.34. This, combined with the fact that only 15% of the word senses defined in LDOCE are used as genus terms, indicates that a relatively small number of concepts are subdivided a large number of times.

It is interesting to note that the median number of descendants for each genus term is 1.0, and that the distribution of descendants (i.e., number of descendants per genus term) closely parallels the distribution of direct children. This seems to indicate a clumping of children about relatively few genus terms.

In summary, the statistics support two conclusions regarding the relationships and distribution of concepts in the NounSense network. First, it appears that the division between concepts is somewhat skewed. A relatively small number of very general terms are immediately divided into a large number of direct children without identifying the more specific properties that the children share (i.e., by introducing intermediate levels). Another way of viewing this problem is to say that concepts are attached too high in the network (Ide and Veronis 1990a). The genus terms used in this capacity are occasionally pronouns, which provide less information than the associated top-level semantic primitive. One possible explanation for this situation is that the lexicographers who wrote the definitions of LDOCE had important restrictions on their choices of genus terms.

The second view of the network supported by the statistics is somewhat more favorable. On average, the bottom-level words in the network have been associated with at least three more general terms, including the semantic primitives. This seems to indicate that some meaningful amount of association between concepts has occurred. But, taken in combination with the first result, it is not clear that the associations defined would result in an adequate set of properties for each bottom-level word sense.

Automatic techniques for selecting the genus term in an LDOCE definition and disambiguating it relative to the senses in LDOCE have proved very effective. A hierachy of 39,000 nouns and phrases defined in LDOCE was constructed using these results. Analysis of this hierarchy shows that it is relatively shallow (the median depth of a node is two levels down), but this is mostly a consequence of restricting the defining vocabulary to a small set.

Chapter 11

Numerical Methods for Language Processing

There have been great advances recently in the application of numerical techniques to natural language processing (NLP). We limit ourselves in this chapter to those techniques which are related in some way to dictionaries. We include numerical techniques for processing dictionaries and creating information for the construction of new dictionaries, as well as numerical techniques for language processing which incorporate information from dictionaries. It is not surprising that these strategies have a common thread: lexical disambiguation.

Lexical ambiguity pervades language and lexical ambiguity is pervasive in most forms of text, including dictionary definitions themselves. The words used in dictionary definitions of words, and their senses, are themselves lexically ambiguous. Ambiguity and arbitrariness are observable within a single dictionary when the sense distinctions made for the definition of a word cannot be made to match with the uses of that word in the definitions of other words in the same dictionary.

For those engaged in transforming machine-readable dictionaries (MRDs) into machine-tractable dictionaries (MTDs), it follows that the language in MRD definitions needs to be analyzed down to the word sense level before we can benefit fully from the information implicit in them.

Researchers in NLP and information retrieval need automatic methods of disambiguation. In machine translation (MT), for example, one must disambiguate the input text in order to yield a correct translation to another language. Information retrieval systems might be more effective if they were able to disambiguate the words in a query and in stored documents, and corpus analysis and lexicography could become more automated if words in the corpora were disambiguated.

The concept of disambiguation, however, is nebulous. Humans often cannot agree about which of a given collection of senses is being used in a particular sentence (Lorge 1938, West 1953) Lexicographers themselves do not agree about the number of senses for a given word, or about the way a word should be divided into senses. Research to automate the task of disambiguation (Hearst 1991, Zernik and Jacobs 1990, Veronis and Ide 1990, Guthrie et al. 1991, Cowie, Guthrie, and Guthrie 1992, McDonald et al. 1990, Wilks et al. 1990, Dagan, Itai, and Schwall 1991, Tsutsumi 1991, Yarowsky 1992, Schutze 1992) is still in a primitive stage and the granularity of the senses used in experiments varies. Senses are often chosen in an ad hoc way, usually with fewer and broader senses than would be found in most standard dictionaries, but ones which the researchers feel are adequate for their purposes, capturing the distinctions in the texts they are processing. Often they eliminate the anachronistic or rare senses found in standard dictionaries.

Although these techniques, based on researcher-defined division of senses, are promising, there are definite drawbacks; each researcher faces a massive job of constructing sense distinctions for each word in the text (essentially creating a new dictionary). Furthermore, this leads to a lexical Tower of Babel. The sense distinctions of one researcher seldom correspond to those of another, so research cannot easily be compared or shared by others. One might argue that a similar situation exists when researchers use different standard dictionaries as the basis of their disambiguation algorithms, but this does lead to some standardization.

Techniques for Aiding in the Construction of Dictionaries

The work of Church and Hanks (1990) suggests a lexicon-corpus compromise for the future. They suggest the need for a principled and consistent numerical analysis of a very large corpus to identify the distinct word senses present and that this information be used to augment the lexicographer's knowledge and intuition. A dictionary constructed in this way might give us a standard dictionary well suited for use in language processing. (See chapter 14 for a discussion of new dictionaries under construction.)

Church and Hanks, with their expertise in computation and lexicography respectively, have in many ways legitimized the use of numerical techniques in language processing. The NLP community now readily incorporates statistical methods (often imported from research in speech processing) into their analysis of texts.

The widely cited Church and Hanks (1990) use the descriptive statistic of "mutual information" to measure the degree of relatedness among words that appear close together in text. They show how this can be used to derive significant collocates and lists of associated words from a corpus. In addition, they describe several applications of this technique to lexicography. They note that, up to now, lexicographers have relied on citations collected by humans, or on "small" corpora of only a million words or so. As the analysis of a much larger corpus is now possible (they analyze several corpora: the 1987 Associated Press corpus of 15 million words, the 1988 Associated Press corpus of 36 million words, and 8.6 million words of tagged text), they suggest augmenting the somewhat primitive computational tools of lexicographers to allow the automated or semiautomated analysis of much larger amounts of text.

Their overall aim is to aid the lexicographer in identifying the senses of a word present in a corpus and to maintain consistency in the dictionary. Lexicographers commonly use concordance programs, which as Church and Hanks (1990) note are "basically KWIC (key word in context) indexes with additional features such as the ability to extend the context, sort leftward as well as rightward, and so on." As they observe, it is easy to identify the senses of a word in the corpus if the concordance for that word is only a few lines; however, when the concordance consists of thousands of lines from a "large" corpus, the lexicographer must resort to techniques such as printing out pages and pages of concordance lines and marking the various senses on the page with different color pens!

They describe methods for semiautomating this process by using the mutual information statistic to suggest significant associations which may be grouped in the concordance. Interestingly, their association ratios work well for function words as well as content words, which may aid in defining verbs and the prepositions which commonly follow them in a more consistent way. In addition, the statistic may be applied to text which augments certain words with their semantic categories. They cite examples of the word "save" and observe significant patterns such as "save PERSON from BAD," "save INSTITUTION from BAD," "save ANIMAL from DESTRUCTION," etc. These patterns are then used to group the concordance lines,thus aiding the lexicographer in the analysis of the corpus.

Attempts have been made to acquire subcategorization information (e.g., typical subjects and objects of verbs) from corpora (Brent 1991), sometimes done under the name of preferences (Lehnert 1990; Grishman and Sterling 1992), as well as verb-preposition dependence information based on co-ocurrence or "mutual information" (Hindle 1983).

Attempts to derive semantically related classes of words directly from corpora by co-ocurrence information based on common neighborhoods have been done for syntagmatic classes within the Pathfinder paradigm (McDonald et al. 1990) and for paradigmatic classes (of similar meaning) by New York University, University of Manchester Institute of Science and Technology, and IBM. Many of these classes at the bottom level are striking.

From the IBM group come such clusters as Christian, Jew, Buddhist, Catholic, Muslim, and Monday, Tuesday, Wednesday, Thursday, etc. Many of these are willy-nilly reimplementations of the early work of Sparck Jones (1964) who did not have the computer power to carry out her statistical algorithms 20 years ago.

We see this trend in research as very important for the construction of the dictionaries of the future (see also Smadja and McKeown 1989), and we are confident that this will lead to better and more consistent dictionaries for language processing.

Limited Domains

Effective specialized disambiguation techniques for a particular application often rely on the hypothesis that, if we limit the domain of discourse, then lexical ambiguity is greatly reduced. Given that most existing applications of NLP are domain-specific, to what extent is lexical ambiguity really a problem? Gale, Church, and Yarowsky (1992) give compelling evidence for the thesis that, within one discourse, words are not ambiguous. That is, in almost all cases, a given word is used in the same sense throughout a given text. One might conclude from this that within a certain type of text there should be little need for word sense disambiguation. In fact, analysis of the Canadian Parliament proceedings show that "bank" appears 99% of the time in its "money" sense and only 1% in its "river" sense. Similarly, "commute" refers to a criminal's sentence and almost never to a drive to work (Klavans and Tzoukermann 1990a,b). However, despite these striking examples, words can still be highly ambiguous within a certain type of document.

The TIPSTER project in the United States (described in chapter 7) provides evidence to support this. In this project, the domains for processing have been very restricted (e.g., microelectronics articles) and the task, at least on the surface, is not as ambitious as many tasks in NLP. One might expect a class of texts such as English newspaper articles on microelectronics to fit the concept of Gale et al. of a single discourse unit. However, very recent investigations in the microelectronics texts provided by the TIPSTER text project suggest that this is really not the case.

The availability of very good automatic part-of-speech tagging programs (Weischedel et at. 1993) allows some lexical ambiguity to be resolved using the parts of speech. However many nouns exist in several senses even in a domain as restricted as microelectronics, as we can see in figure 11.1.

```
2888096: ier firms to meet leading edage      production specifications

2888259: inue to be on the leading edge       of development of innovat

2891821: light which passes by the edge       regions of the shifter fi

2891821: put the shifter along the edge       of the chromium pattern t

2891821: y taking advantage of the edge       characteristics of the ph

2944268: allows Aspen to tune the edge        rates of its drivers for

2948174: kagawa explained. To gain edge       enhancements, Fujitsu's r

3142340: ler that eliminates wafer edge       contact. Specifications f

3818635: data transferred on each edge        of the clock pulse to pro

3576531: ng them the technological edge       over competitors that the
```

```
2528439: 8-bit and 16-bit product line        manager. Intel said five

2528795: ling off its new six inch line       in Carrolton.

2528851: ary distributes Applies's line       of English made ion impla

2532247: r. Rose said. "The bottom line       is more competition." The

2544803: vice being produced, with lines      of 0.5 micron and below.

2673965: on packaging and assembly lines      to evaluate actual condit
```

Figure 11.1
Concordance from the TIPSTER microelectronics texts.

Note that "edge" appears in at least three noun senses: the physical edge ("wafer edge" and "edge of a pattern"), in the competitive edge sense ("leading edge" and "technological edge"), and in a metonymical sense ("the edge of a clock pulse"). The word "line" is also highly ambiguous. The above examples include "assembly line," "product line," "bottom line," and the wire sense of "line" on a microchip. These are characteristic of many technical terms that occur in these texts.

Clearly, lexical ambiguity is a real, not imagined, problem. As builders of large-scale NLP systems, we need methods for resolving ambiguity, and these must be methods that do not require a human to identify the senses of each word used in a domain.

Disambiguation Relative to Translations into Another Language

Several effective procedures have been reported for the lexical disambiguation necessary for choosing the correct translation of a word. Brown et al. (1991) and Gale et al. (1992) derive the set of translations of a given word as well as a model of the corresponding context for each translation from automatically aligned bilingual corpora in French and English. This information is then used to determine the correct translation of the word in a new text. This definition of senses is certainly well motivated and sufficient for automatically disambiguating words with respect to word forms in another language, but the data do depend on the existence of large parallel texts of that type and seem to be applicable only for MT, where equivalences in another language can serve as an effective sense specification.

Dagan et al. (1991) report similar experiments for the translation of German and Hebrew into English. Their method does not rely on the existence of large parallel texts to identify the possible senses of a word, but rather on the translations of that word in a bilingual dictionary. They suggest this method can be used to disambiguate words in a single language or to identify the correct choice for MT. In both cases, the "senses" of a word are defined by its possible translations into another language. In the case of MT, the method considers translations of words appearing in the context of the source language word with all possible translations of the word to be disambiguated. The candidate in the target language "most likely" to appear in this lexical relation is judged to be the correct translation. The judgment of what is "most likely" is based on a statistical model of the target language and a statistical test for the decision. Although this method was tested on a somewhat small sample size and definitions from the bilingual dictionary were filtered manually, and did not always consider all of the translations available in the dictionary, the method has an advantage over those requiring large parallel texts and certainly shows promise for MT.

Disambiguation Relative to a Single Language

Schutze (1992) defines an effective method of word sense disambiguation whereby the senses of a word are defined by a clustering algorithm and the word is disambiguated by identifying the cluster to which the word belongs (or is "closest" to). In particular, the word to be disambiguated is assigned a context vector (which sums the word vectors in the context of that word). The context vectors of all occurrences of the word in the training set are clustered. The word is assigned the sense of the training cluster that is closest to its context vector. Computation of the word vectors is based on a co-occurrence of four-grams of letters and a linear dimensionality reduction. Disambiguation experiments (relative to the clusters) were performed on 10 words with excellent results.

Yarowsky (1992) reports a disambiguation scheme which sense-tags words with their corresponding Roget's category (one of 1042 categories). For each category, contexts representative of that category are gathered from the 10-million word *Grolier's Encyclopedia* (50 words to each side of a word in the category). Salient words are identified statistically and weights are determined for these salient words. The weights are then used to predict the category of a polysemous word in a new text. This experiment was performed on 12 polysemous words that have been used in previous experiments by other researchers. The results of this disambiguation technique are very good. They are extensible to a larger experiment and present a reasonable compromise between ad hoc user-defined senses and the fine-grained distinctions exhibited in dictionaries.

Hearst (1991) suggested adding syntactic information to co-occurrence information and automated the part-of-speech tagging to aid in the disambiguation. She gathered co-occurrence data about the senses of a certain word from text in which the word had been manually sense-tagged. The senses are rather broad and referred to by the author as homographs. Experiments were then conducted to test the effectiveness of the method in disambiguating the given word.

Another technique of disambiguation has been developed by Zernik and Jacobs (1990). This also relies on training text which has been sense-tagged by hand and incorporates other information about the word in question which comes from its morphology or from part-of-speech tagging. They reported on experiments in which the three words "interest," "stock," and "bond" are disambiguated with respect to a restricted set of senses. For example, they defined four senses of "interest," while LDOCE has 10.

Rather than redefining senses for experimental purposes, many researchers have found that a standard dictionary, with its distinctions made by professional lexicographers, is still the most attractive option for use in disambiguation.

Veronis and Ide (1990) described a way to create very large neural networks automatically from MRDs to use for disambiguation. However, the experiments were actually very small, and disambiguated 23 words in small hand-constructed contexts relative to the *Collins English Dictionary*. This work is discussed in more detail below.

Tsutsumi (1991) applied local context in a different way. He extracted hundreds of sentences containing the word "take" from a corpus, automatically tagged each word with its part of speech, and disambiguated the word "take" by hand relative to a restricted set of 12 senses taken from *Webster's Seventh New Collegiate Dictionary*. These processed sentences were then stored in a database. To disambiguate "take" in a new sentence, the system chooses the sentence in the database which most closely matches (in some defined sense) the new sentence and assigns the sense of "take" in the old sentence to the new.

The fact that word senses can be experimentally determined from context by humans was established at least as early as 1985 by Choueka and Luisgnan in an experiment in which human subjects disambiguated words in test sentences by taking into account the surrounding words. There had been much work in AI on automatic sense determination, but the use of standard dictionaries for the purpose can be attributed to Lesk (1986) who suggested how this might be done automatically, using the overlap of words between the definitions of the context words and the sense definitions of the word being disambiguated.

For example, to disambiguate "bank" in the sentence "We got a bank loan to buy a house," the method looks at all the sense definitions of "bank" in a standard dictionary. Each dictionary sense definition of "bank" is then intersected with the union of all senses of the local context {we, got, a, loan, to, buy, house} of "bank," and the number of words in the overlap is counted. The sense definition with the largest overlap with the context is the winner.

There are various problems with this method, and various low-level matters can affect performance, such as fine sense distinctions, or senses defined by synonyms. Further, all implementations of this technique and its extensions must consider how to deal with stop lists and inflected forms. A "stop list" usually means taking out certain commonly occurring closed-class words on the assumption that, since they often appear in both the context and the sense definition, their appearance contributes nothing. Inflected forms can be used to assure that "banking" matches "bank" and "got" matches "get." These enhancements are generally necessary.

This is an elegant technique in its simplest form, although somewhat prone to ungraceful degradation. Nonetheless, Lesk's work forms the basis of all of the approaches described below.

CRL Techniques for Word Sense Disambiguation in Dictionaries

Several automatic methods for lexical disambiguation relative to a standard dictionary are under investigation at the Computing Research Laboratory (CRL) of New Mexico State University. The goal of these methods is to disambiguate words in text relative to the LDOCE. All these methods attempt to use the context of a word to determine its sense.

One class of techniques gathers information about word associations from text and then uses that information for disambiguation. This work uses the LDOCE definitions and example sentences as a text of about 1 million words from which to gather information about word associations, but the methods are easily extensible to gathering information from a large corpus (see chapter 9 for more details).

Associated word sets gathered from a general corpus may contain words that are associated with many different senses. For example, vocabulary associated statistically with the word "bank" includes "money," "rob," "river," "sand," and others. In this section, we describe an additional method for obtaining subject-dependent associated word sets, or "neighborhoods" of a given word, relative to a particular domain. Using the subject classifications of the LDOCE, we have established subject-dependent co-occurrence links between words of the defining vocabulary to construct these neighborhoods. We describe a method of word sense disambiguation based on these co-occurrences. (Guthrie et al. 1991)

Co-occurrence Neighborhoods

Words that occur frequently with a given word may be thought of as forming a "neighborhood" of that word. If we can determine which words (i.e., spelling forms) co-occur frequently with each word sense, we can use these neighborhoods to disambiguate the word in a given text. Assume that we know only the two classic senses of the word "bank": (1) a repository for money, and (2) piled earth at the edge of a river.

We can expect the "money" sense of bank to co-occur frequently with such words as "money," "loan," and "robber," while the "river" sense would be more frequently associated with "river," "bridge," and "earth." In order to disambiguate "bank" in a text, we would produce neighborhoods for each sense, and intersect them with the text, on the assumption that the neighborhood which shared more words with the text would determine the correct sense. Variations of this idea appear in Lesk (1986), McDonald et al. (1990), and Veronis and Ide (1990).

As we noted in chapter 9, McDonald et al. used all the LDOCE definitions as their text, in order to generate co-occurrence data for the 2187 words in the LDOCE control (defining) vocabulary. They used various methods to apply this data to the problem of disambiguating control vocabulary words as they appear in the LDOCE example sentences. In every case, however, the set of associated words for a given word was a co-occurrence neighborhood for its spelling form over all the definitions in the dictionary, though the hope was that these would fall into subnets corresponding to senses.

Subject-Dependent Neighborhoods

The study of word co-occurrence in a text is based on the aphorism (attributed to Firth) that "a word is known by the company it keeps." Guthrie et al. (1991) hold that it also makes a difference where that company is kept, since a word may occur with different sets of words in different contexts, and thus they construct word neighborhoods which depend on the subject of the text in question: "subject-dependent neighborhoods." A unique feature of the electronic version of LDOCE is that many of the word sense definitions are marked with a subject field code which tells us which subject area the sense refers to.

For example, the "money"-related senses of bank are marked EC (Economics) and, for each such main subject heading, the subset of LDOCE definitions that consists of those sense definitions which share that subject code are collected into one file, and co-occurrence data for their defining vocabulary are generated. Word x is said to co-occur with word y if x and y appear in the same sense definition and the total number of times they co-occur is denoted as fxy. A matrix (2,187 × 2,187) is constructed where each row and column corresponds to one word of the defining vocabulary, and the entry in the xth row and yth column is the number of times the xth word co-occurred with the yth word. (This is a symmetric matrix, and therefore it is only necessary to maintain half of it.) We denote by fx the total number of times word x appeared. While many statistics may be used to measure the relatedness of words x and y, we used the function

$$r(x, y) = fxy/fx + fy - fxy$$

in this study. The neighborhoods of the word "metal" in the category "Economics" and "Business" are presented in figures 11.2 and 11.3 and contain the 10 words with the highest value of $r(x, y)$ to "metal" for each category:

	Subject Code EC = Economics			
metal	idea	coin	them	silver
	real	should	pocket	gold
	well	him		

Figure 11.2
Economics neighborhood of "metal."

	Subject Code BU = Business			
metal	bear	apparatus	mouth	inside
	spring	entrance	plate	brass
	tight	sheet		

Figure 11.3
Business neighborhood of "metal."

In these examples, the fact that the neighborhoods are so different illustrates how the subject matter of the context can affect the co-occurrence. Perhaps the presence in the Economics neighborhood of words like "idea," "gold," and "silver," reflects the fact that Economics deals with theoretical issues, while in the more practical domain of Business, we find the words "brass," "apparatus," "spring," and "plate." Consider the neighborhoods of our original example, bank (figures 11.4 and 11.5).

Note that even though the 20 most closely related words are included in each of these neighborhoods, they are still unrelated or disjoint, although

Subject Code EC = Economics				
bank	account	check	money	by
	into	have	keep	order
	out	pay	at	put
	from	draw	an	busy
	more	supply	it	safe

Figure 11.4
Economics neighborhood of "bank" (short stop list).

Subject Code EG = Engineering				
bank	river	wall	flood	thick
	earth	prevent	opposite	chair
	hurry	paste	spread	overflow
	walk	help	we	throw
	clay	then	wide	level

Figure 11.5
Engineering neighborhood of "bank."

many of the words which appear are indeed suggestive of the sense or senses which fall under that subject category. In this experiment the stop list of common words to be ignored was very short. Thus the words "an," "at," "by," and "it" appear in a neighborhood although it seems likely that they contribute little information. In LDOCE, 3 of the 11 senses of bank are marked with the code EC for Economics, and these represent the "money" senses of the word. It is a quirk of the classification in LDOCE that the "river" senses of bank are not marked with a subject code. This lack of a subject code corresponding to a word sense in LDOCE is not uncommon, however, and as was the case with bank, some senses of a given word may have subject codes, whereas others do not.

One may label this lack of a subject code the "null code," and form a neighborhood of this type of sense by using all sense definitions without code as text. This "null code neighborhood" can reveal a common, or "generic" sense of the word (see also Fontenelle 1990a). The 20 most frequently occurring words with bank in definitions with the null subject code form the neighborhood shown in figure 11.6.

It is obvious that about half of these words are associated with the two main senses of bank, but a new element has crept in: the appearance of four out of eight words which refer to the money sense ("rob," "criminal," "police," and "thief") reveal a sense of bank which did not appear in the Economics neighborhood. In the null code definitions, there are quite a few references to the potential for a bank to be robbed. Finally, consider a neighborhood for "bank" which uses all the LDOCE definitions (McDonald et al. 1990, Wilks et al. 1990) (figure 11.7).

Subject Code NULL = no code assigned				
bank	rob	river	account	lend
	overflow	flood	money	criminal
	lake	flow	snow	cliff
	police	shore	heap	thief
	borrow	along	steep	earth

Figure 11.6
Null code neighborhood of "bank" (short stop list).

Subject Code All				
bank	account	bank	busy	check
	criminal	earn	flood	flow
	interest	lake	lend	money
	overflow	pay	river	rob
	safes	and	thief	wall

Figure 11.7
Unrestricted neighborhood of "bank."

Only four of these words ("bank," "earn," "sand," and "thief") are not found in the other three neighborhoods, and the number of words in the intersection of this neighborhood with the Economics, Engineering, and Null neighborhoods are 6, 4, and 11, respectively. Recalling that the Economics and Engineering neighborhoods are disjoint, these data support the hypothesis that the subject-dependent neighborhoods help to distinguish senses more easily than neighborhoods that are extracted from the whole dictionary. There are over 100 main subject field codes in LDOCE, and over 300 subdivisions within these. For example, "medicine-and-biology" is a main subject field (coded "MD"), and has 22 subdivisions such as "anatomy" and "biochemistry." These main codes and their subdivisions constitute the only two levels in the LDOCE subject code hierarchy, with the result that main codes such as "golf" and "sports" are not related to each other.

There are certain drawbacks in using LDOCE to construct the subject-dependent neighborhoods; the amount of text in LDOCE about any one subject area is rather limited. It consists of a control vocabulary for dictionary definitions only, and uses sample sentences that were concocted with non-native English speakers in mind.

Word Sense Disambiguation in General Texts

In this section, we describe an application of subject-dependent co-occurrence neighborhoods to the problem of word sense disambiguation. The subject-dependent co-occurrence neighborhoods are used as building blocks for the neighborhoods used in disambiguation. For each of the subject codes (including the null code) which appear with a word sense to be disambiguated, one intersects the corresponding subject-dependent co-occurrence neighborhood with the text being considered (the size of text can vary from a sentence to a paragraph). The intersection must contain a preselected minimum number of words to be considered. But if none of the neighborhoods intersect at greater than this threshold level, the neighborhood N is replaced by the neighborhood N(1), which consists of N together with the first word from each neighborhood of words in N, using the same subject code. If necessary, add the second most strongly associated word for each of the words in the original neighborhood N, forming the neighborhood N(2).

We continue this process until a subject-dependent co-occurrence neighborhood has intersection above the threshold level. Then, the sense or senses with this subject code is selected. If more than one sense has the selected code, use their definitions as cores to build distinguishing neighborhoods for them. These are again intersected with the text to determine the correct sense. The following two examples illustrate this method. Note that some of the neighborhoods differ from those given earlier since the text used to construct these neighborhoods includes any example sentences that may occur in the sense definitions. Those neighborhoods presented earlier ignored the example sentences. In each example, the task is to disambiguate the word "bank" in a sentence which appears as an example sentence in the Collins *COBUILD* dictionary. The disambiguation consists of choosing the correct sense of "bank" from among the 13 senses given in LDOCE. These senses are summarized below.

bank(1): [ ]: land along the side of a river, lake, etc.

bank(2): [ ]: earth which is heaped up in a field or garden.

bank(3): [ ]: a mass of snow, clouds, mud, etc.

bank(4): [AU]: a slope made at bends in a road or racetrack.

bank(5): [ ]: a sandbank in a river, etc.

bank(6): [AU]: to move a car or aircraft with one side higher than the other.

bank(7): [ ]: a row, especially of oars in an ancient boat or keys on a typewriter.

bank(8): [EC]: a place in which money is kept and paid out on demand.

bank(9): [MD]: a place where something is held ready for use, such as blood.

bank(10): [GB]: (a person who keeps) a supply of money or pieces for payment in a gambling game.bank(11): [ ] : break the bank is to win all the money in the bank(10).

bank(12): [EC] : to put or keep (money) in a bank.

bank(13): [EC] : to keep one's money in a bank.

Example 1   The sentence is "The aircraft turned, banking slightly." The neighborhoods of "bank" for the five relevant subject codes are given in figures 11.8 through 11.12.

Subject Code AU = Automotive			
bank	make	go	up	move
	so	they	high	also
	round	car	side	turn
	road	aircraft	slope	bend
	safe			

Figure 11.8
Automotive neighborhood of "bank."

Subject Code EC = Economics			
bank	have	it	person	out
	into	take	money	put
	write	keep	pay	order
	another	paper	draw	supply
	account	safe	sum	check

Figure 11.9
Economics of neighborhood of "bank."

```
┌─────────────────────────────────────────────────┐
│         Subject Code GB = Gambling              │
│                                                 │
│  bank   person    use      money    piece       │
│         play      keep     pay      game        │
│         various   supply   chance               │
└─────────────────────────────────────────────────┘
```

Figure 11.10
Gambling neighborhood of "bank."

```
┌─────────────────────────────────────────────────┐
│      Subject Code MD = Medicine and Biology     │
│                                                 │
│  bank   something   use       place    hold     │
│         medicine    ready     blood    human    │
│         origin      organ     store    hospital │
│         treatment   product   comb              │
└─────────────────────────────────────────────────┘
```

Figure 11.11
Medical neighborhood of "bank."

```
┌─────────────────────────────────────────────────┐
│      Subject Code NULL = No code assigned       │
│                                                 │
│  bank   game     earth      stone      boat     │
│         river    bar        snow       lake     │
│         sand     shore      mud        framework│
│         flood    cliff      heap       harbor   │
│         ocean    parallel   overflow   clerk    │
└─────────────────────────────────────────────────┘
```

Figure 11.12
Null code neighborhood of "bank."

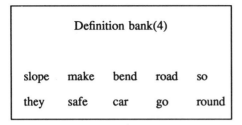

Definition bank(4)

slope   make   bend   road   so

they   safe   car   go   round

Figure 11.13
Words in sense 4 of "bank."

Definition bank(6)

car   aircraft   move   side

high   make   turn

Figure 11.14
Words in sense 6 of "bank."

The Automotive neighborhood contains two words, "aircraft" and "turn," which also appear in the sentence. Note that all forms of turn (turned, turning, etc.) are considered to match "turn." Since none of the other neighborhoods have any words in common with the sentence, and since the threshold value for this short sentence is 2, AU is selected as the subject code. One must now decide between the two senses which have this code. At this point, remove the function words from the sense definitions and replace each remaining word by its root form, obtaining the neighborhoods given in figures 11.13 and 11.14. Since bank(4) has no words in common with the sentence, and bank(6) has two ("turn" and "aircraft"), bank(6) is selected. This is indeed the sense of "bank" used in the sentence.

Example 2 The sentence is "We got a bank loan to buy a car."

The original neighborhoods of "bank" are, of course, the same as in Example 1. The threshold is again 2. None of the neighborhoods has more than one word in common with the sentence, so the iterative process of enlarging the neighborhoods is used. The Automotive neighborhood is expanded to include "engine" since it is the first word in the Automotive neighborhood of "make." The first word in the Automotive neighbor-hood of "up" is "increase," so "increase" is added to the neighborhood. If the word to be added already appears in the neighborhood of "bank," no word is added. On the 15th iteration, the Economics neighborhood contains "get" and "buy." None of the other neighborhoods have more than one word in common with the sentence, so EC is selected as the subject code. Definitions 8, 12, and 13 of bank all have the EC subject code, so their definitions are used as cores to build neighborhoods to allow us to choose one of them. After 23 iterations, bank(8) is selected.

Although the words in the LDOCE definitions constitute a small text (almost 1 million words, compared with the megatexts used in other co-occurrence studies), the unique feature of subject codes, which can be used to distinguish many definitions, and LDOCE's small control vo-cabulary make it a useful corpus for obtaining co-occurrence data. The development of techniques for information retrieval and word sense dis-ambiguation based on these subject-dependent co-occurrence neighbor-hoods seems promising.

Lexical Disambiguation Using Simulated Annealing

In the above methods, since the senses are computed one word at a time, the question arises as to whether and how to incorporate the fact that a sense has been chosen for one word when attempting to disambiguate the next. Should this first choice be changed in light of how other word senses are selected? Although these problems were pointed out in Lesk's original paper (1986), they have been addressed only in the following two methods.

A method of word sense disambiguation that is designed to operate on a large scale and simultaneously for several words was suggested by Ver-onis and Ide (1990). The basis of this method is the construction of large neural networks which have words and word senses (chosen from the machine-readable version of the Collins dictionary) as nodes. Links are established from a word to each of its senses, and from each sense to every word in its definition. Inhibiting links are constructed between senses of the same word. In order to disambiguate a sentence, the words in the sentence are activated in the network, and this activation is allowed to spread with feedback. This cycle is repeated a preselected number of times, for example, 100. At the end of this process, each word in the sentence is disambiguated by choosing its sense which is most highly activated.

The authors report encouraging results on word pairs such as "page" and "pen" and "pen" and "goat." The only complete sentence reported on was "The young page put the goat in the pen," in which "page" and "pen" might be expected to work together to cause the wrong sense of each to be chosen. The inclusion of the word "young" overcomes this problem, and both "page" and "pen" are correctly disambiguated.

The authors report that problems arise from such factors as maintaining a balance between the activation of a word and its senses and the fact that a word with many senses tends to have more connections than one with fewer senses. They indicate that matters such as setting thresholds and rates of decay also present difficulties.

Another possibility is the application of a computational optimization called simulated annealing to this general class of methods (including some of the numerical methods referenced above) to allow all senses to be determined at once in a computationally effective way. We describe the application (Metropolis et al. 1953, Kirkpatrick, Gelatt, and Vecchi 1983) of simulated annealing to a basic method similar to that of Lesk (1986), which also uses the subject area markings in LDOCE, but does not make use of other features such as part-of-speech tagging. The simplicity of the technique makes it fully automatic, and it requires no hand-tagging of text or handcrafting of neighborhoods. When this basic method operates under the guidance of the simulated annealing algorithm, sense selections are made concurrently for all ambiguous words in the sentence in a way designed to optimize their choice. The system's performance on a set of test sentences was encouraging and can be expected to improve when some of the refinements mentioned above are incorporated.

Simulated Annealing

Simulated annealing (Metropolis et al. 1953, Kirkpatrick et al. 1983) is a technique for solving large-scale problems of combinatorial minimization. It has been successfully applied to the famous traveling salesman problem of finding the shortest route for a salesman who must visit a number of cities in turn, and is now commonly used for optimizing the placement of circuit elements on large-scale integrated circuits. Simulated annealing was applied to parsing by Sampson (1986), but since the method has not yet been widely applied to computational linguistics or NLP, we describe it briefly.

The name of the algorithm is in analogy to the process by which metals cool and anneal. A feature of this phenomenon is that slow cooling usually allows the metal to reach a uniform composition and a minimum energy state, while fast cooling leads to an amorphous state with higher energy. In simulated annealing, a parameter T which corresponds to temperature is decreased slowly enough to allow the system to find its minimum.

The process requires a function E of configurations of the system which corresponds to the energy. It is E that we seek to minimize. From a starting point, a new configuration is randomly chosen, and a new value of E is computed. If the new E is less than the old one, the new configuration is chosen to replace the older. An essential feature of simulated annealing is that even if the new E is larger than the old (indicating that this configuration is farther away from the desired minimum than the last choice), the new configuration may be chosen. The decision of whether or not to replace the old configuration with the new inferior one is made probabilistically. This feature of allowing the algorithm to "go uphill" helps it to avoid settling in a local minimum which is not the actual minimum. In succeeding trials, it becomes more difficult for configurations that increase E to be chosen, and finally, when the method has retained the same configuration for long enough, that configuration is chosen as the solution. In the traveling salesman example, the configurations are the different paths through the cities, and E is the total length of his trip. The final configuration is an approximation to the shortest path through the cities. We now describe how the algorithm has been applied to word sense disambiguation. (Cowie et al. 1992)

Word-Sense Disambiguation with Simulated Annealing

Given a sentence with N words, let $s_{i1}, s_{i2}, \cdots s_{ik_i}$, represent the senses of the ith word where k_i is the number of senses of the ith word which appears in LDOCE.

A configuration of the system is obtained by choosing a sense for each word in the sentence. The goal is to choose that configuration which a human disambiguator would choose. To that end, define a function E whose minimum we may reasonably expect to correspond to the correct choice of the word senses.

The value of E for a given configuration is calculated in terms of the definitions of the N senses which make it up. All words in these definitions are stemmed, and the results stored in a list. If a subject code is given for a sense, the code is treated as a stemmed word. The redundancy R is computed by giving a stemmed word form which appears n times a score of $n - 1$ and adding up the scores. Finally, E is defined to be $1/1 + R$.

The rationale behind this choice of E is that word senses that belong together in a sentence will have more words and subject codes in common in their definitions (larger values of R) than senses that do not belong together. Minimizing E will maximize R and determine the choice of word senses.

The starting configuration C is chosen to be that in which sense number 1 of each word is chosen. Since the senses in LDOCE are generally listed with the most frequently used sense first, this is a likely starting point. The value of E is computed for this configuration. The next step is to choose at random a word number i and a sense S_{ij} of that ith word. The configuration C' is constructed by replacing the old sense of the ith word by the sense S_{ij}. Let ΔE be the change from E to the value computed for C'. If $\Delta E < 0$, then C' replaces C, and a new random change is made in C'. If $\Delta E \geq 0$, change to C' with probability $P = e^{-}\Delta E/T$. In this expression, T is a constant whose initial value is 1, and the decision of whether or not to adopt C' is made by calling a random number generator. If the number generated is less than P, C is replaced by C'. Otherwise, C is retained. This process of generating new configurations and checking to see whether or not to choose them is repeated on the order of 1000 times; T is replaced by $0.9T$, and the loop entered again. Once the loop is executed with no change in the configuration, the routine ends, and this final configuration tells which word senses are to be selected.

Experiments

To evaluate a method of word sense disambiguation it is necessary to check the results by hand or have text that has already been disambiguated by hand to use as test data. Since there is no general agreement on word senses, each system must have its own test data. Thus, even though the algorithm we have described is automatic and has coverage of the 28,000 nouns in LDOCE, the evaluation is the tedious handwork the system is meant to ease or eliminate.

In one experiment, the algorithm described above was used to disambiguate 50 example sentences from LDOCE. A stop list of very common words such as "the," "as," and "of" was removed from each sentence. The sentences then contained from 2 to 15 words, with an average of 5.5 ambiguous words per sentence. Definitions in LDOCE are broken down first into broad senses which are called "homographs," and then into individual senses which distinguish among the various meanings. For example, one homograph of "bank" means roughly "something piled up." There are five senses in this homograph which distinguish whether the thing piled up is snow, clouds, earth by a river, etc.

Results of the algorithm were evaluated by having a reasonably skilled human disambiguate the sentences and compare the choices of word senses with the output of the program. Using the human choices as the standard, the algorithm correctly disambiguated 47% of the words to the sense level, and 72 to the homograph level.

Later, a software tool was developed to improve the process of manual disambiguation of test sentences. Slight modifications to the software allow it to be used in conjunction with the algorithm as a computer-aided disambiguation system. The software displays the text to be disambiguated in a window, and when the user chooses a word all its definitions are displayed in another window. The user then selects the appropriate sense, and this selection is added to a file corresponding to the original text. This file is called the key and the results of the algorithm are scored against it.

Using this tool, 17 sentences for the *Wall Street Journal* were disambiguated by hand relative to LDOCE. The same stop list of common words was used as in the first experiment. The algorithm was used to disambiguate the 17 sentences, and the results automatically scored against the key. Results for the *Wall Street Journal* sentences were better, up to 91% for homograph disambiguation.

One difficulty with the algorithm is that long definitions tend to be given preference over shorter ones. Words defined succinctly by a synonym are greatly penalized. The function E must be made to better model the problem to improve performance. On the other hand, the simulated annealing itself seems to do very well at finding the minimum. In those cases where the configuration selected is not the correct disambiguation of the sentence, the correct disambiguation never had a lower value of E than the configuration selected. Experiments in which we varied the beginning temperature and the rate of cooling did not change the configuration ultimately selected seemed to show that those parameters are not very delicate.

This is a method for word sense disambiguation based on the simple technique of choosing senses of the words in a sentence so that their definitions in LDOCE have the most words and subject codes in common. The amount of computation necessary to find this optimal choice exactly and quickly becomes prohibitive as the number of ambiguous words and the number of senses increase. The computational technique of simulated annealing allows a good approximation to be computed quickly, with all the words in a sentence disambiguated simultaneously, in a reasonable time, and automatically (with no hand disambiguation of training text). Results using this technique are comparable to other computational techniques, and enhancements incorporating co-occurrence and part-of-speech information, which have been exploited in one-word-at-a time techniques, may be expected to improve the performance.

Chapter 12

Automatic Processing of Bilingual Dictionaries

Bilingual dictionaries are of computational interest, insofar as they can contribute lexical meanings and associations to the task of machine translation (MT). As we discussed in chapter 5 bilingual dictionaries relate two languages to each other at the level of word senses. They are not dictionaries in the domestic sense, books that associate (sometimes unknown) meanings with words, since the string returned from a bilingual look-up may well be incomprehensible to the user, while the user presumably knew what the source word or phrase meant to begin with.

One interesting point about bilingual dictionaries is their asymmetry. A word in one language often will not correspond to a single word in another, but rather to several words or a phrase. Similarly, a phrase in one language might best resolve to a single word in another, or to several different synonymous words. This creates difficulties in translation, and one of the themes of the work discussed in this chapter is how to deal with these problems.

Bilingual Dictionaries

Machine translation is the oldest problem in natural language processing (NLP). The earliest systems implemented a doomed and straightforward word-for-word strategy. This failed, among other reasons, because so many words in a given source language have mappings to several words or phrases in a given target language. Some of these early systems (Perry 1955) translated by simply listing all the possible word substitutions and left it to the reader to divine the intended sense of the text. As a result, a typical output from (what used to be called) mechanical translation looked like this (Perry 1955):

Paper prepare/produce self principal/main form/fashion of/from wood.

And, it was argued, if you knew what the text was concerned with, or just knew about the industrial world and paper production, and if any translation was better than no translation at all, then this clearly says "Paper is mainly made from wood." A more often reproduced example, however, is this:

(In, At, Into, To, For, On, N) (last, latter, new, latest, lowest, worst) (time, tense) for analysis (and, N) synthesis relay-contact electrical (circuit, diagram, scheme) parallel- (series, successive, consecutive, consistent) (connection, junction, combination) (with, from) (success, luck) (to be utilize, to be take advantage of) apparatus Boolean algebra. (Oettinger 1955, p. 56): [The code N "... means that it *may* be possible to omit the word without injury to the sense of the message (p. 56).]

Which not quite so clearly says,

In recent times Boolean algebra has been successfully employed in the analysis of relay networks of the series-parallel type.

After word-for-word translation was abandoned, the next phase of MT research concentrated on grammatical issues. Various formalisms were proposed (subsequently shown to be equivalent to context-free grammar), and this led to a controversy over the role of the lexicon in language understanding. In those days, an important issue was whether it was necessary to separate the grammar from the lexicon. Since that time, the need for a separable lexicon has been conceded. The issue still simmers in the NLP community, however, and now centers on which semantic codings should reside in the grammar and which in the lexicon.

A printed bilingual dictionary is normally little more than lists of pairs of equivalent strings from different languages, usually with some examples of usage mixed in. Bilingual dictionary research being done today is normally to support what is called "transfer-based" MT (strictly speaking, any MT system with a bilingual lexicon is transfer-based). Transfer-based MT systems are those designed to exploit the lexical and grammatical regularities that exist between particular pairs of languages. That is, certain assumptions can be made when translating from English, say, to German, and this knowledge can be used to improve translation quality and throughput. The price, however, is generality, since a different set of assumptions may apply from German to English. The more general alternative is called "interlingual" MT, where a source text in each language is translated into some other, common, language, and then a target language output is generated from that (there are several survey papers and books on this subject; see Hutchins 1986, Nagao 1989, Wilks 1987). Recent trends have also moved toward statistically based approaches to translation; see Brown et al. (1988), for one recent example.

Much of the European interest in processing bilingual dictionaries has been driven by the EUROTRA MT project, whose goal was a transfer-based system that operates in all directions over the nine European Community languages. This has proved very difficult to achieve since "Current practice in compiling or building bilingual dictionaries basically entails beginning with a set of monolingual dictionary entries and modifying them as problems are encountered" (Warwick 1986, p. 23).

Professional interest in bilingual lexicography has been sporadic, and the MT industry has occupied itself with the more pragmatic concerns of creating products and acquiring funding. This is a perfectly natural course, since MT projects have almost always limited themselves to specialized, technical, domains where some of the more general issues can be avoided and special issues can be focused on. For example, MT is much concerned with naming things (people, places, business entities), and recognizing their names in free text, but lexicography has virtually no interest in this problem. By the same token, there are MT systems that take no particular notice of words at all, except as a recognizable string of characters; these are discussed in chapter 3. In fairness, very recent trends in MT have been more concerned with theoretical and methodological issues than ever before (Nirenburg 1987). Some of the European sites actively working on machine-readable bilingual dictionaries include the University of Liège (Jansen et al. 1985), and Laboratoire d'Automatique Documentaire et Linguistique (LADL) (Gross 1984, 1986).

The ACQUILEX Project

The ACQUILEX Basic Research Action (BRA) involves an initial division of MRD text extraction efforts between Pisa (Italian), Barcelona (Spanish), Cambridge (English), and Amsterdam (Dutch and English). The parsers of lexical definitions were locally adapted to each of the three groups, but all of them concentrated on the FOOD subject area of the lexicon, no matter which MRD was selected. Semantic frames were extracted from syntactically parsed definitions, and during the first stage of extraction, the frames and their contents were specific to the local site, although always expressed in English.

The typed feature structures (TFS) in the lexical knowledge base (LKB) were intended to impose top-down meaning types on these data, so as to extract a maximum frame. In this approach, the main idea was that of inheritance between the nodes of the hierarchically organized types; the bottom-up structures derived were stored along with the level of inheritance structure—the latter was too theoretical to be derived from an MRD (although the type system is consistent with that of the LDOCE sematic classifiers). This complex inheritance structure allowed for non-inheritance, as well as default inheritance.

In this approach, there was also an intermediately derived lexicon which was *not* subject to the TFS constraints, but which retained extracted information that would otherwise have been lost by the top-down filter imposed by the TFS, and was therefore more data-driven. One could argue that this approach combines the best of all possible metaphysical worlds, one of them corresponding more to the cross-linguistic demands of ACQUILEX, with the other, more local, LKB corresponding to its language differences.

Both the control and inheritance aspects of the LKB allowed the lexical entries to be fully expanded, in order to incorporate the content of all its lower nodes in full detail. In this way, the compatibility of data from different sites was guaranteed. The lexical representation language (LRL) can be thought of as a shared metalanguage. However, the type system's rigor and lack of flexibility restricts mapping of ambiguous lower-level data, since lexical information is lost when mapping upward into the TFS. The TFS must be capable of constant revision in order to combine the best empirical and deductive approaches to lexical representation. Collocational information and other syntagmic relations have not yet been incorporated into this system. In the second phase of ACQUILEX, the link to corpora will be vital.

The ACQUILEX LKB was designed to represent syntactic and semantic knowledge as extracted from MRDs. Its syntax is based on a typed, unification-based representation language that incorporates default inheritance (Carpenter 1992). (The details of this language can be found in Copestake and Briscoe 1991). Antonio Sanfilippo's work on verb representation forms the basis of verb semantics in ACQUILEX (Sanfilippo, 1991). Within ACQUILEX, there is a distinction made between "upper model" taxonomies, and taxonomies derived from particular dictionaries.

ACQUILEX's feature structures have to be well formed with respect to types, because the type system constrains both default inheritance and the application of lexical rules. The system makes use of notions found in Pustejovsky's generative lexicon (Pustejovsky, 1991) such as qualia to capture orthogonal multiple inheritance (Touretzky, 1986) within the typing system.

An important notion for the TFS system within ACQUILEX is the extension of sense by means of what they call the "animal grinding" lexical rule. This rule converts the term for an individual physical object into the food substance term derived from that object (Copestake and Briscoe, 1992). Such a rule allows any noun of a certain class to be used with a specific sense extension, independent of its usage motivation. In this way, the "animal grinding" rule adds an edible word sense to every animal word (e.g., human beings), regardless of whether those animals are in fact edible. Similarly, any count noun can be used in a mass sense, an example studied by Givon (1967) in his original sense-extension rules (although he did not generalize his notion for all nouns).

The "grinding" rules comprise a method for adding systematic sense extensions to a lexicon. Although the TFS system is a default inheritance system with specific overrides, as in standard AI systems, the grinding rule does not have such overrides, since it does not have a mechanism for eliminating edible word senses if a particular animal is not edible. At first glance, this would seem to provide us with less helpful and informative entries than would a lexicon that marks words for their edibility (within a given culture group). Copestake and Briscoe argue, however, that the results of "grinding" *are* defeasible, and he cites the entry for "pork" in the lexicon to defend his point (the word "pork" overrides the default-produced "pig" in the edible word sense, indicating that the word "pig" is not marked edible, although the word "cat" is). In short, grinding rules emphasize lexical compactness and succinctness, as opposed to wide coverage of linguistic and cultural data.

Support for the "mass" grinding rule is given by means of example sentences such as:

"There was car all over the road."

These inferences are indefeasible, not because they are used in spoken or written English, but because they could be expressed at all. Whether or not one believes that (Givon did not intend the rule to be applied that way, but only to record systematicities in actual sense extension, as in the word "grain" going from object to mass term), the question as to why such a rule should be operated as a form of forward inferencing remains. After all, it greatly increases the number of useless entries in the lexicon (as there are far fewer edible than inedible animals). Why then, one might ask, aren't all liquids terms marked "potable" as a rule, since it is possible (even if foolish) for a person to drink sulfuric acid, let us say?

It is not easy to understand which selection processes such a structure of rules suggests to us. Briscoe writes of a process of elimination that combs the entire lexicon, removing those entries which have duplicate meanings (e.g., removing [edible] "pig" in favor of "pork"). But what criterion would it use to determine which item in such a pair should be removed? In current British English, the forms [edible] *Lamb*, *Mutton* and the Eurospeak term *Sheepmeat* (and presumably, [edible] *Sheep*), are all attested to. Which term should be eliminated, if any?

In this system compaction is all. Facts are not. The resultant lexicon structure not only expresses Carpenter's notions (and owes the most, perhaps, to Gazdar's DATR [Evans and Gazdar 1990, 1991]), but is also intended to express Asher and Morreau's (1991) commonsense entailment (normally used to describe conflicting inferences, as in the famous "penguin and Nixon" cases). Briscoe argued that regular and tolerated dual plurals in the lexicon can be sorted out using a "logic of blocking" in which, for instance, the terms "lighted" and "lit," or "dreamed" and "dreamt" are tolerated, whereas "sleeped" is not.

The contradictions in all these ACQUILEX structures are readily apparent; they claim to be based on high-level theoretical motives, but in fact their final product is shot through with arbitrary choices (e.g., "animal" is a derived, not a basic category in the type hierarchy). The purported benefits of systematicity offered by the constraints and types are less than apparent. Any standard dictionary information system that includes category names (like the unreconstructed LDOCE) could have its inconsistent application analyzed and corrected in principle, but most such apparent inconsistencies will turn out to be caused by the untidy distribution of properties that exist in the real world, a problem that no formal system can remedy.

Catizone, Russel, and Warwick

Catizone, Russel, and Warwick, (1989) describe a statistical method to establish correspondences between bilingual texts automatically, based on an algorithm attributed to Martin Kay. Different potential sentence pairings are evaluated by detecting multiple word co-occurrences throughout the parallel texts. The result is a sentence-by-sentence alignment of the two texts, with a listing of words which are assumed to correspond. The purpose of this work is to provide tools for computational lexicographers and linguists studying translation equivalence.

The system assumes that parallel texts in different languages will be provided in more or less the same sentence order, and this allows it to account for those cases where a sentence in one language is translated as two sentences in the other, or where two sentences in one are collapsed into a single sentence in translation. However, there is no assumption about the ordering of words or phrases within sentences.

The sentence order assumption also allows the program to execute without recourse to a bilingual dictionary. Although there is a run-time option that takes account of dictionary information, the calculations that produce the text alignment are designed to be based solely on "word" co-occurrence, where a word is any string surrounded by white space that has survived the preprocessing and filtering that removes function words and prepositions from both texts.

On the face of it, this would seem to be an application custom-made for dictionary access, since that knowledge should provide substantial speedup and efficiency of processing (i.e., the number of co-occurrence calculations could be reduced to a fraction by letting the dictionary filter the pairs to be considered). Since dictionary reference is only an option to be exploited by this procedure, and not a central component of the system, this does not strictly qualify as a dictionary project. One potential problem with using a dictionary to filter co-occurrences is the very real possibility that equivalent words or phrases might be overlooked, since the dictionary will doubtless fail to list them all. Since the goal of the procedure is simply alignment of texts, it is an empirical matter whether dictionary access is worthwhile, that is, whether the increased efficiency is worth the potential loss of coverage. Presumably, the ultimate aim of a system of this sort would be word alignment within aligned sentences, which would conceivably be of utility in MT systems and the training of human translators. This methodology can be contrasted with two other successful methods for sentence alignment in corpora (Church 1991, Brown et al. 1988) which make use of only corpus-bound features like sentence length, etc. (see chapter 14).

White

White (1988) reviews the methods employed to construct a "tangled hierarchy" from the *Merriam-Webster Pocket Dictionary* (Amsler and White

1979, Amsler 1980), and makes a key observation putting that work in perspective. The methodology was designed to avoid imposing categories and relations on the content of the dictionary, but rather to discover them through an exhaustive study of the dictionary corpus. The motivation for this approach derived from the belief that "a dictionary is a naturally occurring linguistic artifact [that reflects] the lexicographer's intuitive grasp of the lexical semantics of the language" (White 1988, p. 3). The implication of this appeal to intuition, however, is that the lexical semantic relations present among and between the elements of the dictionary are bound to be "somewhat inexact in random ways" (p. 3). White argues that imposing an external, albeit theoretically motivated, system of categories and relations on the lexicon (as is done whenever an NLP system is built) unavoidably introduces another level of intuition and inexactitude, and this can only serve to increase the preexisting problems of correctness.

In order to reduce these difficulties, White argues against imposing relations on lexical entries, since they are bound to result in errors unless they are completely well-founded. He concedes the merits of the various parsing and pattern-matching efforts (see chapter 7), but argues for relegating these to a subsidiary status, as methods of optimizing search procedures by codifying representational elements. To make his case, White describes a word sense disambiguation scheme that depends on a sort of "minimalist" rendering of the dictionary: the senses in the MRD are associated only with their taxonomic structure, as derived from the tangled hierarchy procedures, and collocationally with the words of their own definitions.

With only these two structures, the collocational set and the taxonomic hierarchy associated with senses in the dictionary, sense disambiguation in free text is accomplished by comparing a collocational structure built for an unknown word against the collocational and taxonomic structures for each sense of that word in the dictionary, a scheme similar to Lesk (1986). A fairly simple metric would then be employed for rating the candidates, and the best could be chosen. It is an appealing scheme that would appear to be both simple and robust. White goes on to argue that this procedure, given the addition of a bilingual dictionary, could serve as the heart of a transfer-based system for MT.

Although he does not claim it, White's scheme could be extended to another language, given a sense-tagged bilingual dictionary (these are usually just lists of target or source word associations, but without definition text). If all these pieces were in place, the sense disambiguation scheme would start in the source language, finding the proper senses as described above, and then the bilingual dictionary would provide the proper senses in the target language. The unexamined assumption is that sense-tagging a bilingual dictionary is accomplished in a straightforward way (where the tags must, crucially, align with the word sense entries of the source language dictionary). White was able to circumvent this difficulty by making reference to the TEAM terminological database, the lexicon for the METAL English-German translation system (Slocum 1985a), which effectively collapses source and bilingual dictionaries into a single monolithic database structure.

Klavans and Tzoukermann

Klavans and Tzoukermann (1990a,b) have used a bilingual English-French, French-English dictionary (the *Collins Robert*) in conjunction with the Hansard corpus (see below) as the basis for the creation of a bilingual lexical database (BLDB). The IBM BICORD system is designed to probe corpora for verb correspondences, and to expand and rebuild the bilingual dictionary with collocation and frequency information. The end goal is to establish lexical correspondences with associated translations and then attach frequencies to the translations for the purpose of mixed probabilistic and transfer-based MT.

The Hansard corpus consists of 85 million English and 95 million French words from the Canadian Parliamentary proceedings. Of these, about 80% are aligned by sentence. A small set of "motion" verbs were chosen, that is, "ascend," "commute," "drift," "dance," etc., and the corpus was searched to find English sentences containing these words. For example, the word "dance" (and morphological variants: "dances," "danced," etc.) was found in 293 sentences, which contributed about 12,000 words to the "probe" corpus.

The motion verbs in English often have no direct translations in French; for example, a verb like "to stroll" is translated to a french equivalent of "to walk in a leisurely manner (*se promener nonchalamment*). The bilingual dictionary often renders the verbs in other forms than are used in the corpus, and vice versa, and so combining corpus and MRD data will, it is hoped, contribute to producing a bilingual lexicon better suited to MT.

Their method, once the corpus was collected, was to use a part-of-speech tagger to separate the verbs usage from the nouns, and the verb sentences were selected (those sentences in Hansard that contained "ascend," "commute," "dance," etc. used as a verb), along with their equivalent, aligned French sentences. Using the tagged probe corpus, alignments in the corpus were then checked against the *Collins Robert*, looking for both translations and collocations. When a match was found, the record for that MRD entry was extended with frequency information for use by a transfer-type MT system.

This method appears to show great promise, although it depends to some degree on an initial understanding of the various "verb types," which are used to cut the procedure into tractable segments. There are theoretical assumptions here that are outside the procedures being described and which are attributed to Levin (1993). As always, the devil is in the details, and the ongoing process of choosing a verb type, applying the BICORD procedures, and iterating through all the various verbs in the language will undoubtedly reveal both the strengths and the weaknesses of both the procedures and the theory driving it.

Neff and McCord

Neff and McCord (1990) use the *Collins English-German* (CEG) bilingual dictionary, in conjunction with other monolingual sources, for building frames automatically for IBM's LMT machine translation system (McCord 1989). The frames are derived from CEG and augmented by frames taken by IBM's UDICT, a large encoded lexicon built over the years from several sources, including LDOCE. The transfer process includes sense disambiguation of the source terms (in English), selection of German target terms, and further representational augmentations taken from various LDBs created from LDOCE, *Webster's Seventh New Collegiate Dictionary*, and the *Collins Synonym Dictionary*.

Conceptually, the lexical access component of LMT works over three separate entities: the source lexicon, the transfer lexicon, and the target lexicon. There is a one-to-one correspondence between disambiguated source terms and elements of the transfer lexicon. Source terms are chosen by the LMT parser which operates using the slot grammar formalism (McCord 1980). The task then is to construct a frame to be used to match the target lexicon. These frames are built by analyzing the definitions and example sentences of the transfer lexicon, looking for optional and obligatory complements to record in the frame. Once this frame has been constructed, a unification algorithm is used to select the correct senses in the target lexicon.

The problem this procedure seeks to solve is an old one. It is no more than the multilingual equivalent of what has been variously called the "resolution" problem, or the "conflation" problem. In short, there are many different lexical resources in the world, and no two agree precisely as to sense distinction and definition. All the machinery described here (in what is a complex procedure involving reference to several different lexical resources, parsing of source language and of dictionary text, frame building and unification), is necessary because there is no direct correspondence between the entries in monolingual and bilingual dictionaries, and neither contains enough information to support translation by itself. The procedures described here are designed, as a byproduct, to create a lexical database that encodes these correspondences, and that, we must believe, will be a good thing.

The NMSU Computing Research Laboratory

Research is being conducted at the NMSU Computer Research Laboratory (CRL) toward automatically creating individual language lexicons for the ULTRA (Universal Language Translator) interlingual MT system (Farwell and Wilks 1990, Farwell and Guthrie 1991). To a great extent, the researchers have already succeeded in automating the construction of one type of lexical entry in the system (those of the interlingual, or concept, lexicon), using an MRD (Farwell and Guthrie 1991). Work is now going on toward automating the creation of the other type of lexical entry in ULTRA, those for the individual language lexicons. To date, such lexicons for MT systems have had to be handcrafted by fluent speakers of that language.

The procedures for creating these can be thought of in the following way. Bilingual dictionaries (e.g., English-Spanish, or vice versa) normally give a simple list of Spanish equivalent words or phrases for a given English word, and an unskilled user of the dictionary usually does not know enough to select among them. The CRL approach employs an algorithm that, using LDOCE, makes that selection based on context, and does it so as to build up automatically a whole lexicon for processing Spanish or doing translation between English and Spanish.

There are two types of lexical entries in the ULTRA system: those for the intermediate representation (IR) lexicon, and those for the individual language lexicons. Each entry in the IR lexicon can be thought of as an interlingual concept, and is associated with at least one entry in each of the specific language lexicons. Each language entry corresponds to the graphic form used to express the word sense in the language, whereas the IR entry corresponds loosely to a word sense token for the sense expressed. Progress in automating the construction of the IR lexicon (Farwell and Guthrie 1991) has greatly decreased construction time for these lexical entries (see chapter 13).

Efforts are continuing toward the automation of the construction of the specific language lexicons which are necesary in ULTRA's interlingual approach. Each entry in the interlingual lexicon for ULTRA corresponds to exactly one word sense in LDOCE. The initial phase of the process concentrates on a sample of noun senses which appear in the interlingual lexicon, in order to construct the corresponding lexicon entries in Spanish. The CRL method uses previous work in automatically selecting the hypernym, or genus word, from a noun definition in LDOCE, and disambiguating it (Guthrie et al. 1990, Bruce and Guthrie 1992). For example, the program already developed can take the definition of "viaduct":

viaduct—a long high bridge which carries a road or railway line across a valley

and will correctly identify the genus "bridge," and the fact that *bridge* is used in the sense "*bridge* over a river or valley," as opposed to the sense of the card game *bridge*, *bridge* of your nose, or *bridge* of a guitar, and so forth (see chapter 10).

To create individual language lexicons for MT entails developing a method that constructs the correspondence from LDOCE senses to the words in Spanish, using this genus disambiguation program. The basis of this method is the assumption that the English definition's genus word is indicative of the meaning of that sense, and that we may well expect the translation of that genus to appear in the definitions of the most closely corresponding Spanish word.

The first step is to find the correct correspondence for the genus words in LDOCE. Appropriate Spanish translations are then chosen for each of these genus senses (it may be possible to choose these automatically, but, if necessary, they can be correlated by hand). This core correspondence is used to obtain the correspondence over all the noun senses by the following bootstrapping method.

Next, we choose automatically (from machine-readable sources) the Spanish noun that is the most suitable translation, given a particular sense of an English noun. In the easiest case, an English noun has only one sense, and we may expect to be able to use a simple strategy such as choosing the first of the Spanish translations given in the English-Spanish dictionary. Indeed, in many cases there may be only one Spanish word listed: Tuesday, *martes*; hat, *sombrero*, etc. When there is more than one noun sense for the English word, several variations and refinements of the following basic technique for handling this case are tested.

For example, suppose the English noun to be translated is "coach." The definitions of its noun senses are given below. The genus word in each definition is in boldface.

coach1—a large enclosed 4-wheeled horse-drawn **carriage** ...
coach2—a **bus** used for long-distance travel or touring.
coach3—a **person** who trains sportsmen for games, ...
coach4—a farm **cow** used for attracting wild cattle into a trap.

The genus words will not only be identified automatically, but will also be tagged to tell which sense is being used. For each sense of the genus word we will have already prepared a list of translations. For example:

carriage—{carruaje}
bus—{autobus}
person—{persona, el que, un que}
cow—{vaca}

The next step is to consult the English-Spanish dictionary for the translations of "coach."

coach—coche, entrenador, maestro particular.

The three Spanish words are looked up in the Spanish monolingual dictionary, and each defintion is checked to see if it contains a word that is a translation of one of the genus words. The pertinent parts of the definitions are:

coche—**carruaje** generalmente de quatro ruedas.
entrenador—**el que** entrena.
maestro—**un que** ensena un arte o ciencia o es ...

Note that *carruaje*, the translation of "carriage", appears in the definition of *coche*, but in neither of the other Spanish definitions. Note also that this is the only translation of a genus word which appears in this definition. Therefore, we translate coach1 quite correctly as *coche*. Both the remaining Spanish definitions contain translations of "person," and either *entrenador* or *maestro particular* is a possible translation of coach3. However, we expect modifications of the basic technique, such as those suggested below, to allow the method to choose *entrenador*, which is the more common translation. Since neither "bus" nor "cow" has a translation in the Spanish definitions, the two remaining senses of "coach" are not translated.

The basic algorithm can be described as follows: Suppose we have a sense E_n of an English word E, and an English-Spanish dictionary lists all given Spanish translations of E as $(S_1, S_2, \cdots S_n)$. Also, the genus G of E_n translates as certain Spanish words $(H_1, H_2, \cdots H_m)$. In order to choose from among the Spanish spelling forms $(S_1, S_2, \cdots S_n)$, we look up their definitions in a machine-readable Spanish monolingual dictionary to determine which (if any) of the definitions include words from the list $(H_1, H_2, \cdots H_m)$. The spelling form S_{i0} which uses the most of the H_i's is then chosen.

Refinements to this basic algorithm include searching for translations of the noun that is the head of the first noun phrase following the genus (as well as translations of the genus terms themselves), and utilizing the parenthetical indications in the English-Spanish bilingual dictionary to determine the subject area of the Spanish word. It may also be possible to exploit the Spanish-English part of the bilingual dictionary when choosing the Spanish word. The exact form of our final algorithm will depend on the results of experiments.

CRL has designed effective software for assigning a valid Spanish translation to LDOCE noun senses, and for incorporating that translation into the Spanish lexicon of ULTRA. Future work could either extend this method to include selection of Spanish translations for other parts of speech, or be adapted (along with its extensions as they are developed) to the task of building lexicons for other languages.

This lexical acquisition method appears to be a quite general one for the automatic construction of lexical entries from existing MRDs. Indeed, the technique developed at CRL could also be applied to the problem of "mapping across dictionaries." That is, given a word sense in LDOCE, one could use a modification of this algorithm to select the most closely corresponding sense from another *English* MRD. This method of lexicon building could thus be used in an MT system that does not include LDOCE.

NORM: The CRL Translator's Assistant

The NMSU Computing Research Laboratory has begun a project, NORM, to implement a translation support system to assist professional translators in doing their work (Ogden 1993). The goal is to apply NLP technology in ways that will assist in translation and to make electronic media available to facilitate search and look-up.

One of the common problems in translation is encountering an unfamiliar verb in an inflected form. In order to look the word up in a standard dictionary, it is first necessary to know the uninflected form, which entails knowing the rules for doing that. However, in some languages there are many irregular verbs, and the rules for deriving an uninflected form can be numerous and complex. For example, in Spanish there are more than 60 of these rules. To help translators solve this problem, the Collins Spanish-English dictionary is used to generate a table of derived forms by using the headword entry for the irregular verb and generating alternative forms on the basis of conjugation codes found in the dictionary. This table allows the translator to search directly for the unknown inflected verb, which is difficult or impossible with a standard dictionary.

Currently, NORM provides a multiwindowed side-by-side presentation of source and target language texts with editing capabilities in both. To support editing of text displayed in both ascii and non-ascii languages (e.g., Chinese), NORM was developed using new X-windows graphical user interface capabilities. The prototype also allows access to a number of on-line resources such as the Collins Spanish-English bilingual dictionary, the WordNet thesaurus, and a database of aligned parallel Spanish-English texts. To help translators find useful information in these resources, NORM implements a number of lexical information retrieval techniques using full text indexing, morphological processing, and contextual vector-based searching.

NORM was designed through a user-centered empirical approach, and user analysis guided the development of the techniques to retrieve the types of lexical information that best support the translation task. The data collected so far suggest that the database of aligned parallel texts is the most useful source of information for these translators.

As NORM moves closer to the translator's actual working environment, a number of additional capabilities have been identified. New online resources (such as other bilingual and technical dictionaries) are being added, and made easily accessible. A procedure is being developed that will enable a translator using NORM to store the results of the translation into the parallel bilingual text database, which can later be used for the detection and reuse of previously translated material. Concurrent with these efforts, protocol data collected while translators use the system are being analyzed to detect and eliminate usability problems.

Chapter 13

Consumer Projects Using Machine-Readable Dictionaries

Lexicons for NLP systems traditionally have been handcrafted, a process which consumes a large part of development time and effort in any research project. Many researchers believe that because of the effort needed to construct system lexicons, most NLP systems have only been able to process a trivial amount of text, and it is this "lexical bottleneck" that one aims to overcome with automatic or semiautomatic methods for constructing lexicons. The section below describes several systems which have made use of the information in an MRD for the construction of their lexicons. We conclude with a description of a general tool for constructing lexicons in any formalism.

MRDs have been used for everything from stemmers and morphological analyzers to language generation (Krovetz 1989), text critiquing (Heidorn et al. 1982), machine translation (Slocum and Morgan 1986), and speech recognition (Carter 1989). In this chapter we describe computational applications of a novel, experimental kind and, in particular, we describe efforts to use dictionary-extracted lexical entries in large-scale working NLP systems.

The Automatic Creation of Lexical Entries for Machine Translation

We describe in this section a method of applying the information extracted from the LDOCE-based MTD to the construction of lexical entries for two MT systems. We have been able to generate lexical entries automatically for interlingual concepts corresponding to nouns, verbs, adjectives, and adverbs. Although several features of these entries continue to be supplied manually, we have greatly decreased the time required to generate each entry and see this as a promising method for the creation of large-scale lexicons.

This description augments that in chapter 12 above where we described some automation of the lexical entries for individual language tokens using a bilingual dictionary; the description here is of automating the construction of the core, interlingual, lexicon. We are perfectly aware that basing, as we do, those interlingual structures on a particular MRD for English (LDOCE) could be thought biased and a classic case of "linguistic imperialism." However, our position of the essentially practical role of interlingual codings (chapter 4) and on semantic representation in general (chapter 3) leads us to a position where an interlingual coding, like any semantic coding, must inevitably have many of the features of a natural language. Our position differs from that of more rigorous theorists in AI and knowledge representation only in that we recognize this obvious truth and they deny it, even while they continue to write their representations in what are plainly unconstrained English words functioning as predicates. Our recognition of the real state of affairs enables us to be on guard against its dangers (as in the major discussions in this book on sense resolving or tagging the primitives or descriptors in a meaning representation).

ULTRA

ULTRA is a multilingual, interlingual machine translation system which currently translates between five languages (Chinese, English, German, Japanese, Spanish) with vocabularies in each language based on about 10,000 word senses (Farwell and Wilks 1990). It makes use of recent AI, linguistic, and logic programming techniques, bringing current research into product form. The system's major design criteria are that it be robust and general in purpose, with simple-to-use utilities for customization.

Its special features include:

• A multilingual system with a language-independent system of intermediate representations (interlingual representations) for representing expressions as elements of linguistic acts
• Bidirectional Prolog grammars for each language incorporating semantic and pragmatic constraints
• Use of relaxation techniques to provide robustness by giving preferable or "near miss" translations
• Access to large MRDs to give rapid scaling up of size and coverage
• Multilingual text editing within an X-windows interface for easy interaction and document preparation in specific domains (e.g., business letters, proforma memoranda, telexes, parts orders)

Below is a sample screen from the ULTRA system (figure 13.1). Each of the Spanish sentences in the SOURCE TEXT window have been translated into Japanese. The system has "cut-and-paste" facilities which allow a sentence from the source text to be moved to the bottom left SOURCE SENT window where it can then be translated by selecting a target language from the choices above the TRANSLATION window (bottom right) and choosing the TRANSLATE button at the bottom of the screen. The translation then appears in the bottom-right TRANSLATION window. From there, the translation can then be moved to the TARGET TEXT window.

The System of Intermediate Representation
The system of intermediate representation (IR) has been designed to reflect our assumption that what is universal about language is that it is used to perform acts of communication: asking questions, describing the world, expressing one's thoughts, getting people to do things, warning them not to do things, promising that things will get done, and so on. Translation, then, can be viewed as the use of the target language to perform the same act as that which was performed using the source language. The IR serves as the basis for analyzing or for generating expressions as elements of such acts in each of the languages in the translation system. The representation has been formulated on the basis of an ongoing cross-linguistic comparative analysis of hand-generated translations with respect to the kinds of information necessary for selecting the appropriate forms of equivalent expressions in the different languages in the system. We have looked at a number of different types of communication including expository texts, business letters, and e-mail messages and dialogues. This, coupled with the fact that the languages selected for the initial development stage are of different historical and typological background, has led to a solid foundation for developing a flexible and complete descriptive framework.

The Language Components
Each individual language system is independent of all other language systems within ULTRA. Corresponding sentences in different languages must produce the same IR and any specific IR must generate corresponding sentences in the five languages. However, the particular approach to parsing or generation that is used in each of the languages may differ. Each language has its own procedures for associating the

ULTRA TRANSLATION SYSTEM

TEXT FILE TO BE LOADED:

| ENG TEXT | JAP TEXT | CHI TEXT | SPA TEXT | GER TEXT | OTHER |

SOURCE TEXT:	TARGET TEXT:
la mayoria de la sustentacion se produce por la presion relativamente baja sobre la forma aerodinamica.	殆んど の 上昇力 は 機翼 上部 の 比較的 低い 圧力 に よるものである
el ala no se empuja hacia arriba desde abajo.	翼 は 下 から 押し上げられない
se puede aumentar la sustentacion en dos maneras.	上昇力 は 二つ の 方法 で 上げられる 事が 出来る
un aumento del angulo de ataque incrementa la sustentacion hasta cierto nivel.	迎え角 の 増加 は 上昇力 を ある 所 迄 上げるしょう
el aire sobre la forma aerodinamica va una distancia mas larga.	機翼 上部 の 空気 は より 遠くの 距離 にわたり移動する
la mayor parte del ala pierde su sustentacion y ocurre una condicion de perdida.	殆んど の 翼 は その 上昇力 を 失う そして 失状態 が 生じる
el avion desciende porque no hay suficiente sustentacion para mantener el avion arriba.	そこ には 機体 を 高く 保つ のに 充分 な 上昇力 が ない 為 飛行機 は 下降する
esto rebaja el angulo de ataque y permite que el paso de aire sobre las alas se normalize.	これ は 迎え角 を 減少させる そして それ は 翼上方 の 気流 を 滑らかにする のを ゆるす

SOURCE SENT: ENG JAP CHI **SPA** GER   TRANSLATION: ENG **JAP** CHI SPA GER

| la mayoria de la sustentacion se produce por la presion relativamente baja sobre la forma aerodi namica | 殆んど の 上昇力 は 機翼 上部 の 比較的 低い 圧力 に よるものである |

CLEAR CLEAR

TRANSLATE   HALT TRANSLATION   RETRANSLATE

LEXICON CHECK   TOOL BOX   IR   SAVE   HELP   CLEAR   QUIT

Figure 13.1
A sample screen from the ULTRA system.

expressions of the language with the appropriate IRs. These independent systems communicate by handing each other IRs, and no actual transfer takes place. Independence of the language-particular systems is of both theoretical and practical interest. Given the required equivalence of the input-output behavior of each of the language systems, this paradigm is excellent for comparing various approaches to parsing or generation for their coverage and efficacy.

ULTRA's Lexicons
There are two types of entries related to the specification of a lexical item in the ULTRA system: those for IR word sense tokens, and those for the words of the individual languages. Currently, there are eight IR word sense categories, including entities (often corresponding to nouns), relations (often corresponding to verbs and adjectives), entity specifiers (often corresponding to determiners), relation specifiers (often corresponding to auxiliaries), case relations (often corresponding to prepositions), proposition specifiers (often corresponding to complementizers), proposition modifiers (often corresponding to sentential adverbials), and conjunctions. Each category is associated with a special set of constraints which ranges in number from 1 for sentential adverbs, to 9 for relations. The number of lexical categories for the individual language lexicons varies from 8 to 14. There is no simple correspondence between the language-particular lexical categories and the IR categories, although the gross relationships stated above appear to hold. All entries take the general form of simple Prolog unit clauses in (1):

(1) category (Form, F1, F2, ...).

where **F1, F2,** and so on, are constraints. For language-particular entries, these are generally syntactic constraints associated with an orthographic form, **Form**, such as the gender of a noun, whether a verb is reflexive, and so on. For example, (2) is a simplified and readable version of a Spanish entry for the noun *banco*.

(2) noun (banco, third_singular, masculine, bank4_1).

Similarly, (3) is a Spanish entry for the verb *ingresó*.

(3) verb (ingresó, third_singular, finite, past, simple, indicative, active, deposit1_3).

The final argument represents the IR word sense the Spanish form is used to express. This sense token is associated with a sense definition in

LDOCE and is used to index the corresponding IR entry. For IR entries, the features **F1, F2,** and so on, correspond to universal semantic and pragmatic constraints on the word sense, **Form,** such as the classification of an entity as countable or not, the semantic case structure of a relation, and so on. For example the IR entry for **bank4_1** would look something like:

(4) entity (bank4_1, class, countable, institution, abstract_object, economics_banking).

while the IR entry for **deposit1_3** would look like:

(5) relation (deposit1_3, dynamic, placing, agent, patient, human, amount, human, abstract_object, economics_banking).

The Automatic Construction of Lexical Items
Much of the core IR lexicon has been derived from the 72,000 word senses in LDOCE. Codings from the dictionary for such properties as semantic category, semantic preferences, and so on have been used, either directly or indirectly, to generate partial specifications of some 10,000 IR tokens for the system.

The mapping process from LDOCE to ULTRA word sense entries assumes a particular linguistic context. All the information contained in the LDOCE definition is automatically extracted and used in the appropriate ULTRA specification. For some parts of speech (e.g., nouns), most of the information stored in the interlingual entry can be extracted automatically; for others (e.g., verbs and adjectives), only a portion of the information is available. To date, information from LDOCE nouns has been used for specifying IR entries for entities, from verbs and adjectives for specifying IR entries for relations, and from adverbs for specifying IR entries for relation modifiers and proposition modifiers. These are the major open class categories of IR word sense tokens and constitute over 95% of the tokens defined thus far. Details of the information extracted and the process of extraction are given in Farwell et al. (1993).

Approaches to Achieving Full Specification

It was clear at the outset of this project that a great deal of lexical acquisition could be done automatically and we have initiated projects to discover how much of the missing information can be identified automatically through further analysis of the definitions, examples, grammatical categories, etc. Finally, in order to automate the construction of lexical items during translation, procedures must be defined to select specific senses on the basis of the source language linguistic context of the item being defined. Similarly, procedures must be developed to specify the different language-particular lexical entries automatically (these procedures have been completed for English to a limited extent), and these will have to be adapted to other languages.

Pangloss

Currently, CRL is working together with the Center for Machine Translation at Carnegie Mellon and the Information Sciences Institute at the University of Southern California on *Pangloss*, a Department of Defense–funded MT project. One of the goals of that project is to use MRDs in the construction of its lexicons, to improve the techniques used in the ULTRA system described above, and to develop techniques for using bilingual dictionaries to construct the individual language lexicons automatically.

The *Pangloss* project is founded on an interlingual, knowledge-based approach combined with statistical methods. Automatic acquisition of lexical information is used at all three levels of the initial system: analysis (Spanish), interlingual/ontological, and generation (English). For this extraction/acquisition task we have used both LDOCE and Collins Spanish-English and English-Spanish bilingual dictionaries.

Lexical Levels: An Overview of the Lexicons
The interlingual nature of the *Pangloss* system lends itself to a stratified approach to lexicon building. Lexical information, for both English and Spanish, contains primarily syntactic and morphological information, together with a pointer to an interlingual conceptual token containing semantic information. In the initial system there are three levels for which automated acquisition has been useful: the IR lexicon based on ULTRA (Farwell and Wilks 1990), the Spanish lexicon for analysis (also originally based on ULTRA), and the English lexicon used by the generator, Penman (Mann 1983).

During the first year of the project, automated acquisition has been used only for English and the IR. Below, we show Spanish lexical entries to indicate how lexical tokens in Spanish are connected with IRs.

I. Spanish Lexical Entries

Nouns
se_form(san,josé,ts,f,_A,san_jose_x).
se_form(abarrote,ts,m,_A,groceries0_0).
se_form(abarrotes,tp,m,_A,groceries0_0).
se_form(abrigo,ts,m,_A,coat1_1).
se_form(abrigo,tu,m,_A,shelter1_2).
se_form(abrigos,tp,m,_A,coat1_1).

Spanish entries for nouns and pronouns use a five-tuple to encode the lexical item, person and number information, gender information, case information, and the corresponding interlingual token. Noun and pronoun senses make up more than half the senses in a standard dictionary and will be a large part of the *Panglosss* Spanish lexicon. The entries were created in a semiautomatic way, using the Collins Spanish-English dictionary as an aid. We are developing procedures to create these entries entirely automatically from the machine-readable version of the Collins dictionary. The procedures for supplying the first four components from the dictionary have been developed and we are investigating techniques for associating the correct interlingual token.

Verbs
sr_form(identifica,dyn,ts,_A,fin,prs,simp,indic,actv,identify_1).
sr_form(identifica,dyn,tu,_A,fin,prs,simp,indic,actv,identify_1).
sr_form(identificada,dyn,ts,f,psp,_A,_B,_C,pasv,identify_1).
sr_form(identificadas,dyn,tp,f,psp,_A,_B,_C,pasv,identify_1).
sr_form(identificado,dyn,_A,_B,psp,_C,perf,_D,actv,identify_1).
sr_form(identificado,dyn,ts,m,psp,_A,_B,_C,pasv,identify_1).
sr_form(identificados,dyn,tp,m,psp,_A,_B,_C,npasv,identify_1).
sr_form(identifican,dyn,tp,_A,fin,prs,simp,indic,actv,identify_1).
sr_form(identificando,dyn,_A,_B,prp,_C,prog,_D,actv,identify_1).
sr_form(identificar,dyn,_A,_B,inf,_C,simp,_D,actv,identify_1).
sr_form(identificaron,dyn,tp,_A,fin,pst,simp,indic,actv,identify_1).
sr_form(identificará,dyn,ts,_A,fin,fut,simp,put,actv,identify_1).
sr_form(identificará,dyn,tu,_A,fin,fut,simp,put,actv,identify_1).
sr_form(identificarán,dyn,tp,_A,fin,fut,simp,put,actv,identify_1).
sr_form(identificó,dyn,ts,_A,fin,pst,simp,indic,actv,identify_1).
sr_form(identificó,dyn,tu,_A,fin,pst,simp,indic,actv,identify_1).

Verbs as well as adjectives are represented in the Spanish lexicon of *Pangloss* using the sr_form (for Spanish relations) above. The ten-tuple representation encodes the following information whenever it is appropriate and uses a Prolog-style variable (A for example) for any components that are not relevant to the entry: the lexical token; whether the verb is stative or dynamic; agreement information (person and number); agreement information (gender); morphological information; information on tense; information on aspect; information on mood; information on voice; and the corresponding interlingual token. At present, these entries were created interactively, with the use of the Collins bilingual dictionary. Procedures are being developed to create entries automatically from the dictionary. We have completed procedures to derive automatically the agreement information (person, number, and gender), tense, aspect, mood, voice, and morphological information. We are investigating methods for deriving the remaining features as well as techniques for associating the interlingual token.

II. Intermediate Representations

Entities
ir_spec_ent(san_jose_x,prop,loc,c,_Lc,_Ld).
ir_spec_ent(groceries0_0,nrm,p_obj,c,sol_or_liq,open).
ir_spec_ent(grocery0_0,nrm,place,m,abstract,open).

The entries corresponding to nouns and verbs in the IR are based on the IR of ULTRA. The entity entries above have been derived entirely from the machine-readable version of LDOCE, except for the third component which is a manually assigned semantic category. The ir_spec_ent entries correspond roughly to nouns and encode a semantic category, whether the noun is proper or common, mass or count, the LDOCE semantic category (provided from the machine-readable version of the dictionary), and the LDOCE domain category (provided for some senses in the version of LDOCE). For nouns that do not appear in LDOCE (such as San Jose above), the entries were created manually. The first component represents the headword, homograph, and sense in LDOCE.

The entries in the IR that correspond roughly to verbs and adjectives were also generated semiautomatically.

III. English Lexical Entries for Generation

Penman noun   See figure 13.2.

Penman verb   See figure 13.3.

```
(lexical-item
  :name LOS-ANGELES
  :spelling "Los Angeles"
  :sample-sentence   ""
  :features   (NOUN NOINFLECTIONS PROPERNOUN COUNTABLE NOT-PERIOD
              NOT-DETERMINERREQUIRED NOT-PROVENANCE)
  :comments  "city"
  :date  "10/24/88 10:21:02"
  :editor  "HOVY")
```

Figure 13.2
A Penman noun.


```
(lexical-item
  :name IDENTIFY
  :spelling "identify"
  :sample-sentence  "The navy identified the new Russian ship as the
                    Gorky."
  :features   (VERB INFLECTABLE LEXICAL NOT-CASEPREPOSITIONS
     OBJECTPERMITTED NOT-TOCOMP QUESTIONCOMP PARTICIPLECOMP
     NOT-MAKECOMP BAREINFINITIVECOMP NOT-COPULA PASSIVE
     THATCOMP NOT-THATREQUIRED NOT-SUBJUNCTIVEREQUIRED NOT-ADJECTIVECOMP
     NONE-OF-BITRANSITIVE-INDIRECTOBJECT EXPERIENCEVERB
     PERCEPTION MIDDLE OBJECTNOTREQUIRED NOT-SUBJECTCOMP
     UNITARYSPELLING VISUAL IRR PLURALPASTFORM SECONDSINGULARPASTFORM
     PLURALFORM FIRSTSINGULARFORM EDPARTICIPLEFORM THIRDSINGULARFORM
     INGPARTICIPLEFORM PASTFORM SECONDSINGULARFORM FIRSTSINGULARPASTFORM
     THIRDSINGULARPASTFORM)
  :properties  ((INGPARTICIPLEFORM "identifying")
                (EDPARTICIPLEFORM "identified")
                (PLURALPASTFORM "identified")
                (THIRDSINGULARPASTFORM "identified")
                (SECONDSINGULARPASTFORM "identified")
                (FIRSTSINGULARPASTFORM "identified")
                (PASTFORM "identified")
                (PLURALFORM "identify")
                (SECONDSINGULARFORM "identify")
                (FIRSTSINGULARFORM "identify")
                (THIRDSINGULARFORM "identifies"))
  :comments  "process"
  :date  "10/26/88 12:08:51"
  :editor  "HOVY")
```

Figure 13.3
A Penman verb.

As the entries for Penman are more readable, we will not describe their content in detail. At this point in the project, procedures have been developed for deriving the inflected forms of nouns, verbs, adjectives, and adverbs.

Interdependence and Uniformity of Representations

For theoretical reasons, these different lexical representations are kept separate. The representations differ according to the type of information contained (syntactic vs. semantic) and use (analysis vs. generation).

Use of Automated Procedures

In addition to the automated procedures described above, we have created phrasal lexicons for English-Spanish, and Spanish-English. A lexicon of English phrases and idioms was extracted from LDOCE and, in conjunction with the network of noun senses (NounSense) described in chapter 10, results in over 30,000 nouns being used in an ontology for *Pangloss*.

Part of the *Pangloss* effort has been directed to extracting information from MRDs on-line for the specific purposes of the project. Another part of the effort, however, has been directed to the general problem of making on-line dictionary information more accessible: processing each dictionary and its entries into a format that makes extraction of *any* information much simpler and faster. For each dictionary, of course, this format differs. And lexical databases are being constructed which eliminate inconsistencies in format.

The Collins Spanish-English dictionary has provided useful information in this project. Monolingual information, such as morphological information and syntactic information, is extensive, and monolingual semantic information in the form of synonyms, subject areas, and preferred collocations is perhaps more accessible than in LDOCE. Phrasal lexicons have been extracted for both example-based translation and for coding multiword lexical items for the *Pangloss* parser/analyzer.

Conclusion

The (semi-)automatic use of MRDs for applications like MT remains a desirable goal, and we have given what we believe to be the first operational proof of the concept. We do not suppose that very general MRDs (like LDOCE and Collins) will suffice in the absence of domain-specific

lexicons described from bilingual corpora (parallel and, more intrigu-
ingly, nonparallel) by empirical methods. What we have described here is
no more than a core lexicon. In a separate project described in chapter 7
(TIPSTER), we are investigating not only how to join MRD-derived to
corpora-derived lexicons but how to obtain the latter by "tuning" the
former against the domain corpus itself (Wilks, Pustejovsky, and Cowie
1993).

As is well known, there is at the moment no way of evaluating the performance of a lexicon separately from the whole project of which it is a part,
other than by comparing final output performance with different versions
of a lexicon at different times (while the rest of the system is kept fixed).
We believe fuller evaluation methods for lexical systems will be derived, but
at the moment this project of automatic lexical requisition for *Pangloss* is
subject to the evaluation of *Pangloss* itself, which is conducted periodi-
cally against other MT systems funded under the same overall scheme.

It is clear that not all the properties that researchers would like to include in their lexicons appear in any given dictionary, yet our experience
at CRL has been that a sizable portion of what is needed in the lexicon for
a system can be found in the lexical database. With each project we have
been prompted to enrich the database based on analysis of information in
one of the fields of each entry.

The realization that the information in the lexical database at every
stage has proved to be useful in the constuction of lexicons for a range of
natural language sytems has led to the development of a general-purpose
tool for lexicon building called LEXI-CAD/CAM. In each of the systems
we worked with, the lexical database was used to automatically create
partially or fully filled lexical entries for the systems. Our experience with
these projects has allowed us to create a flexible tool for lexicon building.
The lexicons that were generated for the projects above were recreated
automatically using the new tool, LEXI-CAD/CAM. We can now create
lexicons in any format (e.g., any LISP list, Prolog fact, or framelike structure) for new applications in the LEXI-CAD/CAM system. The lexicon
builder need only to specify the words, phrases, or word senses to be included in the lexicon, and the format of the lexical entries to be generated.

Slator's PREMO: Knowledge-Based Parsing

The knowledge base constructed by the lexicon provider (chapter 9) was
designed to be used by a preference semantics parser for text. Preference

semantics is a theory of language in which the meaning of a text is represented by a complex semantic structure that is built up out of smaller semantic components. Knowledge is required to compute preferences for deciding lexical ambiguity, constituent attachment, and reference, and LDOCE is a rich source of such information. In a preference semantics system the primary focus is on semantic knowledge, such as the preferred types for the subjects and objects of verbs, and the preferred types of modifiers for heads, and heads for modifiers. Grammatical information is secondary but also useful, particularly for the predictions of later grammatical constructions that are made possible by the LDOCE comprehensive grammar for English (Quirk et al. 1972, 1985).

PREMO (**PRE**ference **M**achine **O**rganization) is an architecture for parsing natural language texts modelled as an operating system. Each "ready process" in the system captures the state of a partial parse in a "process control block" structure called a *language object*. Global system data structures include a *text lexicon*, a *phrase grammar*, and a *pragmatic context structure*. The control structure is a priority queue of competing parses, with priority given to each parse process on the basis of a preference semantics evaluation. The "time slice" for each process is whatever is needed to move forward one word in a local process text buffer (where each process operates on a private copy of the current sentence). After every time slice, the preference priority for the currently "running" parse is recomputed and the language object for that process is returned to the priority queue. The first process to emerge from the queue with its sentence buffer empty is declared the winner and is saved (becoming part of the pragmatic context), the other processes are flushed from the queue, and a new sentence is started. This cycle is continued until the entire text has been processed and inserted into the pragmatic context structure.

Language Objects

The basic data structure manipulated by the preference machine is a *language object*. Each language object is a complex structure containing at least: (1) NAME and TYPE—where every object is named by a word from the lexicon, every word is typed by the phrase it appears in, and the *head* of a phrase has its comembers subordinated to it; (2) SCORE—a preference priority computed for the object; (3) SUBORDINATES—a LIFO stack of language objects linguistically subordinate to the current object; (4) PREDICTIONS and REQUIREMENTS—grammatical constraints, both of the object itself, and as synthesized from subordinated objects; (5) SURROUNDING TEXT—the sentential context of the current language object, those words that precede and follow in the sentence; and (6) LEXICAL FRAME—a lexical semantic frame instantiated to a single sense of the language object NAME.

Control Structure

The basic control structure of the preference machine is a priority queue of language objects. The high-priority objects are those with the highest scores as computed by a preference metric that includes consideration of grammatical predictions, semantic type matching, and pragmatic cohesion. The language object at the front of the queue is the partial parse that is currently most preferred; the others represent less preferred readings. These others are still "alive," but are not being actively pursued. Each iteration of the PREMO algorithm (1) retrieves the highest priority language object from the queue; (2) creates language objects for all senses of the next word in that object's sentence buffer, (3) coalesces these pairs (subordinating one to the other), according to rules of phrase grammar, (4) computes a new preference priority for each coalesced pair, and (5) inserts each into the priority queue.

Text Structure

The global pragmatic structure produced by the lexicon provider (and discussed in chapter 7) is used for computing preferences as well as serving as a central organizing principle for the emerging text structure. Every sentence in a text is eventually represented by a single language object. This language object is named for the word seen to be the head of the dominating phrase in the sentence. Each of the subordinated phrases in the sentence is stacked within this dominating language object. All of these language objects are stored in the global pragmatic context structure under a unifying principle of text structure.

Text Lexicon

Dictionary definitions from a large machine-readable source (LDOCE) are converted into semantic structures (a frame-based knowledge representation), suitable for knowledge-based parsing (Slator and Wilks 1987, Wilks et al. 1987). Besides exploiting the special encodings contained in the dictionary, the text of the definition entry itself is analyzed, with a chart parser and a pattern matcher, to extract *genus* and *differentia* terms. This additional information further enriches the semantic structures. The output of the program is a lexicon of word sense frames, with each frame explicitly or implicitly positioned in multiple, preexisting, hierarchies. These frames constitute a text-specific knowledge source used by the **PREMO** preference semantics parser for text. Other, more pragmatic, information, such as the typical discourse domain for content words, is also available (e.g., that "ammeter" is a technical term typically encountered in an electrical engineering context). All these sorts of information are made available to PREMO through the lexicon provider (see chapter 9).

IBM: Deciding Attachments

Attachment decisions are among the hardest unsolved problems in natural language understanding. For example, understanding the meaning of a sentence like "A man ate a fish with a fork," depends crucially on deciding whether it is the man, or the fish, who has possession of the fork. Jensen and Binot (1987, Binot and Jensen 1987) take an approach to making these decisions that centers on interpreting definition parse trees and applying heuristic rules about definition patterns using *Webster's Seventh Collegiate Dictionary* as a knowledge base.

The first step in the process is to parse a sentence syntactically. The PEG grammar is used to do this, with the IBM PLNLP system (Heidorn 1975) returning parse trees with potential attachment ambiguities marked. Each of the competing attachment decisions is then evaluated, and the results are returned in order of their likelihood. In this example, plausibility evaluations are made for both (with fish fork) and (with eat fork), which amounts to deciding whether it is more likely to find a fish in possession of a fork, or to eat a fish with a fork. The evaluations are made in terms of specific relations, and the results of the evaluation give a ranking for each of these.

The mechanism for attachment evaluation, after the sentence has been syntactically parsed, is to look up the definitions of the target word, in this case "fork," and parse all its definitions. The system has a set of patterns associated with each of the relations it knows about: patterns for INSTRUMENT, such as "used for" and "a means for"; patterns for PART-OF, such as "part of" and "arises from," and so on. These patterns are applied to each definition's parse tree and a score is assigned to the match that depends on the difficulty of the matching.

One definition of "fork" is "an implement with two or more prongs used especially for taking up, pitching and digging" and "take" is in the genus of one sense of "eat." Therefore, an INSTRUMENT connection is established between "eat" and "fork," because of the indirect link between them, and because the pattern that revealed this connection is an INSTRUMENT pattern that depends on the "used especially for" part of the definition of "fork." As a consequence of the evaluation procedure, the (with eat fork) alternative returns an INSTRUMENT rating of 0.72 and the (with fish fork) reading of the attachment returns values below 0 for all its possible relations.

The system depends on a rule-based inference mechanism to assign MYCIN-like probabilities (Shortliffe 1976) to attachment alternatives, the numbers arrived at by intuition and tuning. This imposes a significant interactive effort on the ultimate implementation, although far less than hand-coding the information instead of using the dictionary. The algorithm, as described in Jensen and Binot (1987), sounds quite inefficient, since it depends on repeatedly looking up the words that appear and then parsing their definitions. Binot and Jensen (1987) propose a scheme for ameliorating the procedure, the weakest part of which is that there is no account of word sense distinctions: "fish" is associated with "bone" because they both have relations to the word "skeleton," but there is built-in potential for error because a "ship" or a "bridge" can also have relations to "skeleton," but of another type and defined in another sense. All this notwithstanding, this is one of the more original and practical applications of computational lexicography.

Chapter 14

The Present

In this chapter we describe two quite different kinds of future developments in lexically related areas. First, new developments in the construction of MRDs from corpus and other sources, using partial computational methods, of the kind described in this book, and being in some cases dictionaries intended for computational linguistics (CL) purposes, in addition to the normal printed (or CD-ROM) forms. We describe the Electronic Dictionary Research (EDR) effort in Japan, the new Cambridge dictionary by Procter, and the Oxford University Press–Digital Equipment Corporation (OUP-DEC) dictionary by Hanks. Second, new developments of an organizational type: a brief survey of cooperative efforts in the research, development, survey, and distribution of lexical materials, all designed in their different ways to speed up the construction of lexical systems as the basis of NLP. We mention the ACQUILEX project, the Linguistic Data Consortium, and the Consortium for Lexical Research.

Piggybacking a Dictionary from a Corpus and a "Seed" MRD

The following ingenious method is due to Jim Cowie at CRL-NMSU and is one of many possible algorithms for classifying the occurrences of a word in a corpus into sense groups so as to construct a dictionary from a corpus, and doing so by means of an ultimately dispensible seed MRD. This task is the one almost all corpus-oriented lexicographers want to perform, though none have succeeded yet. It also enshrines, in an interesting and novel way, the manner in which all existing dictionaries piggyback upon existing ones, though in this case in a perspicuous and straightforward manner, one in which the "seed" MRD is ultimately dispensed with and superseded by the dictionary under construction.

We would like to classify all the occurrences of a word in a corpus as belonging to one of a set of senses defined by a lexicographer who has examined a subset of the occurrences of the word using a KWIC (key word in context) indexing system (see the OUP-DEC dictionary enterprise described below). It would seem that after a sufficient number of example senses have been marked it should be possible to classify the remaining instances of a word using overlap techniques. More interestingly, it may be possible to highlight unusual usages (or different "unclassified" senses) by identifying instances where the overlap occurrence is low. Cases where the overlap is high may indicate archetypical example usages.

To allow the overlap technique to work optimally we need to disambiguate the surrounding words. Cowie (unpublished data; 1992) proposes doing this initially relative to an already existing MRD, using its definitions to provide the words to be overlapped. Any words already disambiguated by the lexicographer relative to the corpus would be used in their new sense. Thus the initial step would be to disambiguate the words in individual lines of the KWIC index using the overlap of their definitions by some method like Lesk's, possibly optimized as in the last section. This would give us the following list of KWICS:

S0_0 S1_0 S2_0 W0 S3_0 S4_0 S5_0
S0_1 S1_1 S2_1 W0 S3_1 S4_1 S5_1
        .
        .
S0_2 S1_2 S2_2 W1 S3_2 S4_2 S5_2
        .
        .
S0_z S1_z S2_z Wx S3_z S4_z S5_z

where Sj_k is a disambiguated word sense, $W0$ .. Wn are the assigned senses of the word being examined, and Wx are all the unresolved instances of the word.

This tagged KWIC can now be used to classify all the Wx's as one of $W0$ to WN using the overlap of all the Sj_k's. If low overlap occurs, then it is necessary to examine this instance manually. As more and more senses are tagged in the corpus, these will be used instead of the MRD senses in computing new overlaps. Thus the corpus will be gradually converted to the new set of senses.

We anticipate other advantages in the above method, for example, identifying words which are specified as single sense in several MRDs. The use of multiple MRDs could also be used to highlight words on which there exist poor levels of agreement.

The increasing availability of large corpora in machine-readable form and the computing power to manipulate such huge chunks of data make increasing use of numerical techniques inevitable. Such methods have clearly progressed beyond the simple word counting of a few years ago, as is shown by the fact that in this book we have referred to recent work using statistics, neural nets, and simulated annealing. The MRD itself represents a controlled text of manageable (a few million words) size which can be used as a test bed in the development of techniques which may be then applied to more general text. This has been the case with the co-occurrence techniques described here.

New Modes of Dictionary Construction

As we have noted many times, lexicographers want to derive their dictionaries from corpora, which are seen as representing living, developing, as opposed to fossilized, language. As we also saw in discussing the construction of COBUILD (see chapter 7), each sense was supported (sometimes in error, inevitably) by a genuine example sentence drawn from corpus (in a way that LDOCE with its much lower quality of example sentences was not), yet there is no procedure at all, in the sense of a computation, by which the occurrences of a word in the corpus are divided into or matched against any particular sense taxonomy. It is this enormous barrier—from corpus direct to dictionary—that lexicographers would dearly love to leap if only they knew how.

Three current large-scale dictionary construction efforts are underway, all of which hope to see a much closer use of the corpus in the construction of the dictionary: (1) the EDR project in Japan; (2) the Cambridge University Press dictionary project: and (3) the Oxford-DEC project.

The Japanese EDR Project

The Japan Electronic Dictionary Research Institute (JEDR 1990) has several research initiatives going forward in parallel, all directed toward the global goal of NLP: "to enable computers to understand and process languages used by humans" (EDR-TR-024 1990, p. 1). In order to accomplish this, the institute has begun the development of several complementary, full-sized dictionaries: an English word dictionary, a Japanese word dictionary, a concept dictionary, and a bilingual dictionary, as well as associated English and Japanese interfaces. With these, they hope to make significant inroads into the problems of natural language interface (NLI) and MT before the project ends.

The EDR word dictionaries for English and Japanese are a combination of both general word lists and specialized vocabulary from the information-processing domain. Each contains grammatical information for the words (from a finely grained set of grammatical categories), combined with information on usage and frequency, and the usual notation for syllabification. One interesting feature is that compound words and phrases have a syntactic parse tree stored with them, to represent the constituent structure of the compound. The meaning of each entry is encoded as a "head-concept," which is a pointer to an entry in the concept dictionary. Using a nonstandard term, EDR refers to the sense division by headword, in English, along with the associated definitions in English, as the English interface.

The EDR concept dictionary is a multiply partitioned network of concept labels and relations between them, including simple concepts, like

⟨bird⟩,

relations between simple concepts, like

⟨bird⟩—kind-of → ⟨food⟩,

as well as compounds to represent phrasal and sentential level concepts, which appear, in the printed description, to be recursively defined and infinitely extensible. One section of the concept dictionary provides compound concepts defined by two or more concept entries consisting of head concepts and a relation. For example, the concept "Sumo wrestlers drink much liquor," is represented as

[⟨to drink⟩—agent → ⟨wrestlers of Japanese wrestling⟩
⟨to drink⟩—object → ⟨liquor⟩
⟨to drink⟩—quantity → ⟨a large amount⟩]

The EDR bilingual dictionary is a three-column list, of which the two outer columns contain source and target words, and the middle column contains an "interlingual correspondence label" which is either "equivalent relation," "synonymous relation," "subset relation," or "superset relation." The bilingual dictionaries are of the unidirectional transfer type, and are constructed by reference to the previously constructed monolingual dictionaries. That is, the bilingual dictionaries only have headword entries if these headwords already exist in one of the monolingual dictionaries (which solves one of the correspondence problems that other bilingual dictionary users have faced).

The interlingual correspondence labels are an attempt at solving the other correspondence problems, that is, when a single word in the source language translates to several more specific words or phrases in the target language, or when a specific word or phrase in the source language has only general equivalents in the target language. For example, there are three Japanese expressions for "eraser": "keshi gomu," "kokuban keshi," and "inu keshi," which refer to erasers of pencil, chalk, and ink, respectively. Meanwhile both "hat" and "cap" in English translate to the Japanese word "booshi." The interlingual correspondence labels are intended to inform the generation component of a machine translation (MT) system that some form of supplementary explanation needs to pass through to the translation: either a modifier to narrow down the meaning of the corresponding word, or to explain the meaning of the corresponding headword.

Unlike most other dictionary projects, the EDR initiative is intended to be text-driven. A large part of the effort has been to gather a 20-million sentence corpus from which the word and concept dictionaries could be built. After that, a great deal of the effort has been tackled by hand, using various interactive software tools. The texts of definitions in the interface which are encoded in the concept dictionary appear to be typical lexical entries, but it is not clear where these were gathered from, or whether they too have been generated by hand. Taking the approach of letting the text drive the lexical efforts has certain advantages, including closing off the domain to eliminate unknown words, and reducing spurious senses that appear in traditional lexical resources. In this way, the EDR project avoids having to account for the obscure English sense of "buttery," an archaic word for a certain room in an English university, and can simply account for the adjective derived from the dairy product.

There has never been any precise method defined by which the original entries were gathered—some clearly owe a strong debt to exisiting MRDs, but we have argued that that is always the case everywhere—nor has there been a method by which they are attested or verified in the corpus. However, the enterprise is vast and a great deal of effort has gone into building the interfaces and making them available at low cost to researchers everywhere.

The New Cambridge Dictionary
It is said that Cambridge once turned down the enterprise that later became the OED at Oxford, and Cambridge University Press has never published a full English dictionary. Paul Procter, who masterminded

LDOCE, is currently remedying that by means of a large dictionary, nearing completion, which is closely linked to a corpus, at least in the COBUILD sense above, and also contains what is very like a vastly reformed and improved top-down LDOCE-style taxonomy of the semantic and pragmatic universe. The whole enterprise is far more computer-controlled and is designed from the beginning to be widely available as a linguistic knowledge base tool for NLP.

The Cambridge University Press (CUP) team have worked within the ACQUILEX project, most closely with the Cambridge University group (see chapter 12). The dictionary is intended from the beginning as an electronic reference tool for research in the widest sense, and its relationship with corpora is intended to be not just data gathering but to include the use of software associated with the building of the corpora in a range of languages; the gathering aspect is called the Cambridge Language Survey.

The Oxford-DEC dictionary: The Hector Project

Patrick Hanks, who led the Collins and COBUILD teams, is managing a collaboration to explore a quite new type of dictionary between Oxford University Press and Digital Equipment Corporation in Palo Alto, California. With this, he is attempting to realize his dream that actual computations over a corpus (especially statistical ones; see chapter 11) can provide direct input to dictionary construction, a gap no one has so far bridged in the lexicographic world.

The methodology is essentially an extension of the COBUILD one, augmented by enormously powerful corpus-processing tools constructed by DEC. That is to say, the example sentences used are all attested from real corpora, and the lexicographer is able to make sense-clusterings of very large numbers of examples at the screen displayed in KWIC-like formats. There is frequency information (of the chosen word with collocates) available to the lexicographer, but no statistical computations play any direct role in the sense divisions or other aspects of the dictionary construction. Hector, then, was an OUP-DEC collaborative project and has yielded about 200,000 sense-tagged corpus items for about 1000 lexical entries (a total of 1% of the nonbalanced pilot corpus).

Organizational Developments

A substantial range of initiatives are currently being supported by the Commission of the European Community (CEC) and its European Special Project for Research in Information Technology (ESPRIT) and Language Research and Engineering (LRE) programs, and by Eureka. The various information technology projects and the language engineering project, funded by the Thirteenth Directorate of the Commission of European Communities (CEC DG-XIII) in Luxembourg, can be considered as a follow-up to the Eurotra MT project in a effort to make some use of the lexicons constructed as part of that enormous enterprise.

ACQUILEX I and II (basic research initiatives under ESPRIT) were discussed earlier in detail. They are directed toward the acquisition of lexical information from monolingual and bilingual MRDs and from text corpora for NLP applications, and to create a prototype of a lexical knowledge base.

Multilex (ESPRIT) was to establish a standard for multilingual and multifunctional lexicons for the CEC languages, and to implement a common core demonstration lexicon.

Genelex (Eureka) was to produce generic and application-specific lexicons according to a unified lexical model.

NERC is a feasibility study for the creation of a *n*etwork of *E*uropean *r*eference *C*orpora (CEC).

ET-6 and **ET-9** (CEC) are studies and an implementation of a common computational framework for the development of a variety of software tools for NLP.

ET-7 (CEC) involved studying the feasibility of building large-scale reusable lexical and terminological resources.

ET-10 63 (CEC) was to enhance the Eurotra system by speeding up processes such as lexicon construction, or by partially solving problems such as overgeneration, and to show the value of a mixed approach in NLP which consists in fine-tuning rule-based systems through statistical extraction of information from textual data.

ET-10 85 (CEC) was research on the characterization and analysis of collocations, on representation of collocations, and implementation of a prototype lexicon system for collocational information.

ET-10 51 (CEC) was to devise a route from dictionary definition to a formal representation of word meaning, using the COBUILD dictionary.

ELSNET (European Network of Excellence for Natural Language and Speech) is a task group for reusable linguistic resources (ESPRIT).

Delis (CEC-LRE) aims at producing descriptive lexical specifications and acquisition and representation tools for corpus-based lexicon building.

Onomastica (CEC-LRE) has the objective of making available, for wide-scale exploitation for speech and NLP, quality-controlled pronunciation lexicons in machine-readable form for use in automated language systems (city and town names, street names, family names, product names).

EAGLES (CEC-LRE) aims at accelerating the provision of common functional specifications for the development of large-scale language resources. Five working groups have been set up dealing with corpora, lexica, formalisms, evaluation and assessment, and speech.

ACQUILEX

As part of the ESPRIT initiative, the ACQUILEX project is a broadly ambitious approach to creating lexical resources that will serve many purposes. It seeks to generalize over many different dictionaries in community languages (two English dictionaries, two Italian, one Spanish, one Dutch, one Italian-English, and one Dutch-English) in order to create a set of common templates for different types of lexical items. These templates will form an interlingual inheritance hierarchy, and the lexical items from the different languages will nestle together in coherent relation to one another. The project can be seen as a fulfillment of the plan to construct a lexical knowledge base (LKB) in the sense of Calzolari (1990).

The thrust of the effort is toward reusability, since potential clients range from a variety of NLP systems builders to linguists and lexicographers. The plan is to construct an overarching conceptual structure that will draw together definitional material with the world knowledge implicitly encoded there, and to formalize all this in the form of concepts and semantic relations. Like most projects of this sort, the first steps involve building taxonomies from the dictionaries in the usual ways, since this is now a fairly well-understood, although not a solved, problem. For ACQUILEX there is an extra level of difficulty though, since it is hoped that the process of taxonomizing the individual dictionaries will lead to the insights required to "normalize" the abstraction hierarchies (in order to have the different conceptual structures, represented in the different dictionaries, coalesced into one).

The normalizing step will provide the set of attributes and relations necessary for the LKB, and the plan is then to implement an inheritance network where the nodes are framelike entities (Minsky 1975) whose internal structure explicitly acknowledges the influence of the lexical semantics theories of Pustejovsky 1989, Pustejovsky and Boguraev 1993). In this instance, the theory translates to a system of "meaning types" and the notion of a template to structure semantic information. The templates are intended to form the nodes that appear in the upper reaches of the taxonomy, and to provide abstract knowledge about entire classes of words. So, for example, a template would be filled out for concepts like SUBSTANCE, which would be placed in an abstract relation to other templates for LIQUID and GAS.

The templates will most probably be constructed by hand, although a method has been suggested for constructing the SUBSTANCE template by reference to all the dictionary entries for words defined by the word "substance" or hyponyms of "substance." The templates are constructed with slots for function (i.e., the substance is "used for" certain things, and "used by" certain agents), property (i.e., the substance has certain origins, a certain color, shape, and taste), and so on.

The principal problem that an ambitious project like this faces is one of knowledge representation. We would like to think that our knowledge of language and of the world is, in some way, neat and packageable. Unfortunately, the world and the languages of the world are messy and inconsistent, and it is practically impossible to predict in advance how a thing will be used, and hence what properties need to be accounted for in its definition (see Cohen and Margalit 1972). This is not a damning theoretical point at all, but merely the observation that a hammer can be used as a paper weight, and a rock can be, and traditionally was, used as a hammer when of the appropriate heft. A more technical description of the system of ACQUILEX-typed feature structures was given in chapter 12.

The "Survey of NLP Lexicons"
Bob Ingria proposed a common format for lexicon transfer that he presented to the American Research Projects Agency (ARPA) common lexicon working group (1986). The goals of the common lexicon working group are to specify both the general structure of a lexical entry for Defense Advanced Research Projects Agency (DARPA) speech and language systems sites, and the format of information that appears in each entry slot. He has given a BNF description of the proposed common lexicon format, and proposals for a category system, morphological features, and a subcategorization system. Three examples were chosen from lexical items collected by the Text Encoding Initiative (TEI) Lexicon Working Group from the Information Services Institute (ISI)–Penman Lexicon, the UMIST Eurotra UK Monolingual English Lexicon, and the University of Helsinki/IBM Finland MENTOR/F System Lexicon. They were specified in their original format, and in their proposed interchange format.

Ingria noted that interchange via the lexicon is most likely to succeed if
it is limited to open-class items, and he suggested that interchange of information about closed-class items be done via grammatical descriptions,
or grammar fragments, since the treatment of closed-class items is highly
dependent on a system's grammar. Ingria believes that existing systems
tend to make fine-grained distinctions for closed class items, and that it
would be difficult to reconcile these differences. He therefore suggested
that closed class items be made available as a resource for new projects
rather than for interchange among fairly advanced projects.

The Linguistic Data Consortium
The Linguistic Data Consortium (LDC) at the University of Pennsylvania has been set up by ARPA to remedy a crisis in the provision of lexical
materials on a large scale to researchers and developers. It is intended to
be a "data factory" that will provide much larger amounts of data than
any one group can afford, by sharing those costs widely. The resulting
data will be true national assets, enabling a great deal of valuable research
and product development while simultaneously serving important government needs. The data envisioned include large quantities of raw and
annotated text and speech (billions of words of text and thousands of
hours of speech), a large lexicon, and a broad-coverage grammar of English. The data will also include whatever additional materials (including
foreign-language materials) the consortium can obtain by exchange or on
other reasonable terms. Where feasible, the consortium will acquire existing data (such as naturally occurring text) and put it in a standard format; in other cases it will produce data from scratch. The consortium will
also negotiate with foreign entities to make even larger and more varied
amounts of data available to members. Although the consortium does not
need exclusive rights to donated data, ARPA does intend to make its
growing holdings available exclusively through the consortium. Potential
members include many companies and universities plus several government agencies. General membership fees will be set at affordable levels,
and foreign members will be considered if access to foreign data can be
assured. Senior members (i.e., organizations willing to contribute significant sums of money) will have votes on the consortium's governing
board. The actual work will be done by various organizations (companies
and universities) under contract to the consortium.

Over the past 15 years, systematic use of linguistic data has been the
main engine of progress in speech research, and recent developments in

MT full-text information retrieval and text understanding tend in the same direction. However, no single organization has been able to afford to create enough linguistic data to satisfy its researchers, and many smaller groups have been seriously starved. In addition, wide-sharing of data has an added value due to its role in permitting quantitatively scored competition among research groups, as shown by the history of examples such as the Texas Instruments (TI) digits database, the ARPA resource management database, and the Brown corpus.

The LDCs goals are to acquire or create linguistic data according to the evolving needs of its members; transform these data into a consistent, accessible form; establish the right of consortium members to use these data in research and in appropriate product development; and distribute these data to its members in a timely way.

The LDC has recently funded the construction of COMLEX, a project that will create a moderately broad-coverage computational lexicon of English (beginning with a vocabulary of 35,000 headwords), to be used in a variety of research and commercial text analysis tasks. Its initial focus will be on syntactic information, because of the greater consensus that exists regarding how to encode this information. Other, mainly semantic, information may be added later.

All the verbs in the lexicon will have detailed subcategorization, as well as adjectives and nouns with complements. To ensure that the lexicon can be widely used, the COMLEX subcategorization frames are being compared and cross-referenced to other subcategorization systems, such as the Brandeis verb lexicon, the AQUILEX lexicon, the New York University (NYU) Linguistic String Project, OALD, and LDOCE codes. COMLEX's syntactic lexicon specifications (now being developed at NYU) are nearly complete. The current plan is to populate this dictionary by hand, with reference to a large corpus and several existing dictionaries, starting at NYU in 1993.

LDC Contact: Mark Liberman, myl@unagi.cis.upenn.edu.

The Consortium for Lexical Research

The Association for Computational Linguistics (ACL) proposed that a Consortium for Lexical Research (CLR) be established, and ARPA agreed to fund this. It was sited at the Computing Research Laboratory, Las Cruces, New Mexico, under its director, Yorick Wilks, and an ACL committee consisting of Roy Byrd, Ralph Grishman, Mark Liberman, and the late Don Walker.

The CLR is an organization for sharing lexical data and tools used to perform research on natural language dictionaries and lexicons, and for communicating the results of that research. Members of the consortium contribute resources to a repository and withdraw resources from it in order to perform their research. There is no requirement that withdrawals be compensated by contributions in kind.

A basic premise of the proposal for cooperation on lexical research is that the research must be "precompetitive." That is, the CLR does not have as its goal the creation of commercial products. The goal of precompetitive research is to augment our understanding of what lexicons contain and, specifically, to build computational lexicons having those contents.

The task of the CLR is primarily to facilitate research, making available to the whole NLP community certain resources now held by only a few groups that have special relationships with companies or dictionary publishers. The CLR, as far as is practically possible, accepts contributions from any source, regardless of theoretical orientation, and makes them available as widely as possible for research. There is also an underlying theoretical assumption or hope that the contents of major lexicons are very similar, and that some neutral, or "polytheoretic," form of the information they contain can be at least a research goal, and would be a great boon if it could be achieved. A major activity of the CLR is to negotiate agreements with "providers" on reassuring and advantageous terms to both suppliers and researchers. Major funders of work in this area in the United States have indicated interest in making participation in the CLR a condition for financial support of research.

Resources and Services of the Consortium

Data
1. Word lists (proper nouns, count/mass nouns, causative verbs, movement verbs, predicate adjectives, etc.)
2. Published dictionaries
3. Specialized terminology, technical glossaries, etc.
4. Statistical data
5. Synonyms, antonyms, hypernyms, pertainyms, etc.
6. Phrase lists

Tools
1. Lexical database management tools
2. Lexical query languages

3. Text analysis tools (concordance, KWIC, statistical analysis, collocation analysis, etc.)
4. Standard generalized markup language (SGML) tools (particularly
tuned to dictionary encoding)
5. Parsers
6. Morphological analyzers
7. User interfaces to dictionaries
8. Lexical workbenches
9. Dictionary definition sense taggers

Services
Repository management involves cataloging and storing material in dis-
parate formats, and providing for their retransmission (with conversion,
where appropriate tools exist). In addition, there is a library of documentation describing the repository's contents and containing research
papers resulting from projects that use the material. A brief description of
the services to be provided is as follows:
1. CRL will provide a catalog of, and act as a clearinghouse for, utilities
programs that have been written for existing on-line lexical data.
2. CRL will compile a list of known mistakes, misprints, etc. that occur
in each of the major published sources (dictionaries, etc.).
3. CRL will set up a new memorandum series explicitly devoted to the
lexical center.
4. CRL will also be a clearinghouse for preprints and hard-to-find re-
prints on MRDs.
5. CRL also expects to continue to conduct workshops in this area, following inaugural workshops in 1992 and 1993.
6. CRL would provide a catalog for access to repositories of corpus-
manipulation tools held elsewhere.

During 1992 the repository grew significantly to about 100 items and
the consortium membership quadrupled in that year. Information about
the CLR, including the catalog of offerings, the membership or provider
agreements, or any back numbers of the newsletter can be obtained from
lexical@nmsu.edu.

Conclusion: Evaluating Lexicons?

An important question everywhere in NLP these days is how one eval-
uates what one does. Until recently this was a question that could only

really be asked of MT, but the climate and methodology of evaluation has now spread over the whole terrain. Much NLP is undoubtedly "lexically driven," but the lexicon can never be more than a component in an NLP system, and the question naturally arises as to whether the lexicon can be evaluated separately from the whole application of which it is a part.

Some would argue that any lexicon evaluation must be piggybacked on one of the existing text evaluation schemes, since it would be difficult to get participants to devote their resources to an entirely separate evaluation method. A "glass box" evaluation might be one that looked explicitly at the information contained in lexicons. Yet, as we have seen, lexicons are created for specific grammars and grammar formalisms, so the types of information they contain may not be commensurate. A "black box" evaluation would keep the system constant, and swap various lexicons, and examine how well the system performed on the given task with each lexicon separately. The problem with this method is that using multiple lexicons involves a great deal of work to translate from the lexicon's representation to that used by the general linguistic system. In the meantime, the problem presented by the glass box proposal remains insuperable.

Ingria (1986) has reported on a "lexical ablation" experiment performed with the Bolf-Berunek and Newman Corp. PLUM system in the MUC-3 domain. Various percentages of the system's semantic lexicon were reduced, showing a steady decrease in recall with decrease in lexicon size.

Is the MRD Era Over?

The trends described briefly in this final chapter suggest that MRD-related work may be at a turning point. No one doubts the value of lexicons in NLP work except the most unrepentant "statistics alone" (Brown et al. 1988, 1991) theorist. Nor does anyone question that lexicons should be derived by the most automatic possible means. Dispute centers on two issues. First, are existing MRDs played-out, in that what can be extracted from them has been, and in any case are they out of date and defective? Those who answer yes to this may go on to support either the construction of new dictionaries and lexicons by a mixture of traditional and automatic methods, or may wish to go directly to a lexicon derived from a corpus if they believe that methodology has been, or can be, fully defined. Those who take these views tend to be less patient with enterprises such as SGML formats for dictionary interchange, or any format for lexicon interchange, since they believe those will only be used for out-of-date dictionaries and lexicons.

Second, a related but independent issue is the legal and copyright one. Many researchers and consortia like LDC have grown increasingly frustrated at dealing with the publishers of MRDs and attempting to get permission from them to use those works for research, for later commercial applications, and for further distribution in different formats to the research community (e.g., by the CLR as described above).

Publishers, naturally, have profits to make and precious resources to safeguard, and see themselves as being as flexible as they can be in a difficult world. Some publishers have indeed made MRD materials widely available for research and struck a number of commercial deals for incorporation of MRDs in software products.

However, problems undoubtedly remain. Publishers' positions are being undermined by the promised easy availablity of large dictionary-lexicons like the EDR interfaces and lexicons, and the CUP enterprise can be seen as an attempt to take up a position of open access (or as open as possible) from the beginning so as to deal with these issues.

The COMLEX lexicon construction project funded by LDC can be seen as a response to what it perceives as the intransigence of publishers and an attempt to set up a lexicon project free of legal constraint. Again, the risk is that just another dictionary will be produced, one with no special status or authority.

So much good software has been built to access MRDs like LDOCE that it is hard to believe they will not remain valuable to the research community, whatever their faults. No existing extraction of them to an LKB can ever be definitive, and there will always be a need to transfer the original MRD in a relatively unprocessed format. In the programming language world, ADA was an unfortunate precedent where a standard was imposed on the research community too soon.

Whatever the longevity of MRDs or otherwise, much NLP will need larger technical and domain-specific lexicons and these can probably only be gathered from corpora, so the lexicon-corpus effort and attention balance will inevitably shift more and more toward the corpus as time goes on. Discussion will continue as to whether the dictionary-lexicon should be (1) wholly derived from the corpus, as Hanks has promised with the OUP-DEC project (but no one can see quite how that could be achieved), or (2) constantly "tuned" to it, so as to remain up to date, or (3) at least containing attested sentences, as in COBUILD.

There is no doubt that a number of independent forces are moving us beyond reliance on MRDs, not only for contractual reasons and the perceived (by some) rebarbativeness of publishers but also because of their inadequacies from the point of view of certain theories of lexical content and structure (as with the Typed Feature Structures school and the new producers, like CUP), and because of the dynamic primacy of text vs. the derivative passivity of dictionaries. Time will tell, as empiricists often add at this point, often without any great optimism.

What is occasionally overlooked in these sometimes pessimistic assessments are the fundamental assumptions driving MRD work in the first place. These assumptions being, not coincidentally, the major themes of this book: sufficiency, extricability, and bootstrapping.

Do MRDs contain sufficient information to do all we need done to texts? After many years of hard work, amid considerable progress, the jury is still out. Clearly, no dictionary will supply all the information required for every linguistic theory, but that was never a serious requirement. Nobody knows what "pragmatic force" is, to choose a random example, and one would not expect MRDs to provide lexical entries coded for that. The sufficiency question is a different one: Do MRDs provide enough to make MTDs that are useful, robust, and extensible?

The extricability question is very much related: Given there is information in there, can we get at it? And will it come along quietly, or will it be more trouble than it is worth? Experience tells us guarded optimism is appropriate here. If anything, this book is a monument to extricablity, and its pages are filled with success stories of various sorts.

The final component of our triad, bootstrapping, is the most interesting question, and the one that will take us into the twenty-first century. The NMSU lexical research program has always held bootstrapping as a central tenet, and the most promising work in our worldwide survey has that flavor. The key to maintaining a lexical knowledge base is extensibilty: the will to keep up with the languages of the world as they change day by day. Corpora keep us current, and the world is going toward corpora-based studies of various sorts. Moving in that direction from an MRD foundation, as many seem to be, is a bootstrapping strategy in the finest tradition.

The other bootstrapping direction lies toward coalescing MRDs with other sorts of formatted texts, the encyclopedia being the obvious choice.

This is one avenue that has not been explored extensively, but it makes so much sense that it cannot be far away. There is no easy way to distinguish word knowledge from world knowledge, and no principled reason for dictionaries to remain distinct from encyclopedias.

Johnson wrote at the end of his labors that his dictionary "fell from him with frigid tranquility." We hope that, at the end of this much lighter task, we have conveyed something of the great energy and cheerfulness of this new field.

References

Aarts, J. H. 1985. Computational tools for the syntactic analysis of corpora. *Linguistics*, 23, pp. 303-335.

Abney, S. 1990. Rapid incremental parsing with repair. *Proceedings of the Sixth Annual Conference of the Centre for the New Oxford English Dictionary.* Waterloo, Ontario: University of Waterloo, pp. 1-9.

Ahlswede, T., and M. Evens. 1988. Generating a relational lexicon from a machine-readable dictionary. Edited by W. Frawley and R. Smith. *Problems in Lexicographic Form. International Journal of Lexicography*, 1:214-238. [Also presented at the Workshop on Machine Readable Dictionaries, SRI, Menlo Park, Calif., April 1983.]

Akkerman, E. 1989. An independent analysis of the LDOCE Grammar Coding System. In *Computational Lexicography for Natural Language Processing.* Edited by B. K. Boguraev and T. Briscoe. Essex, UK: Longman Group, pp. 65-84.

Alexandrosen, R., E. Hajicova, and H. Janajic. 1992. Derivation of underlying valency frames from a learner's dictionary. *Proceedings of the 15th International Conference on Computational Linguistics*, August 1992. Nantes, France.

Alshawi, H. 1987. *Memory and Context for Language Interpretation.* Cambridge, England: Cambridge University Press.

Alshawi, H., B. K. Boguraev, and T. Briscoe. 1985. Towards a dictionary support environment for real time parsing. *Proceedings of the Second European Conference on Computational Linguistics.* Cambridge, England: Computer Laboratory, Cambridge University, pp. 171-178.

Alty, J. L. and M. L. Coombs. 1984. *Expert Systems: Concepts and Examples.* Manchester, UK: National Computer Centre.

Amsler, R. A. 1980. *Dictionary Databases.* Cambridge, England: Computer Laboratory, Cambridge University.

Amsler, R. A. 1980. The structure of the Merriam-Webster Pocket Dictionary. *Technical Report*, TR-164. University of Texas at Austin.

Amsler, R. A. 1982. Computational lexicology: a research program. *AFIPS Conference Proceedings, 1982 National Computer Conference*, pp. 657-663.

Amsler, R. A. 1989. Third generation computational lexicography. *Proceedings of the First International Lexical Acquisition Workshop.* Edited by U. Zernick. Detroit: Artificial Intelligence and Information Research Group.

Amsler, R. A., and J. White. 1979. Development of a computational methodology for deriving natural language semantic structures via analysis of machine-readable dictionaries. *NSF Technical Report*, MCS77-01315, Washington, D.C.

Anick, P., and J. Pustejovsky. 1990. *An Application of Lexical Semantics to Knowledge Acquisition from Corpora.* 13th International Conference COLING-90, Helsinki, pp. 1–6.

Antal, L. 1963. *Questions of Meaning.* The Hague: Mouton.

Asher, N. and M. Morreau. 1991. Commonsense entailment. In *Proceedings of the Twelfth International Joint Conference on Artificial Intelligence.* Sydney, Australia, pp. 387–392.

Atkins, B., and B. Levin, 1990. Admitting impediments. In *Using On-Line Resources to Build a Lexicon.* Edited by U. Zernik. Hillsdale, N.J.: Lawrence Erlbaum.

Atkins, B. T., J. Kegl, and B. Levin. 1986. Explicit and implicit information in dictionaries. *CSL Report 5.* Princeton, N.J.: Princeton University.

Atkins, B. T. S., and A. Zampolli (Eds.). 1994. *Computational Approaches to the Lexicon.* New York: Oxford University Press.

Austin, J. 1962. *How to do Things with Words.* Cambridge, Mass.: Harvard University Press.

Ayer, A. J. 1946. *Language, Truth and Logic.* London: Gollancz.

Bahl, L., P. Brown, P. DeSouza, and R. Mercer. 1989. A tree-based statistical language model for natural language and speech recognition. *IEEE Transactions on Acoustics, Speech and Signal Processing*, 37:7.

Ballim, A. and Y. Wilks. 1991. *Artificial Believers.* Hillsdale, N.J.: Lawrence Erlbaum.

Barnett, J. E., E. Rich, and D. Wroblewski. 1991. Functional interface to a knowledge base for use by a natural language processing system. *MCC Technical Report Series*, ACT-NL-019-91.

Beckwith, R., C. Fellbaum, D. Gross, and G. A. Miller. 1989. Word Net: a lexical database organized on psycholinguistic principles. *Proceedings of the First International Lexical Acquisition Workshop (IJCAI-89).* Detroit.

Belew, R. 1986. Adaptive information retrieval. Ph.D. thesis, University of Michigan.

Bierwisch, M. 1970. Semantics. In *New Horizons in Linguistics.* Edited by J. Lyons. Harmondsworth, England: Penguin Books.

Binot, J. L., and K. Jensen. 1987. A semantic expert using an online standard dictionary. *Proceedings of the 10th International Joint Conference on Artificial Intelligence*, vol. 2. Milan: pp. 709–714.

Birkhoff, G. 1961. *Lattice Theory.* Providence, R.I.: American Mathematical Society.

Bobrow, D., and T. Winograd. 1975. An overview of KRL: a knowledge representation language. *Cognitive Science*, 1:29–42.

Bobrow, D., and T. Winograd. 1977. KRL: another perspective. *Cognitive Science*, 3:29–43.

Boguraev, B. K. 1987. *A Description of the Cambridge "Lispfied" Version of the LDOCE Master Tape.* Cambridge, England: Cambridge University.

Boguraev, B. K. 1989. *Building a Lexicon: The Contribution of Computational Lexicography.* Yorktown Heights, N.Y.: IBM Research.

Boguraev, B. K., and T. Briscoe. 1987. Large lexicons for natural language processing: exploring the grammar coding system of LDOCE. *Computational Linguistics*, 13:203–218.

Boguraev, B. K., T. Briscoe, J. Carroll, D. Carter, and C. Grover. 1987. The derivation of a grammatically indexed lexicon from the Longman Dictionary of Contemporary English. *Proceedings of the 25th Annual Meeting of the Association for Computational Linguistics.* Stanford, Calif.: Stanford University, pp. 193–200.

Boguraev, B. K., and T. Briscoe (Eds.). 1989. *Computational Lexicography for Natural Language Processing.* London: Harlow.

Boguraev, B. K., R. J. Byrd, J. L. Klavans, and M. S. Neff. 1989. From structural analysis of lexical resources to semantics in a lexical knowledge base. *Proceedings of the International Joint Conference on Artificial Intelligence.* Detroit.

Boguraev, B. K., and B. Levin. 1990. Models for lexical knowledge bases. *Sixth Annual Conference of the UW Centre for the New Oxford English Dictionary and Text Research.* Waterloo, Ontario, Canada: University of Waterloo.

Boguraev, B. K., and J. Pustejovsky. 1990. Lexical ambiguity and the role of knowledge representation in lexicon design. *Proceedings of the 13th International Conference on Computational Linguistics (COLING-90)*, vol. 2. Helsinki, pp. 36–41.

Boguraev, B. K., and J. Pustejovsky. 1993. A richer characterization of dictionary entries. In *Towards a Lexicographer's Workstation.* Edited by A. Zampolli and N. Calzolari. Oxford, England: Oxford University Press.

Bolinger, D. 1965. The atomization of meaning. *Language*, 41:555–573.

Braithwaite, R. B. 1962. Models in the empirical sciences. *Proceedings of the 1960 International Congress on Logic, Methodology and Philosophy of Science.* Edited by E. Nagel, P. Suppes, and A. Tarski. Stanford, Calif.

Brent, M. 1991. Automatic acquisition of subcategorization frames from untagged free-text corpora. In *Proceedings of the Twenty-ninth Annual Meeting of the Association for Computational Linguistics.* Berkeley, Calif.: Association for Computational Linguistics, pp. 305–333.

Bridgman, P. 1936. *The Nature of Physical Theory.* Princeton. N.J.: Princeton University Press.

Brouwer, L. 1952. Historical background, principles and methods of intuitionism. *South African Journal of Science*, 49:136–150.

Brown, P., J. Cocke, S. Della Pietra, V. Della Pietra, F. Jelinek, R. Mercer, and P. Roossin. 1988. A statistical approach to language translation. *Proceedings of the 12th International Conference on Computational Linguistics.* Budapest, pp. 71–74.

Brown, P., A. D. Pietra, V. J. Pietra, and R. Mercer. 1991. Word sense disambiguation using statistical methods. *Proceedings of the 29th Annual Meeting of the Association for Computational Linguistics.* Berkeley, Calif., pp. 264–304.

Bruce, R., and L. Guthrie. 1992. Genus disambiguation: a study in weighted preference. *Proceedings of the 16th International Conference on Computational Linguistics (COLING-92).* Nantes, France, pp. 1187–1191.

Bruce, R., Y. Wilks, and L. Guthrie. 1992. *NounSense.* MCCS-92-246. Las Cruces N.M.: Computing Research Laboratory.

Burgess, C. and G. B. Simpson. 1989. Neuropsychology of lexical ambiguity resolution: the contribution of divided visual field studies. In *Lexical Ambiguity Resolution.* Edited by S. L. Small, G. W. Cottrell, and M. K. Tannenhaus. San Mateo, Calif.: Morgan Kaufmann, pp. 411–430.

Byrd, R. J. 1989. Large-scale cooperation on large-scale lexical acquisition. In *Proceedings of the First International Lexical Acquisition Workshop.* Edited by U. Zernick. Detroit, Michigan. [Revised version of a paper originally presented at the 1989 IJCAI Lexical Acquisition workshop, Detroit.]

Byrd, R., N. Calzolari, M. S. Chodorow, J. L. Klavans, M. S. Neff, and O. A. Rizk. 1987. Tools and methods for computational lexicology. *Computational Linguistics*, 13:219–240.

Calzolari, N. 1977. An empirical approach to circularity in dictionary definitions. *Cahiers de Lexicologie*, 31:118–128.

Calzolari, N. 1984. Machine-readable dictionaries, lexical databases and the lexical system. *Proceedings of the 10th International Conference on Computational Linguistics.* Stanford, Calif.

Calzolari, N. 1988. The dictionary and the thesaurus can be combined. In *Relational Models of the Lexicon.* Edited by M. Evens. *Studies in Natural Language Processing.* Cambridge, England: Cambridge University Press, pp. 75–96.

Calzolari, N. 1990. Lexical databases and textual corpora: perspectives of integration for a lexical knowledge-base. *Proceedings of a Workshop on Lexical Acquisition, Detroit.* Cambridge, Mass.: MIT Press. [also ESPRIT BRA-3030 ACQUILEX WP NO.006].

Calzolari, N., and R. Bindi. 1990. Acquisition of lexical information from a large textual Italian corpus. *Proceedings of COLING 1990*, vol. 3. Helsinki, pp. 54–59.

Calzolari, N., and A. Zampolli. 1989. Lexical data bases and textual corpora: a trend of convergence between computational linguistics and literary and linguistic computing. *Association for Literary and Linguistic Computing/Association for Computing in the Humanities Conference.* Toronto.

Carnap, R. and Y. Bar-Hillel. 1952. An outline of a theory of semantic information. *Technical Report No. 247.* Cambridge, Mass.: Massachusetts Institute of Technology.

Carpenter, B. 1992. Typed feature structures. *Computational Linguistics,* 18:121–141.

Carter, D. 1989. LDOCE and speech recognition. In *Computational Lexicography for Natural Language Processing.* Edited by B. K. Boguraev and T. Briscoe. Harlow, England: Longman, pp. 135–152.

Catizone, R., G. Russell, and S. Warwick. 1989. Deriving Translation Data from Bilingual Texts. Edited by U. Zernik. In *Proceedings of the First International Workshop on Lexical Acquisition.* Detroit.

Charniak, E. 1975. A brief on case. *Institute for the Study of Semantics and Cognition memo,* 22. Castagnola, Switzerland.

Chodorow, M., R. Byrd, and G. Heidorn. 1985. Extracting semantic hierarchies from a large on-line dictionary. *Proceedings of the 23rd Annual Meeting of the Association for Computational Linguistics.* Chicago, pp. 299–304.

Chomsky, N. 1965. *Aspects of the Theory of Syntax.* Cambridge, Mass.: MIT Press.

Chomsky, N. 1970. Remarks on nominalization. *Readings in English Transformational Grammar.* Edited by R. Jacobs and P. Rosenbaum. Waltham, Mass.: Ginn, pp. 184–221. [Reprinted in Chomsky, N. 1972. *Studies on Semantics in Generative Grammar,* The Hague: Mouton, pp. 11–61.]

Chomsky, N. 1981. *Lectures on Government and Binding.* Dordrecht, Netherlands: Foris.

Chomsky, N. 1986. *Knowledge of Language: Its Nature, Origin and Use.* New York: Praeger.

Choueka, Y., and S. Luisgnan. 1985. Disambiguation by short context. *Computers and the Humanities,* 19:147–157.

Church, K., W. Gale, P. Hanks, and D. Hindle. 1989. Parsing, Word Associations and Typical Predicate-Argument Relations. *International Workshop on Parsing Technologies,* Carnegie-Mellon University, August 28–31.

Church, K. W., and P. Hanks. 1990. Word association norms, mutual information, and lexicography. *Computational Linguistics,* 16, pp. 22–29.

Cohen, L. J., and A. Margalit. 1972. The role of inductive reasoning in the interpretation of metaphor. In *Semantics of Natural language.* Edited by D. Davidson and G. Harman. Dordrecht, Netherlands: Reidel.

Collins, A. M., and E. F. Loftus. 1975. A spreading activation theory of semantic processing. *Psychological Review,* 82, pp. 407–428.

Cooper, W. S. 1969. Is interindexer consistency a hobgoblin? *American Documentation,* 20, pp. 268–278.

Copestake, A. 1990. An approach to building the hierarchical element of a lexical knowledge base from a machine readable dictionary. *Proceedings of the First*

International Workshop on Inheritance in Natural Language Processing, Tilburg, Netherlands, pp. 19–29. [also ESPRIT BRA-3030 ACQUILEX WP NO.008].

Copestake, A. and E. J. Briscoe. 1991. Lexical operations in a unification-based framework. In *Proceedings of ACL SIGLEX Workshop on Lexical Semantics and Knowledge Representation, Berkeley, California*, pp. 88–101. [Also ESPRIT BRA-3030 AC-QUILEX WP NO.021.]

Cottrell, G. W. 1985. A connectionist approach to word sense disambiguation. (TR154). Ph.D. thesis, University of Rochester Computer Science Department.

Cowie, J., J. Guthrie, and L. Guthrie. 1992. Lexical disambiguation using simulated annealing. *Proceedings of the 16th International Conference on Computational Linguistics (COLING-92)*. Nantes, France, pp. 359–365.

Cowie, J., L. Guthrie, Y. Wilks, and J. Pustejovsky. 1992. CRL/NMSU and Brandeis MucBruce: MUC-4 test results and analysis. *Proceedings of the Fourth Message Understanding Conference (MUC-4)*, June 16–18. McLean, Va., pp. 120–123.

Cowie, J., and B. Ogden. 1993. *Workshop summaries for the Symposium on Advanced Information Processing and Analysis.* Tyson's Corner, Va., US Department of Defense.

Croft, W. B. 1986. Boolean queries and term dependencies in probabilistic retrieval models. *Journal of the American Society for Information Science*, 37:71–77.

Cruse, D. A. 1986. *Lexical Semantics.* Cambridge, England: Cambridge University Press.

Dagan, I., and A. Itai. 1990. Automatic acquisition of constraints for the resolution of anaphora references and syntactic ambiguities. *Technical Report*, No. 626. Haifa, Israel.

Dagan, I., A. Itai, and U. Schwall. 1991. Two languages are more informative than one. *Proceedings of the 29th Annual Meeting of the Association for Computational Linguistics.* Berkeley, Calif. pp. 130–137.

Dailey, D. P. 1986. The extraction of a minimum set of semantic primitives from a monolingual dictionary is NP-complete. *Computational Linguistics*, 12:306–307.

Davidson, D. 1959. In defense of convention T. In *Truth, Syntax and Modality*. Edited by H. Leblanc. Amsterdam: North Holland.

Davidson, D. 1970. Semantics for natural languages. *Linguaggi nella Societa e nella Tecnica.* Milan: Visentini, pp. 170–190.

Davies, J., and J. Isard. 1972. Utterences as programs. *Machine Intelligence*, vol. 7. Edited by D. Michie and B. Meltzer. Edinburgh: Edinburgh University Press.

DeJong, G. 1979. *Skimming Stories in Real Time.* New Haven: Yale University Press.

Doreian, P. 1974. On the connectivity of social networks. *Journal of Mathematical Sociology*, 3:245–258.

Dorr, B. 1991. Conceptual basis of the lexicon in machine translation. In *Lexical Acquisition: Using On-Line Resources to Build a Lexicon.* Edited by U. Zernik. Hillsdale, N.J.: Lawrence Erlbaum, pp. 263–307.

Dowty, D. R. 1979. *Word Meaning and Montague Grammar.* Dordrecht, Netherlands: Reidel.

Dreyfus, H. L. 1979. *What Computers Can't Do: The Limits of Artificial Intelligence,* ed. 2. New York: Harper & Row.

Evans, R. and G. Gazdar (Eds.). 1990. The DATR Papers. *Cognitive Science Reports,* vol. 1. (CSRP 139) University of Sussex.

Evens, M. (Ed.). 1988. *Relational Models of the Lexicon.* Cambridge, England: Cambridge University Press.

Evens, M., and S. Conlon. 1990. Generating a lexical database for adverbs. *Sixth Annual Conference of the University of Waterloo Centre for the New Oxford English Dictionary and Text Research.* Waterloo, Ontario: University of Waterloo.

Farwell, D., L. Guthrie, and Y. A. Wilks. 1993. Using machine readable dictionaries for the creation of lexicons. *Proceedings of the AAAI Spring Symposium on BUILDING Lexicons for Machine Translation.* Stanford University.

Fass, D. C. 1988. An account of coherence, semantic relations, metonymy, and lexical ambiguity resolution. In *Lexical Ambiguity Resolution in the Comprehension of Human Language.* Edited by S. L. Small, G. W. Cottrell, and M. K. Tannenhaus. Los Altos, Calif.: Morgan Kaufmann, pp. 151–178.

Fidel, R. 1986. Towards expert systems for the selection of search keys. *Journal of the American Society for Information Science,* 37:37–44.

Fillmore, C. J. 1968. The case for case. In *Universals in Linguistic Theory.* Edited by E. Bach and R. Harms. New York: Holt, Rinehart, & Winston, pp. 1–88.

Firth, J. 1957. A synopsis of linguistic theory 1930–1955. In *Selected Papers of J. R. Firth.* Edited by F. Palmer. *Studies in Linguistic Analysis.* London: Longmans.

Fodor, J. 1975. *The Language of Thought.* New York: Thomas Crowell.

Fodor, J. A. 1980. Methodological solipsism considered as a research strategy in cognitive psychology. *Behavioral and Brain Sciences,* 3:63–73. [Reprinted in *Mind Design,* 1981. Edited by J. Haugeland. Cambridge, Mass.: MIT Press.]

Fodor, J. A. 1983. *The Modularity of Mind: An Essay on Faculty Psychology.* Cambridge, Mass.: MIT Press.

Fodor, J. 1988. Why there still has to be a language of thought. In *The Foundations of AI: A Source Book.* Edited by D. Partridge and Y. Wilks. Cambridge, England: Cambridge University Press. [Originally published in 1987 in *Psychosemantics* Cambridge, Mass.: MIT Press.]

Fontenelle, T. 1990a. Automatic extraction of lexical-semantic relations from dictionary definitions. *EURALEX,* pp. 89–103.

Fontenelle, T. 1990b. Improving the terminological dimension in a computational lexical. *Revue d'Informatique et des Sciences Humaines,* 16, pp. 83–91.

Fontenelle, T., and J. Vanandroye. 1989. Retrieving ergative verbs from a lexical database. *Dictionaries: Journal of the Dictionary Society of North America,* 11, pp. 11–39.

Fowler, H. 1926. *A Dictionary of Modern English Usage.* Oxford, England: Clarendon Press.

Fowler, R. H., and D. W. Dearholt. 1989. Pathfinder networks in information retrieval. In *Memorandum in Computer and Cognitive Science.* MCCS-89-147. Las Cruces, N.M.: Computing Research Laboratory, New Mexico State University.

Fowler, R. H., and D. W. Dearholt. 1990. Information retrieval using Pathfinder networks. In *Pathfinder Associative Networks: Studies in Knowledge Organization.* Edited by R. W. Schvanevelt. Norwood, N.J.: Ablex.

Fowler, R. H., and B. M. Slator. 1989. Information retrieval and natural language analysis. *Proceedings of the Fourth Annual Rocky Mountain Conference on Artificial Intelligence.* Denver, June 8–9, pp. 129–136.

Frege, G. [1982] 1952. On sense and reference. In *Frege: Philosophical Writings.* Edited by P. T. Geach and M. Black. Oxford, England: Blackwell.

Furnas, G. W., T. K. Landauer, L. M. Gomez, and S. T. Dumais. 1983. Statistical semantics: analysis of the potential performance of keyword information systems. *The Bell System Technical Journal,* 62:1753–1806.

Gale, W., K. Church, and D. Yarowsky. 1992. A method for disambiguating word senses in a large corpus. *AT&T Bell Laboratories Statistical Research Report No. 104.* Murray Hill, N.J.: AT&T Bell Laboratories.

Garside, R. and G. Leech. 1982. Grammatical tagging of the LOB corpus: general survey. In *Computer Corpora in English Language Research.* Edited by S. Johansson. Bergen: Norwegian Computing Centre for the Humanities, pp. 36–42.

Gigley, H. 1989. Process synchronization, lexical ambiguity resolution, and aphasia. In *Lexical Ambiguity Resolution.* Edited by S. L. Small, G. W. Cottrell, and M. K. Tannenhaus. San Mateo, Calif.: Morgan Kaufmann, pp. 229–267.

Givon, T. 1967. *Transformations of Ellipsis, Sense Development and Rules of Lexical Derivation.* SP-2896. Santa Monica, Calif.: Systems Development Corp.

Goodman, N. 1951. *The Structure of Appearance.* Cambridge Mass.: Harvard University Press.

Gove, P. B. (Ed.). 1969. *Webster's Seventh New Collegiate Dictionary.* Springfield, Mass.: Merriam-Webster.

Grice, H. 1957. Meaning. *Philosophical Review,* 56, pp. 76–97.

Grishman R., and J. Sterling. 1992. Acquisition of selectional patterns. *Proceedings of the 14th International Conference on Computational Linguistics (COLING-92).* Nantes, France.

Gross M. 1984. Lexicon-grammar and the syntactic analysis of French. *Proceedings of the Tenth International Joint Conference on Computational Linguistics (COLING-84).* Stanford, Calif., pp. 275–282.

Gross, M. 1986. Lexicon grammar: the representation of compound words. *Proceedings of the Eleventh International Joint Conference on Computational Linguistics (COLING-86).* Bonn, West Germany, pp. 1–6.

Gruber, J. S. 1976. *Lexical Structures in Syntax and Semantics.* Amsterdam: North Holland.

Guha, R. V., and D. B. Lenat. 1990. CyC: a midterm report. *AI*, 11, pp. 32–59.

Guo, C. 1989. Constructing a machine tractable dictionary from Longman Dictionary of Contemporary English. *Memoranda in Computer and Cognitive Science.* MCCS-89-156. Las Cruces, N.M.: Computing Research Laboratory, New Mexico State University.

Guo, C. (Ed.). 1992. *Machine Tractable Dictionaries: Design and Construction.* Norwood, N.J.: Ablex.

Guo, C. M. 1987. Interactive vocabulary acquisition in XTRA. *Proceedings of the 10th International Joint Conference on Artificial Intelligence (IJCAI-87)*, Milan, pp. 715–717.

Guthrie, J., L. Guthrie, Y. Wilks, and H. Aidinejad. 1991. Subject-dependent co-occurrence and word sense disambiguation. *Proceedings of the 29th Annual Meeting of the Association for Computational Linguistics.* Berkeley, Calif., pp. 146–152.

Guthrie, L., B. Slator, Y. Wilks, and R. Bruce. 1990. Is there content in empty heads? *Proceedings of the 13th International Conference on Computational Linguistics (COLING-90)*, vol. 3. Helsinki, pp. 138–143.

Halliday, M. A. 1980. *How is a Text Like a Clause?* Sydney, Australia: University of Sydney.

Hanks, P. 1978. To what extent does a dictionary definition define? Edited by R. K. Hartmann. *Papers from BAAL Lexicography Seminar.* Exeter, England: Exeter University.

Hanks, P. 1986. Typicality and meaning potentials. *ZURILEX-86 Proceedings.* Edited by S. Hornby. Zurich: Franke Verlag, pp. 142–167.

Hanks, P. 1987a. Definitions and explorations. *Looking Up.* Edited by J. M. Sinclair. Glasgow: Collins.

Hanks, P. (Ed.). 1987b. *Collins English Dictionary.* Glasgow: Collins.

Hanks, P. 1990. Towards a statistical dictionary of modern English: some preliminary reflections. *Proceedings BUDALEX-88.* Budapest, Akademiai Kiado.

Hanks, P. 1991. Evidence and intuition in lexicography. *Meaning and Lexicography.* Edited by J. Tomaszczyk and B. Lewardowska. Menlo Park, Calif.: Benjamins.

Hanks, P. W. 1994. Computational analysis and definitional structure. *Lexicographica Series.* Edited by H. Wiegand and F. Dolezal. Berlin: Maior, Neimeyer, pp. 321–333.

Harris, Z. 1957. Co-occurrence and transformation in linguistic structure. *Language*, 33:283–340.

Hart, H. 1961. *The Concept of Law.* Oxford, England: Oxford University Press.

Hayes, P. 1974. Some issues and non-issues in representation theory. *Proceedings of the Artificial Intelligence Society Bulletin Conference.* University of Sussex, England.

Hearst, M. 1991. Toward noun homonym disambiguation—using local context in large text corpora. *Proceedings of the Seventh Annual Conference of the UW Centre for the New Oxford English Dictionary and Text Research Using Corpora*, Waterloo, Ontario, University of Waterloo, pp. 1–22.

Heidorn, G. E., K. Hensen, L. A. Miller, R. J. Byrd, and M. S. Chodorow. 1982. The EPISTLE text-critiquing system. *The IBM Systems Journal*, 21, pp. 305–327.

Heidrich, C. 1973. Should generative semantics be related to intensional logic? *Formal Semantics of Natural Language*. Edited by E. Keenan. Cambridge, England: Cambridge University Press.

Hindle, D. 1983. User manual for Fidditch. *Naval Research Laboratory Technical Memorandum, 7590-142*. Bethesda, Maryland.

Hindle, D., and M. Rooth. 1990. Structural ambiguity and lexical relations. *Proceedings of the DARPA Speech and Natural Language Workshop*. Murray Hill, N.J. AT&T Bell Laboratories.

Hintikka, J. 1973. Language games for quantifiers. *Logic, Language Games and Information*. Oxford, England: Clarendon Press, pp. 56–79.

Hirst, G. 1987. *Semantic Interpretation and the Resolution of Ambiguity*. Cambridge, England: Cambridge University Press.

Hobbs, J. R. 1987. World knowledge and word meaning. *Proceedings of the Third Workshop on Theoretical Issues in Natural Language Processing (TINLAP-3)*. Las Cruces, N.M. pp. 20–25.

Hobbs, J. and S. Rosenschein. 1977. Making computational sense of Montague's intensional logic. *Courant Institute Computer Science Report No. 1*. New York: Courant Institute.

Hornby A. 1963. *The Advanced Learner's Dictionary of English*. Oxford, England: Oxford University Press.

Hornby, A. S. (Ed.). 1974. In *Oxford Advanced Learner's Dictionary of Current English*, 3rd ed. Oxford, England: Oxford University Press.

Horwill, H. 1935. *A Dictionary of Modern American Usage*. Oxford, England: Clarendon Press.

Hutchins, W. J. 1986. *Machine Translation: Past, Present, Future*. New York: Halsted Press, Ellis Horwood.

Ide, N., and J. Veronis. 1990a. Very large neural networks for word sense disambiguation. *European Conference on Artificial Intelligence (ECAI '90)*. Stockholm.

Ide, N. M., and J. Veronis. 1990b. Mapping dictionaries: a spreading activation approach. *Electronic Text Research, Proceedings of the Sixth Annual Conference of the Centre for the New Oxford English Dictionary*. Waterloo, Ontario: University of Waterloo, pp. 52–64.

Ingria, R. 1986. Lexical information for parsing systems: points of convergence and divergence. *Workshop on Automating the Lexicon*. Marina di Grosseto, Italy.

Jackendoff, R. 1972. *Semantic Interpretation in Generative Grammar.* Cambridge, Mass.: MIT Press.

Jackendoff, R. 1976. Toward an explanatory semantic representation. *Linguistic Inquiry,* 7:89–150.

Jackendoff, R. S. 1983. *Semantics and Cognition.* Cambridge, Mass.: MIT Press.

Jackendoff, R. S. 1990. *Semantic Structures.* Cambridge, Mass.: MIT Press.

Jansen, J., J. P. Morgeai, and J. Vanandroye. 1987. Controling LDOCE's controlled vocabulary. *The Dictionary and Language Learner.* Edited by A. Cowie. *Papers from EURALEX Seminar,* University of Leeds, Leeds, England, pp. 78–94.

JEDR. 1990. An overview of the EDR electronic dictionaries. *EDR Technical Report 024.* Tokyo, Japan: Japanese Electronic Dictionary Research Institute.

Jensen, K., and J. L. Binot. 1987. Disambiguating prepositional phrase attachments by using on-line dictionary definitions. *Computational Linguistics,* 13, pp. 251–260.

Johnson, S. [1755] 1827. *A Dictionary of the English Language.* Edited by H. J. Todd. London.

Johnson-Laird, P. 1974. Memory for words. *Nature,* 87, pp. 768.

Johnson-Laird, P. 1978. What's wrong with grandma's guide to procedural semantics. *Cognition,* 6, pp. 101–105.

Johnson-Laird, P. N., and J. Quinn. 1976. To define true meaning. *Nature,* 264, pp. 112–113.

Jones, W. P. 1986. On the applied use of human memory models: the memory extender personal filing system. *International Journal of Man-Machine Studies,* 25, pp. 191–228.

Jones, W. P., and G. W. Furnas. 1987. Pictures of relevance: a geometric analysis of similarity measures. *Information Processing and Management,* 38, pp. 420–442.

Joshi, A. 1974. *Factorization of Verbs.* Edited by C. Heidrich. Amsterdam: North Holland.

Katz, J. 1966. *The Philosophy of Language.* New York: Harper & Row.

Katz, J. 1972. *Semantic Theory.* New York: Harper & Row.

Katz, J., and J. Fodor. 1963. The structure of a semantic theory. *Language,* 39, pp. 170–210.

Kay, M. 1984. The Dictionary Server. *Proceedings of COLING-84.* Stanford, Calif.

Kay, M. 1989. The concrete lexicon and the abstract dictionary. *Proceedings of the Fifth Annual Conference of the University of Waterloo Centre for the New Oxford English Dictionary.* Oxford, England, pp. 35–41.

Kegl, J. 1987. The boundary between word knowledge and world knowledge. *Proceedings of the Third Workshop on Theoretical Issues in Natural Language Processing (TINLAP-3).* Las Cruces, N.M., pp. 26–31.

Kirkpatrick, S., C. D. Gelatt, and M. P. Vecchi. 1983. Optimization by simulated annealing. *Science*, 220, pp. 671–680.

Klavans, J., R. Byrd, N. Wacholder, and M. Chodorow. 1990. Taxonomy and polysemy. Preprint presented at the IBM International Technical Meeting. Paris, France.

Klavans, J., M. S. Chodorow, and N. Wacholder. 1990. From dictionary to knowledge base via taxonomy. *Electronic Text Research, Proceedings of the Sixth Annual Conference of the Centre for the New Oxford English Dictionary.* University of Waterloo, Waterloo, Ontario, pp. 110–132.

Klavans, J., and E. Tzoukermann. 1990a. Linking bilingual corpora and machine readable dictionaries with the BICORD system. *Electronic Text Research, Proceedings of the Sixth Annual Conference of the Centre for the New Oxford English Dictionary.* University of Waterloo, Waterloo, Ontario, pp. 19–30.

Klavans, J., and E. Tzoukermann. 1990b. The BICORD system: combining lexical information from bilingual corpora and machine readable dictionaries. *Proceedings of the 13th International Conference on Computational Linguistics.* Helsinki.

Knight, K. 1989. Integrating knowledge acquisition and language acquisition. Ph.D. thesis, Carnegie-Mellon University, Pittsburgh, Pa.

Krovetz, R. 1989. Lexical acquisition and information retrieval. In *Proceedings of the First International Lexical Acquisition Workshop.* Edited by U. Zernick. Detroit, Michigan.

Kucera, H., and W. N. Francis. 1967. *Computational Analysis of Present-Day American English.* Providence, R.I.: Brown University Press.

Lehmann, Fritz (Ed.). 1992. *Semantic Networks in Artificial Intelligence.* New York: Pergamon Press. [Also in *Computers and Mathematics with Applications: an International Journal (CMAIJ)*, 23 (6–9).]

Lehnert, W. G. 1990. Symbolic/subsymbolic sentence analysis. In *Advances in Connectionist and Neural Computation.* Edited by J. Pollack and J. Barnden. Norwood, N.J.: Ablex, pp. 135–164.

Leibowitz, M., and G. Fjermedal. 1988. Brain trusts. *Omni,* June, pp. 44–50.

Lenat, D. B., and E. A. Feigenbaum. 1987. On the thresholds of knowledge. *Proceedings of the 10th International Joint Conference on Artificial Intelligence (IJCAI-87).* Milan, pp. 1173–1182.

Lenat, D. B., M. Prakash, and M. Shepherd. 1986. CYC: using common sense knowledge to overcome brittleness and knowledge acquisition bottlenecks. *AI* 7, pp. 65–85.

Lesk, M. 1986. Automatic sense disambiguation using machine readable dictionaries: how to tell a pine cone from an ice cream cone. *Proceedings of the ACM SIGDOC Conference,* Toronto, Ontario, pp. 24–26.

Levin, B. 1993. *English Verb Classes and Alternations: A Preliminary Investigation.* Chicago: University of Chicago Press.

Lewis, D. 1972. General semantics. *Semantics of Natural Language*. Edited by D. Davidson and G. Harman. Dordrecht, Netherlands: Reidel.

Longuet-Higgins, C. 1972. The algorithmic description of natural language. *Proceedings of the Royal Society*, 182, pp. 1170–1175.

Lorge, I. 1938. The English semantic count. *Teacher's College Record*, pp. 65–77.

Lyons, J. 1968. *Introduction to Theoretical Linguistics*. Cambridge, England: Cambridge University Press.

Luhn, H. P. 1968. *H. P. Luhn: Pioneer of Information Science; Selected Works*. Edited by C. K. Schultz. New York: Spartan Books.

Mandelbrot, B. 1961. On the theory of word frequencies and on related Markovian models of discourse. In *Proceedings of the Symposia in Applied Mathematics*, vol. XII. Providence, R.I.: American Mathematics Society, pp. 190–219.

Mann, W. C. 1983. An overview of the Penman text generation system. In *Proceedings of the American Conference on Artificial Intelligence*. pp. 261–265.

Markowitz, J., T. Ahlswede, and M. Evens. 1986. Semantically significant patterns in dictionary definitions. *Proceedings of the 24th Annual Meeting of the Association for Computational Linguistics*, New York, pp. 112–119.

Martin, J. H. 1992. *The Meta Bank Project: A Knowledge Base of Metaphoric Language Conventions*. Boulder: Institute of Cognitive Science, University of Colorado.

Martin, W. 1992. Concept-oriented parsing of definitions. *Proceedings of the 15th International Conference on Computational Linguistics*. Nantes, France, August 1992.

Masterman, M. 1957. The thesaurus in syntax and semantics. *Mechanical Translation*, 4, pp. 1–2.

McArthur, T. (Ed.). 1981. *Longman Lexicon of Contemporary English*. Harlow: Longman.

McCarthy, J., and P. J. Hayes. 1969. Some philosophical problems from the standpoint of artificial intelligence. In *Machine Intelligence 4*. Edited by B. Meltzer and D. Michie. Edinburgh: Edinburgh University Press, pp. 463–502.

McCord, M. C. 1980. Slot grammars. *Computational Linguistics*, 6:31–43.

McCord, M. C. 1989. Design of LMT: a Prolog-based machine translation system. *Computational Linguistics*, 15, pp. 33–52.

McDermott, D. 1976. Artificial intelligence meets natural stupidity. *SIGART Newsletter*, 2:4–9. [Reprinted in *Mind Design*. Edited by J. Haugeland. Cambridge, Mass.: MIT Press.]

McDermott, D. 1986/1978. Tarskian semantics, or no notation without denotation. In *Readings in Natural Language Processing*. Edited by B. J. Grosz, K. Sparck Jones, and B. L. Webber. Los Altos: Morgan Kaufmann, pp. 167–169.

McDermott, D. 1987. A critique of pure reason. *Computational Intelligence.*

McDonald, J. E., T. Plate, and R. W. Schvanveldt. 1990. Using Pathfinder to extract semantic information from text. *Pathfinder Associative Networks: Studies in Knowledge Organization.* Edited by R. W. Schvaneveldt. Norwood, N.J.: Ablex.

McDonald, J. E., and R. W. Schvaneveldt. 1988. The application of user knowledge to interface design. In *Cognitive Science and Its Applications to Human-Computer Interaction.* Edited by R. Guindon. Hillsdale, N.J.: Lawrence Erlbaum, pp. 289–338.

Mellish, C. S. 1983. Incremental semantic interpretation in a modular parsing system. In *Automatic Natural Language Parsing.* Edited by K. Sparck Jones and Y. A. Wilks. Chichester, England: Ellis Horwood, pp. 148–155.

Mellor, D. H. 1977. Natural kinds. *British Journal of the Philosophy of Science,* 28, pp. 1–17.

Metropolis, N., A. Rosenbluth, M. Rosenbluth, A. Teller, and E. Teller. 1953. *Journal of Chemical Physics,* 2:1087.

Michiels, A. 1982. Exploiting a large dictionary data base, PhD Thesis, University of Liège, Belgium.

Michiels, A., J. Mullenders, and J. Noel. 1980. Exploiting a large data base by Longman. *Proceedings of the Eighth International Conference on Computational Linguistics (COLING-80).* Tokyo, pp. 374–382.

Michiels, A., and J. Noel. 1982. Approaches to thesaurus production. *Proceedings of the Ninth International Conference on Computational Linguistics (COLING-82).* Prague, Czechoslovakia, pp. 227–232.

Miller, G. 1985. Wordnet: a dictionary browser. *Proceedings of the First International Conference on Information in Data.* Waterloo, Ontario: University of Waterloo Centre for the New Oxford English Dictionary.

Miller, G. A., and P. N. Johnson-Laird. 1976. *Language and Perception.* Cambridge, Mass.: Harvard University Press.

Minsky, M. 1975. A framework for representing knowledge. In *The Psychology of Computer Vision.* Edited by P. H. Winston. New York: McGraw-Hill. [Reprinted in *Readings in Knowledge Representation,* edited by R. J. Brachman and H. J. Levesque. Los Altos, Calif.: Morgan Kaufman, pp. 245–262. 1985; *Mind Design,* edited by John Haugeland. Cambridge, Mass.: MIT Press, 1981; *Frame Conceptions and Text Understanding* edited by Dieter Metzing. Berlin: Walter de Gruyter, 1980.]

Montague, R. 1974. *Formal Philosophy: Selected Papers of Richard Montague.* Edited by R. Thomason. New Haven: Yale University Press.

Morgan, J. 1969. On arguing about semantics. *Papers in Linguistics,* 1, pp. 1–23.

Mott, P. M., D. L. Waltz, H. L. Resnikoff, and G. G. Robertson. 1986. Automatic indexing of text. *Technical Report No. 86–1.* Cambridge, Mass.: Thinking Machines Corp.

Murray J. A. H., et al. (Eds.). 1884–1928. *The Oxford English Dictionary.* Oxford, England: Clarendon Press.

MWPD. 1964. *The New Merriam-Webster Pocket Dictionary.* New York: Pocket Books.

Nakamura, J., and M. Nagao. 1988. Extraction of semantic information from an ordinary English dictionary and its evaluation. *Proceedings of the 12th International Conference on Computational Linguistics.* Budapest.

Neff, M., and B. K. Boguraev. 1989. Dictionaries, dictionary grammars and dictionary entry parsing. *Proceedings of the 27th Annual Meeting of the Association for Computational Linguistics.* Vancouver, Canada.

Neff, M. S., and M. C. McCord. 1990. Acquiring lexical data from machine-readable dictionary resources for machine translation. *Proceeding of the Third International Conference on Theoretical and Methodological Issues in Machine Translation.* Austin, Tex., pp. 85–90.

Newell, A. 1973. Artificial intelligence and the concept of mind. In *Computer Models of Thought and Language.* Edited by R. C. Schank and K. M. Colby. San Francisco: W. H. Freeman, pp.1–60.

Nirenburg, S. 1987. Knowledge and choices in machines translation. In *Machine Translation: Theoretical and Methodolocal Issues.* Edited by S. Nirenburg. Cambridge, England: Cambridge University Press, pp. 1–21.

Nirenburg, S. 1989. Lexicons for computer programs and lexicons for people. *Proceedings of the Fifth Annual Conference of the University of Waterloo Centre for the New Oxford English Dictionary.* Oxford, England: St. Catherine's College, pp. 43–66.

Nomura, N. 1993. Functions of the set of concept explications in an MTD and a methodology for developing bilingual concept explications. *Proceedings of Electronic Dictionary Research Workshops.* Philadelphia: University of Pennsylvania.

Oettinger, A. G. 1955. The design of an automatic Russian-English technical dictionary. In *Machine Translation of Languages: Fourteen Essays.* Edited by W. N. Locke and A. D. Booth. New York: Wiley, pp. 47–65.

Ogden, C. K. 1942. *The General Basic English Dictionary.* New York: W. W. Norton.

Olney, J. 1967. Toward the development of computational aids for obtaining a formal semantic description of English. *SDC Technical Report Series. (SP-2766).* Santa Monica, Calif.: Systems Development Corp.

Parker-Rhodes, F. 1978. *Inferential Semantics.* Hassocks: Harvester.

Partridge, D., and Y. Wilks. 1990. *The Foundations of Artificial Intelligence.* Cambridge: Cambridge University Press.

Perry, J. W. 1955. A practical development problem. In *Machine Translation of Languages: Fourteen Essays.* Edited by W. N. Locke and A. D. Booth. New York: Wiley, pp. 174–182.

Postal, P. 1970. On the surface verb "remind." *Linguistic Inquiry*, 1, pp. 24–43.

Prather, P. A., and D. A. Swinney. 1989. Lexical processing and ambiguity resolution: an autonomous process in an interactive box. In *Lexical Ambiguity Resolution*. Edited by S. L. Small, G. W. Cottrell, and M. K. Tannenhaus. San Mateo, Calif.: Morgan Kaufmann, pp. 289–310.

Procter, P. (Ed.). 1978. *Longman Dictionary of Contemporary English*. Harlow, Essex, England: Longman Group.

Pulman, S. G. 1983a. Generalized phrase structure grammar, Earley's algorithm, and the minimisation of recursion. In *Automatic Natural Language Parsing*. Edited by K. Sparck Jones and Y. A. Wilks. Chichester, England: Ellis Horwood, pp. 117–131.

Pulman, S. G. 1983b. Trace theory, parsing and constraints. In *Parsing Natural Language*. Edited by M. King. London: Academic Press, pp. 171–196.

Pustejovsky, J. 1987. On the acquisition of lexical entries: the perceptual origin of thematic relations. *Proceedings of the 25th Annual Conference of Association for Computational Linguistics*, pp. 172–178.

Pustejovsky, J. 1991. The generative lexicon. *Computational Linguistics*, 17:4.

Pustejovsky, J. and P. Anick, 1988. On the semantic interpretation of nominals. In *Proceedings of the International Conference on Computational Linguistics*. Budapest, pp. 196–201.

Pustejovsky, J., and S. Bergler. 1987. The acquisition of conceptual structure for the lexicon. *Proceedings of the Sixth National Conference on Artificial Intelligence (AAAI-87)*. Seattle, pp. 556–570.

Pustejovsky, J., and B. K. Boguraev. 1993. Lexical knowledge representation and natural language processing. *Artificial Intelligence*.

Putnam, H. 1970. Is semantics possible? *Metaphilosophy*, 1, pp. 187–201.

Putnam, H. 1977. The Meaning of "Meaning". *Mind, Language and Reality*. Cambridge, England: Cambridge University Press.

Quillian, M. R. 1967. Word concepts: a theory and simulation of some basic semantic capabilities. *Behavioral Science*, 12:410–430. [Also reprinted in *Readings in Knowledge Representation*, edited by R. J. Brachman and H. J. Levesque. Los Altos, Calif.: Morgan Kaufmann, 1985, pp. 98–118.]

Quillian, M. R. 1968. Semantic memory. *Semantic Information Processing*. Edited by M. Minsky. Cambridge, Mass.: MIT Press, pp. 216–270.

Quine, W. V. O. 1960. *Word and Object*. Cambridge, Mass.: MIT Press.

Quirk, R., S. Greenbaum, G. Leech, and J. Svartvik. 1972. *A Grammar of Contemporary English*. London: Longman Group.

Quirk, R., S. Greenbaum, G. Leech, and J. Svartvik. 1985. *A Comprehensive Grammar of the English Language*. London: Longman.

Ramsay, A. 1992. Why dictionaries cannot be neutral. In *Machine Tractable Dictionaries: Design and Construction*. Edited by C. M. Guo. Norwood, N.J.: Ablex.

Reichert, R., J. Olney, and J. Paris. 1969. Two dictionary transcriptions and programs for processing them. *The Encoding Scheme. Technical Report*, vol. 1. Santa Monica, Calif.: System Development Corp.

Revard, C. 1968. On the Computability of Certain Monsters in Noah's Ark. (SP-3165). Santa Monica, Calif.: Systems Development Corp.

Robertson, S. E., and K. Sparck Jones. 1976. Relevance weighting of search terms. *Journal of the American Society for Information Science*, 27, pp. 129–146.

Robinson, J. A. 1965. A machine oriented logic based on the resolution principle. *Journal of the Association for Computing Machinery*, 12, pp. 23–41.

Rosch, E. 1976. Classifications of real-world objects: origins and representations in cognition. *Bulletin de Psychologie*, Special Annual, pp. 242–250.

Rumelhart, D. E., J. L. McClelland, and the PDP Research Group. 1986. *Parallel Distributed Processing*. Cambridge, Mass.: MIT Press.

Ryle, G. 1949. *The Concept of Mind*. London: Hutchinson.

Sager, N. 1981. *Natural Language Information Processing*. Reading, Mass.: Addison-Wesley.

Sampson, G. 1975. *The Form of Language*. London: Weidenfield & Nicholson.

Sampson, G. 1986. A stochastic approach to parsing. *Proceedings of the 11th International Conference on Computational Linguistics (COLING-86)*. Bonn: University of Bonn, pp. 151–155.

Sanfilippo, A. 1991. Aspectual aud thematic information in verb semantics. *Belgian Journal of Linguistics*, 6. [Also ESPRIT BRA-3030 ACQUILEX WP NO.033.]

Sanfilippo, A., T. Briscoe, A. Copestake, M. A. Marti, and A. Alonge. 1992. Translation equivalence and lexicalization in the ACQUILEX LKB. *ESPRIT BRA-3030 ACQUILEX WP NO.042*.

Schank, R. C. 1973. Identification of conceptualizations underlying natural language. *Computer Models of Thought and Language*. Edited by R. C. Schank and K. M. Colby. San Francisco: W. H. Freeman, pp. 187–247.

Schank, R. C. 1975. *Conceptual Information Processing*. Amsterdam: North-Holland.

Schank, R. C., and R. P. Abelson. 1977. *Scripts, Plans, Goals and Understanding*. Hillsdale, N.J.: Lawrence Erlbaum.

Schuetze, H. 1992. *Word Space*. Center for the Study of Language and Information, Stanford University, Stanford, Calif.

Schvaneveldt, R. W. (Ed.). 1990. *Pathfinder Networks: Theory and Applications*. Norwood, N.J.: Ablex.

Schvaneveldt, R. W., F. T. Durso, and D. W. Dearholt. 1985. Pathfinder: scaling with network structure. In *Memorandum in Computer and Cognitive Science* MCCS-85-9. Computing Research Laboratory, New Mexico State University.

Scott, D. S. 1987. What should we demand of electronic dictionaries. In *Processings of the Third Annual Conference of the UW Centre for the New Oxford English Dictionary*. Ontario, Canada: University of Waterloo.

Scott, D. S., and C. Strachey. 1971. Towards a Mathematical Semantics for Computer Languages. *Proceedings of the Symposium on Computers and Automata.* Edited by J. Fox. Brooklyn, N.Y.: Polytechnic Institute of Brooklyn, pp. 19–46.

Searle, J. 1969. *Speech Acts.* Cambridge, England: Cambridge University Press.

Searle J. 1979. Literal meaning. In *Expression and Meaning.* Cambridge, England: Cambridge University Press.

Sedelow, S., and W. Sedelow. 1992. Recent model-based and model-related studies of a large-scale lexical resource (Roget's Thesaurus). *Proceedings of the 15th International Conference on Computational Linguistics.* Nantes, France, August 1992.

Shapiro, S. C. (Editor-in-chief) 1992. *Encyclopedia of Artificial Intelligence*, 2nd ed. New York: Wiley.

Shapiro, S. C., and J. G. Neal. 1982. A knowledge engineering approach to natural language understanding. *Proceedings of the Twentieth Meeting of the Association for Computational Linguistics.* Menlo Park, Calif.: Morgan Kaufmann, pp. 136–144.

Shieber, S. M. 1984. Direct parsing of ID/LP grammars. *Linguistics and Philosophy*, 7, pp. 135–154.

Shortliffe, E. H. 1976. *Computer-Based Medical Consultation: MYCIN.* New York: Elsevier.

Simmons, R. F. 1973. Semantic networks: their computation and use for understanding English sentences. *Computer Models of Thought and Language.* Edited by R. C. Schank and K. M. Colby. San Francisco: W. H. Freeman, pp. 63–113.

Simpson, G. B., and C. Burgess. 1989. Implications of lexical ambiguity resolution for word recognition and comprehension. *Lexical Ambiguity Resolution.* Edited by S. L. Small, G. W. Cottrell, and M. K. Tannenhaus. San Mateo, Calif.: Morgan Kaufmann, pp. 271–288.

Sinclair, J. M. (Ed.). 1987a. In *COBUILD Dictionary of the English Language.* Glasgow: Collins.

Sinclair, J. M. (Ed.). 1987b. *Looking Up.* Glasgow: Collins.

Slator, B. M. 1987. *First Thoughts on Lexical Access for a Preference Sematics Parser for Text.* Las Cruces, N.M.: Computing Research Laboratory, New Mexico State University.

Slator, B. M. 1988a. Constructing contextually organized lexical semantic knowledge-bases. *Proceedings of the Third Annual Rocky Mountain Conference on Artificial Intelligence.* Denver, Colo., June, 13–15, pp. 142–148.

Slator, B. M. 1988b. Lexical semantics and a preference semantics analysis, doctoral dissertation. *Memoranda in Computer and Cognitive Science*, MCCS-88-143. Las Cruces, N.M.: Computing Research Laboratory, New Mexico State University.

Slator, B. M., S. Amirsoleymani, S. Andersen, K. Braaten, J. Davis, R. Ficek, H. Hakimzadeh, L. McCann, J. Rajkumar, S. Thangiah, and D. Thureen. 1990. Towards empirically derived semantic classes. *Proceedings of the Fifth Annual Rocky Mountain Conference on Artificial Intelligence*. Las Cruces, N.M., pp. 257–262.

Slator, B. M., and Y. A. Wilks. 1987. Toward semantic structures from dictionary entries. *Proceedings of the Second Annual Rocky Mountain Conference on Artificial Intelligence*. Boulder, Colo., pp. 85–96. [Also *Memoranda in Computer and Cognitive Science*, MCCS-87-96, Computing Research Laboratory, New Mexico State University.]

Slator, B. M., and Y. A. Wilks. 1990. Towards semantic structures from dictionary entries. In *Linguistic Approaches to Artificial Intelligence*. Edited by A. Kunz and U. Schmitz. Frankfurt: Peter Lang, pp. 419–460. [Revision of RMCAI-87 and CRL-MCCS-87-96.]

Slocum, J. 1985a. A survey of machine translation: its history, current status, and future prospects. *Computational Linguistics*, 11, pp. 1–17.

Slocum, J. 1985b. Parser construction techniques: a tutorial. *Tutorial at the 23rd Annual Meeting of the Association for Computational Linguistics*. Chicago.

Slocum, J., and M. G. Morgan. 1986. The role of dictionaries and machine readable lexicons in translation. Unpublished.

Smadja, F., and K. McKeown. 1989. Automatically extracting and representing collocations for language generation. *Proceedings of the 28th Annual Meeting of the Association of Computational Linguistics*. Pittsburgh, Pa., pp. 252–259.

Small, S. L., W. G. Cottrell, and K. M. Tannenhaus (Eds.). 1989. *Lexical Ambiguity Resolution in the Comprehension of Human Language*. Los Altos, Calif.: Morgan Kaufmann.

Smolensky, P. 1987. Connectionist AI, symbolic AI and the brain. *Artificial Intelligence Review*, 1:95–110.

Sparck Jones, K. 1964. Synonymy and semantic classification, Ph.D. thesis, University of Cambridge, Cambridge, England. [Published in Edinburgh Information Technology Series, edited by S. Michaelson and Y. A. Wilks and Studies in Computer-Aided Lexicology, for Sture Allen, Sprakdata, University of Gothenburg, Sweden.]

Sparck Jones, K. 1986. *Synonymy and Semantic Classification*. Edinburgh: Edinburgh University Press.

Stein, G., F. Lin, R. Bruce, F. Weng, and L. Guthrie. 1993. The development of an application independent lexicon: Lexbase. *Memorandum in Computer and Cognitive Science*. (MCCS-93-247). Las Cruces, N.M.: Computing Research Laboratory.

Sterkenburg, J. Van, and W. J. J. Pijnenburg. 1984. *Groot Woordenboek van Hedendaggs Nederlands.* Utrecht, Netherlands: Van Dale Lexicografie.

Stich, S. 1983. *From Folk Psychology to Cognitive Science.* Cambridge, Mass.: MIT Press.

Strunk W. Jr., and E. B. White. 1979. *The Elements of Style,* ed 3. New York: Macmillan.

Swift, J. 1726/1983. *Gulliver's Travels.* London: Penguin Books.

Tannenhaus, M. K., C. Burgess, and M. Seidenberg. 1989. Is multiple access an artifact of backward priming? In *Lexical Ambiguity Resolution.* Edited by S. L. Small, G. W. Cottrell, and M. K. Tannenhaus. San Mateo, Calif.: Morgan Kaufmann, pp. 311–329.

Toma, P. 1976. An operational machine translation system. In *Translation: Applications and Research.* Edited by R. W. Brislin. New York: Gardner.

Touretzky, D. S. 1986. *The Mathematics of Inheritance Systems.* Los Altos, Calif.: Morgan Kaufmann.

Tsutsumi, T. 1992. *Word-Sense Disambiguation by Examples.* Tokyo: IBM Research, Tokyo Research Laboratory.

Van Petten, C., and M. Kutas. 1989. Tracking the time course of meaning activation. In *Lexical Ambiguity Resolution.* Edited by S. L. Small, G. W. Cottrell, and M. K. Tannenhaus. San Mateo, Calif.: Morgan Kaufmann, pp. 431–475.

Veronis, J., and N. M. Ide. 1990. Word sense disambiguation with very large neural networks extracted from machine readable dictionaries. *Proceedings of the 13th International Conference on Computational Linguistics (COLING '90).* Helsinki.

Vossen, P. 1989. Polysemy and vagueness of meaning descriptions in the Longman Dictionary of Contemporary English. In *Topics in English Linguistics.* Edited by J. Svartvik and H. Wekker. The Hague: Mouton de Gruyter. [Also ESPRIT BRA-3030 ACQUILEX WP NO.001].

Vossen, P. 1990. The end of the chain: Where does decomposition of lexical knowledge lead us eventually? *Proceedings of the Fourth conference of Functional Grammar, Copenhagen, June 1990.* [Also ESPRIT BRA-3030 ACQUILEX WP NO.010].

Vossen, P. 1991a. Comparing noun-taxonomies cross-linguistically. *ESPRIT BRA-3030 ACQUILEX WP NO.014.*

Vossen, P. 1991b. Converting data from a lexical database to a knowledge base. *ESPRIT BRA-3030 ACQUILEX WP NO.027.*

Vossen, P., and I. Serail. 1990. Word-devil: a taxonomy-browser for decomposition via the lexicon. *EXPRIT BRA-3030 ACQUILEX WP. NO.009.*

Walker, D. E., and R. A. Amsler. 1986. The use of machine-readable dictionaries in sublanguage analysis. In *Analyzing Language in Restricted Domains.* Edited by I. R. Grishman and R. Kittredge. Hillsdale, N.J.: Lawrence Erlbaum.

Waltz, D. 1987. Connectionist models: not just a notational variant, not a panacea. *Theoretical Issues in Natural Language Processing*, pp. 56–62.

Waltz, L. D., and J. B. Pollack. 1985. Massively parallel parsing: a strongly interactive model of natural language interpretation. *Cognitive Science*, 9, pp. 51–74.

Warwick, S. 1986. *Automated Lexical Resources in Europe: A Survey*. Geneva, Switzerland: ISSCO, University of Geneva.

Weinreich, R. 1966. Explorations in semantic theory. In *Current Trends in Linguistics*, vol. 3. Edited by T. Sebeok. Mouton, Netherlands: The Hague, pp. 212–229.

Weischedel, R., M. Meteer, R. Schwartz, L. Ramshaw, and J. Palmucci. 1993. Copying with ambiguity and unknown words through probabilistic models. *Computational Linguistics*, 19:359–382.

West M. 1953. *General Service List of English Words*. London: Longman.

White, J. 1988. Determination of lexical-semantic relations for multi-lingual terminology structures. In *Relational Models of the Lexicon*. Edited by M. Evens. Cambridge, England: Cambridge University Press.

Wierzbicka, A. 1989. *Semantics, Culture and Cognition*. New York: Oxford University Press.

Wilensky, R. 1987. Primal content and actual content: an antidote to literal meaning. *Report UCB/CSD 87/365*. Berkeley, Calif.: University of California at Berkeley.

Wilks, Y. A. 1968. On-line semantic analysis of English texts. *Machine Translation*, 11:59–72.

Wilks, Y. A. 1971. Decidability and natural language. *Mind*, 80:497–516.

Wilks, Y. A. 1974. One small head: models and theories in linguistics. In *Foundations of Language*, vol. 11, pp. 77–95. [Reprinted in *The Foundations of AI: A Source Book*, 1988. Edited by D. Partridge and Y. Wilks. Cambridge, England: Cambridge University Press.]

Wilks, Y. A. 1975a. Preference semantics. In *The Formal Semantics of Natural Language*. Edited by E. Keenan. Cambridge, England: Cambridge University Press.

Wilks, Y. A. 1975b. An intelligent analyzer and understander of English. *Communications of the ACM*, 18:264–274. [Reprinted in *Readings in Natural Language Processing*, edited by B. J. Grosz, K. Sparck Jones, and B. L. Webber, Los Altos, Calif.: Morgan Kaufmann, 1986, pp. 193–203].

Wilks, Y. A. 1975c. A preferential pattern-seeking semantics for natural language inference. *Artificial Intelligence*, 6, pp. 53–74.

Wilks, Y. A. 1977. Frames, scripts, stories and fantasies. *Pragmatics Microfiche*, University of Sussex.

Wilks, Y. A. 1978. Making preferences more active. *Artificial Intelligence*, 11, pp. 75–97.

Wilks, Y. A. 1981. A position note on natural language understanding and artificial intelligence. *Cognition*, 10:337–340.

Wilks, Y. A. 1992. Review of Jackendoff's semantic structures. *Computational Linguistics*, 18:95–97.

Wilks, Y. A. (Ed.). 1993. *Proceedings of the Second Workshop of the Consortium for Lexical Research. Memoranda in Computer and Cognitive Science, MCCS-93-254*. Las Cruces, N.M.: Computing Research Laboratory, New Mexico State University.

Wilks, Y. A., and D. Farwell. 1990. White paper on research in pragmatics-based machine translation. *Memoranda in Computer and Cognitive Science, MCCS-90-188*. Las Cruces, N.M.: Computing Research Laboratory, New Mexico State University.

Wilks, Y. A., D. C. Fass, C. M. Guo, J. E. McDonald, T. Plate, and B. M. Slator. 1987. A tractable machine dictionary as a resource for computational semantics. *Memoranda in Computer and Cognitive Science (MCCS-87-105)*. Las Cruces, N.M.: Computing Research Laboratory, New Mexico State University. [Also appears in *Computational Lexicography for Natural Language Processing*, 1989. Edited by B. K. Boguraev and T. Briscoe. Harlow, England: Longman.]

Wilks, Y. A., D. C. Fass, C. M. Guo, J. E. McDonald, T. Plate, and B. M. Slator, 1988. Machine tractable dictionaries as tools and resources for natural language processing. In *Proceedings of the 12th International Conference on Computational Linguistics (COLING-88)*. August 22–27. Budapest, pp. 750–755.

Wilks, Y. A., D. C. Fass, C. M. Guo, J. E. McDonald, T. Plate, and B. M. Slator, 1990. Providing machine tractable dictionary tools. In *Semantics and the Lexicon*. Edited by J. Pustejovsky. Cambridge, Mass.: MIT Press. [Also in *Machine Translation*, 1990, 5, pp. 99–151.]

Wilks, Y., J. Pustejovsky, and J. Cowie. 1993. DIDEROT: automatic data extraction from text using semantic analysis. *Proceedings of the ARPA Conference on Human Language Technology*, Princeton, N.J. Menlo Park, Calif.: Morgan Kaufmann, p. 405.

Winograd, T. 1972. *Understanding Natural Language*. New York: Academic Press.

Winograd, T. 1973. A procedural model of language understanding. In *Computer Models of Thought and Language*. Edited by R. Schank and K. Colby. San Francisco: W. H. Freeman, pp. 152–186.

Wisdom, J. 1961. *Philosophy and Psychoanalysis*. London: Routledge.

Wittgenstein, L. 1953. *Philosophical Investigations*. Oxford: Blackwell.

Woods, W. 1978. Procedural semantics as a theory of meaning. *Proceedings of the Sloan Workshop*, June 14, 1978. University of Pennsylvania, Philadelphia.

Workshop, *Tipster* 6 Month. 1992a. Philadelphia Airport Hotel, Philadelphia.

Workshop, *Tipster* 12 Month. 1992b. The Catamaran Resort, San Diego.

Workshop, *Tipster* 18 Month. 1993. The Williamsburg Lodge, Williamsburg, Va.

Yarowsky, D. 1992. Word-sense disambiguation using statistical models of Roget's categories trained on large corpora. *Proceedings of the 15th International Conference on Computational Linguistics.* Nantes, France, pp. 454–460.

Zernik, U., and Michael G. Dyer. 1986. Disambiguation and language acquisition through the phrasal lexicon. In *Proceedings of the 11th International Conference on Computational Linguistics (COLING-86).* Bonn, Germany, pp. 247–252.

Zernik, U., and P. Jacobs. 1990. Tagging for learning: collecting thematic relations from corpus. *Proceedings of the 13th International Conference on Computational Linguistics (COLING-90),* vol. 1. Helsinki, pp. 34–39.

Zwicky, A. 1973. Linguistics as chemistry: the substance theory of linguistic primes. In *Festschrift for Morris Halle.* Edited by J. Anderson and P. Kiparsky. New York: Holt, Rinehart & Winston.

Index